Structure and Development
in Child Language

Structure and Development in Child Language

The Preschool Years

MARION POTTS

PATRICIA CARLSON

RODNEY COCKING

CAROL COPPLE

CORNELL UNIVERSITY PRESS

Ithaca and London

First published 1979 by Cornell University Press.
Published in the United Kingdom by Cornell University Press Ltd.,
2-4 Brook Street, London W1Y 1AA.

International Standard Book Number 0-8014-1184-x
Library of Congress Catalog Card Number 78-10968
Printed in the United States of America
Librarians: Library of Congress cataloging information appears on the last page of the book.

Contents

5

Tables

Preface

The theme of this book is the emergence of structural features in the language that young children produce; we endeavor throughout to show clearly the relationship between features of the linguistic structures and the methods used to tap them. The data we report are examined for what they suggest about the emergence of phonological, syntactic, and semantic structures; about the types of variations that appear in the course of development toward Standard English forms; and about dialect patterns that are variant from Standard English. We attempt to ascertain where our data support or fail to support the results of other child language research.

The data reported in the book are distinctive in several ways. First, they are developmental in nature, and they deal with the language production of 3-, 4-, and 5-year-olds, thus extending well beyond the age limit of much of the developmental language literature. Second, they are concerned, in a strong developmental context, with how language emergence varies across social classes and ethnic groups. Third, the data were collected in a large-scale experimental study, based upon a standardized procedure; thus comparisons both within and among groups are possible.

We have written and organized the book to serve both as a reference work and as a textbook. Using it as a reference work, the reader can find information on selected groups of linguistic constructions and on theoretical comparisons. The various discussion sections are geared to workers and students in psycholinguistics, developmental psychology, and education, as well as to those in child language research itself.

The technique on which the book is based was developed while I was with the Child Study Center of the State University of New York, Cortland. In designing research, it seemed useful to work out a new method to assess children's linguistic development. How this technique emerged from the characteristics of children is described in this manuscript. Later at Cornell, the compelling needs of preschool language programs for a criterion measure suggested using the method to develop such a tool. It was clear that standardization of an evaluation instrument could simultaneously result in a massive body of data on language acquisition, were the research designed to that end too. The proposal I submitted for funding had, therefore, a twofold thrust: (a) to develop an instrument that would reflect children's control of Standard English and (b) to study the emergence of syntactic structures in speakers of that dialect, as well as to explore aspects of linguistic development in children from other language environments. During the academic year 1969–70, the items described in this book were developed and tested, and the first standardization norms were gathered. Diana Chastain joined the project in December of that year and ably assisted in this work; her contribution is gratefully acknowledged. Ursula Bellugi-Klima offered invaluable assistance by listening to tapes, examining the test, and supporting the plan to gather data on dialect groups as well as on speakers of Standard English.

In the fall of 1970 the test was cross-validated on the children whose responses are described in this book. Carol Copple joined the project as research assistant for 1970–71; she made a fine contribution in supervising testers, ensuring the accuracy of our coding, and implementing the free-speech aspect of the proposal. Helen Moyer and Mary Hayter worked with us as full-time research associates, handling innumerable tasks and making possible the smooth functioning of the entire operation. We are deeply indebted to the nursery school and kindergarten teachers of Ithaca, Cortland, and Syracuse, New York. They provided records and made available facilities that helped to make the project fun for our young subjects as well as for us.

The years 1972–74 were spent in detailed and painstaking analysis of this voluminous body of data. Acknowledgment and gratitude are extended to John Harding, Professor of Human Development and Family Studies at Cornell University, and to Harold Mitzel, Associate Dean for Research at The Pennsylvania State University, for their valuable help and insights on statistical matters.

Rodney Cocking had used the test in several of our research projects and had done statistical work for us; his competence was recognized by those of us directly involved with test development. Patricia Carlson had done some first-rate editorial work on related projects. Both agreed to collaborate in the long-planned book on child language. Cocking's major interest was in cognitive development, Carlson's in psycholinguistics. Copple, who had a strong interest in sociolinguistics, later rejoined the project. This four-way collaboration resulted in a set of perspectives that accounts for many of the manuscript's strengths. I would like to add that the book would not yet have been completed had not Carlson, Cocking, and Copple participated as co-authors. Their names appear on the title page (in alphabetical order), reflecting their substantial contributions.

At long last, it seems by now, we have hammered out what is offered here. While the massive amount of research required that many years be spent in a search for relationships, the data seem to provide a base sufficiently sturdy to support the many hypotheses that have emerged. Part of the research culminating in this book was funded by the Office of Education, the National Institute of Education, and the Central Midwest Regional Educational Laboratory. Their contribution to this complex undertaking is gratefully acknowledged.

MARION POTTS

Ithaca, New York

Structure and Development
in Child Language

And neither that boy not eating a cookie too.

—3-year-old child

Chapter 1

Introduction

Most 3- and 4-year-old children are fairly proficient speakers of their native language. We seldom hear a diversity of errors in their speech because they rarely use structures they cannot control. For those of us who study child language, this sets up a waiting game. Young children do not spontaneously emit just the range of structures we are interested in. And rarely will they bestow upon us errors in those they have not yet mastered. Because children have a way of not volunteering structures they cannot handle, there has been a dearth of information on syntactic development in the preschool years. The data we report here explore this range of language development. But to find out what these children know about language, we were compelled to be somewhat wily.

Fortunately, there is something children love to do that played into our hands: When an adult is telling a story to a child and pauses in midsentence, the child will spontaneously fill in the missing phrase. Opening a book to a picture of a kitten, a mother might read, "Once there was a little _____," and the child says "kitty." Turning next to a picture of the cat nestled in a big shoe, she draws the child further into the storytelling:

> Mother: Lucy looked and looked for her kitten but she couldn't find him. That kitty was hiding _____.
> Child: in the shoe!

r

Several years ago, the senior author developed a test to create this kind of interaction with children (Potts, 1970). The items were designed to discover whether or not a child controlled a given syntactic structure. For instance, a picture of two dogs facing each other and barking carries this story:

> Tester: Sometimes when dogs see other dogs, they bark. These dogs are barking at _____.
> Mark (5): each other.

If the child does not yet control the required structure, he does not complete the sentence correctly.

> Tester: These dogs are barking at _____.
> Karen (3): both of them.

This format was successful in eliciting a wide range of structures. And the ease with which such data could be gathered meant also that many more children could be tested than had previously been possible.

The test focused on children 3 through 5 years old. Prior to this, there had been little developmental information on children above 3 years of age even among middle-class speakers of Standard English, except in a few syntactical subsystems that had interested psychologists and psycholinguists, primarily because of the cognitive operations involved.[1] The scarcity of developmental data at all age levels among other social classes and among racial groups was even greater. Certainly many studies have compared the language of lower-class and middle-class children. However, even when concerned with syntax, they have not been developmental, and some have not separated race and social class variables. Those that have investigated Black English Vernacular, such as Labov's, have looked at structures of interest with respect to that dialect, structures for which we have little middle-class information. Thus, despite the interest in dialect and social class differences in language in the past decade, we were still lacking comparable data across social classes, ethnic groups, and developmental levels. To provide a fuller picture of patterns of language acquisition and variability in different

1. Among these were passives (Bever, 1970; Turner and Rommetveit, 1967), negatives (Bellugi, 1967; Bloom, 1970; Klima and Bellugi, 1966; McNeill and McNeill, 1968), and questions (Brown, 1968a; Brown and Hanlon, 1970; Ervin-Tripp, 1970; Holzman, 1972).

groups of children, the research reported here focused on lower-class white, lower-class black, and middle-class white children.

The purpose of this book is to present the results of the testing of several hundred 3- to 5-year-olds and to examine the patterns that emerged in relation to age, social class, and dialect groups. We think that such an extensive body of data may offer the field a new kind of information about the emergence of syntactic development.

CHILDREN'S COMMUNICATION SKILLS

We return now to the test items, juxtaposing a 3-year-old's production with a 5-year-old's to show their contrasting responses for several additional structures.

> Tester: Some children were drawing pictures but they weren't quite finished and it was time to go outside. The teacher said, "In five minutes those pictures have to _____."
> Karen (3): finish.
> Mark (5): be finished.

> Tester: Eddie didn't know how to tie his shoe, so he asked if his mother
> _____.
> Karen (3): tie his shoes.
> Mark (5): could tie them.

> Tester: It was hot out, so Doug put on his bathing suit. What he did then
> _____.
> Karen (3): go in the pool.
> Mark (5): is jumped in his pool.

> Tester: Donna was trying to get her doll's dress clean. What did she do to it?
> Karen (3): She wash it.
> Mark (5): She put it in the water.
> Tester (probing Mark's response): Yes, she did. That's washing. So how did she clean it?
> Mark: She washed it.

> Tester: This baby didn't finish her soup, and neither did this baby. This boy isn't eating a cookie, and neither _____.
> Karen (3): and neither that boy not eating a cookie too.
> Mark (5): is that boy.

Dialogues between an adult and a child of the type we have just been considering are possible because of the amazing adeptness of children at participating in these gamelike verbal exchanges. These story games demonstrate an important characteristic of child language: the early ability of children to communicate and to take part in semantically coherent conversation. When children are engaged in highly constrained story-completion games, we would expect them to employ a variety of both linguistic and nonlinguistic modes of responding, other than the one of completing the story. These varied modes of response seem likely because the sentences that are forced upon the child may be too much for him to handle. As an example, a child might complete stories that involve grammatical structures of which she has control but refuse to respond to those that are too difficult for her. Or she might adopt a completion strategy of simply labeling a prominent aspect of the picture or of the story. Or she might shrug or say "I don't know" or change the subject of discussion to something else, such as "I'm hungry." All of these responses, of course, do occur from time to time; but we found that these side steps constitute a surprisingly small proportion of the total responses of children conversing with adults around these story-completion tasks. The vast majority of the responses are relevant both to the picture and to the meaning of the adult's words, even when the child's own completion statement is not syntactically correct. Let us consider some of the strategies children use as they participate in language games with adults.

The most basic strategy children use, for their own productions as well as for comprehending what is said to them, is the assumption of semantic relevance. For example, as the preceding transcript shows, the children who did not fully produce the syntax of the difficult secondary conjunction item (e.g., *This boy isn't eating a cookie, and neither* _____) did not fail to mention the second figure in the pictures, which the adult had not mentioned. On another item, which depicted a girl eating, many children who did not produce the target *she eats* said something semantically relevant, about food for example.

In addition, children seem to be quite aware of the rules for dialogue. They know that in conversational games, such as these story-completion tasks, the participants alternate utterances. The semantic relevance of their responses to the adult's commentary shows also that the strategy is not simply one of "taking turns." Children, in most cases, attend to the meaning of the adult's statements and are not just waiting for a pause as their signal to begin talking.

Children at these ages are sensitive to another feature, which we will call parallelism. If the adult telling the story refers to two out of three people in a picture, most children will attempt to refer to the third, unmentioned person. This feature is quite apparent in stories that, syntactically, could take a variety of complements. For example, the item testing for the superlative, *His father's the (tallest)*, could be completed as *His father's the (doctor)* or *His father's the (dark-haired one)* or *His father's the (one over there)*. However, if there are two references to height in the frame as the adult presents the story and the picture is of three people of different heights, most children refer to the height dimension in their completions; for example: *This one is tall and this one is taller, but this one is the (tallest)*. This means that most children complete the story with either a correct superlative *(tallest)* or an incorrect one *(most tallest)*. But those who do not supply a superlative still mention something that refers to the height dimension (e.g., *big*). Stories framed by adults in this way, then, are only weakly constrained by the syntactic form itself, and the rules of communication that children control very early are the overriding feature.

In summary, as children play the picture-story games in the situations we have described here, they sometimes mimic portions of the story the adult is telling, and they occasionally enumerate picture elements. However, variations that do not conform to the game demands are relatively rare. Children usually complete the stories, and their principal strategy is an assumption of semantic coherence. That is, even when syntactic elements are not fully comprehended by children, they will comment upon other features of the story or of the picture. They also show an awareness of the rules of dialogue. And, finally, children show an early sensitivity to parallelism.

These impressive language-sensitive strategies are organismic characteristics that certainly can aid anyone wishing to study child language processes. The technique on which this book is based capitalized upon these features of children's language and turned such characteristics to advantage in collecting the information reported here. We will now briefly review the methods of assessing children's syntactic development and indicate why an alternative technique seemed desirable.

Measures of Syntactic
Development

The study of the child's emerging language has been approached through a variety of techniques: those that probe for comprehension, those that elicit imitation, and those that sample the free speech of children. But when the need arose to analyze the production of language by preschool children, it seemed that some other method was required. We did have a measure for studying the comprehension of some structures but could not assume that production would be achieved simultaneously. Several studies have reported that comprehension probably precedes productive ability (McNeill, 1970a; Menyuk, 1971; Cocking and Potts, 1976). Imitation methods were considered, but reports on the correspondence between what children imitate and what they have under productive control were conflicting. Free-speech sampling was an intuitively appealing route, but it is a method that requires an enormous amount of time and training, and too often the structures of interest do not appear.

Any measure of production, as with measures of comprehension, is a test of performance and can reflect underlying competence only indirectly. But a production measure may be more limiting than a test of comprehension. Perhaps, as McNeill hypothesizes, comprehension involves fewer distorting factors between performance and its underlying competence (1966). But a child's language is reflected in both of these aspects of performance—in the encoding, which is reflected in production, as well as in the decoding, which is reflected in comprehension. In an extensive review of comprehension and production, Ingram (1974) has pointed out that the real issue has eluded language-research. We have not seen a thorough study of the *nature* of comprehension and the *nature* of production, nor one that details the nature of the gap between the two. Too much attention, he contends, has been given to trying to prove the precedence of one language function over the other. To obtain a clear picture of a child's language development, both aspects need to be tapped.

Attempts to study language, particularly the longer or more difficult structures involved in syntax, have in fact included measures of both comprehension and production. Various techniques of probing children's comprehension have been designed by Brown (1957); Fraser, Bellugi, and Brown (1963); Shipley, Smith, and

Gleitman (1969); Bellugi-Klima (1971); Wetstone and Friedlander (1973); and Strohner and Nelson (1974).

Among the techniques for measuring productive ability in children is the Berko measure of children's use of morphemes in combination with nonsense syllables (1958). The child completes the missing element in a statement framed by the tester; for example: *Here is a wug* (picture). *Here are two others. There are two* _____ (*wugs*). To study the passive transformation, Brown and Olds (cited in McNeill, 1970a) designed the Alligator Test, a game in which tester and child each have a puppet and the child's task is to have his alligator puppet respond in passive voice statements to the experimenter's bear puppet statements, which are always in active voice. This technique might also be extended to negative and question transformations.

An efficient and often effective technique used by a number of investigators is the method of imitated production. The child is simply told to repeat what the examiner says, for example: *The boy is pushed by the girl*. The literature discussing the effectiveness of this technique is, however, uncomfortably conflicting. Miller and Ervin (1964) reported that, in their sample of five children ranging in age from 22 to 34 months, the capacity for imitation approximated spontaneous productions. The finding supported Menyuk's (1963a) observation. Fraser, Bellugi, and Brown (1963) obtained similar results with 25- to 35-month-old children. However, for the older children of the Fraser, Bellugi, and Brown study (37 to 43 months of age), imitation elicited patterns that could not be produced spontaneously.

Slobin reports a fine-grained analysis of Brown's transcripts of Adam and Eve's speech, an analysis that he interprets as evidence that "imitations *can* be grammatically progressive" [1968:439]. About 15 percent of Adam and Eve's imitations were repetitions of expansions, and in 50 percent of these imitations, the child had added something to his original utterance (something imitated from the adult's expansion). Menyuk (1971) points out that both comprehending and noncomprehending imitation may occur, depending on the length of the sentence and upon the grammatical structure.

These methods for assessing child language are all suited to the purposes for which they were developed. Each focuses upon a particular feature of language development. However, to obtain a composite view of children's language production, one that samples morphemic and syntactic development across a wide range of structures, necessitates a different approach. In considering this problem, it seemed useful to rely on children's characteristic strategies for responding to language.

LANGUAGE OBSERVATIONS: STRUCTURED AND UNSTRUCTURED

We have looked at the characteristics of child language that were built upon in collecting the data to be reported here, and we have set the language production technique into the context of other techniques for assessing children's syntactic development. At this point it seems logical to examine some of the reasons for a structured technique being a useful alternative to the collection of free-speech samples.

There is a characteristic of free speech that we want to demonstrate by a "typical" free-speech protocol. In general, there is no way to select a portion of free speech from a given group of subjects and say that it is typical. Even within the 30-minute conversation of a single child there is such variety in the content, function, and utterance length, as well as in the particular structures used, that looking at any part of it is like feeling only the elephant's tail. But for the one characteristic of free speech that we wish to discuss here, almost any portion of the protocol of any subject would do. This feature is the repetitiveness of structure, the recurrent appearance of certain syntactic structures that appear very commonly in speech.

Lisa (3:5): Peter *lived*$^{(9)}$ in the forest and that—but *he*$^{(4)}$ was a boy. But then *he*$^{(4)}$ *went*$^{(9)}$ out into the forest to *catch*$^{(14)}$ a wolf, hunt for *wolfs*$^{(1)}$. *He*$^{(4)}$ *was going to hunt*$^{(11)}$$^{(14)}$ for a wolf. But then *he*$^{(4)}$ *caught*$^{(9)}$ one and some *hunters*$^{(1)}$ *came*$^{(9)}$ along and *helped*$^{(9)}$ him to *take*$^{(14)}$ it to the zoo. And who *was helping*$^{(11)}$ him?

The numbers, indicating the corresponding items on the production test, show the recurrence of structures. Structures 1, 4, 9, 11, and 14 (plural, subject pronoun-gender, past tense, past progressive, and infinitive complement) each show up several times, even in this short segment. From the fact that not everything in the protocol is marked, we see the predominance in free speech of syntactical features that emerge very early and thus were not even included in the test, for example, articles, prepositional phrases, conjunctions, and the use of subject, verb, and object. There are always many of these. Throughout a 100-utterance segment, a 3-year-old would typically use about ten of the syntactic structures that do appear on the test, but each one might appear several times. Most of the remaining structures used would be the very basic ones, which are solidly controlled before the period of language development presently under consideration.

What is to be concluded about structures that are not used? If, in the course of a 10-minute conversation, an adult friend did not use a future tense verb, we would not assume that the poor individual did not know how to use it. Rather, we would conclude that it "didn't come up." Perhaps, if we were really curious about his ability, we could change the subject to plans for summer vacation, to increase the likelihood of his need to employ a future tense verb. This is one way of looking at what the production technique does; in a 10-minute period, it makes sure that the need to use certain structures "comes up."

Now, suppose that we have generated this conversation loaded with the expression of things yet to come, but instead of providing us with the "will" usage we are interested in, the adult friend says things like, "After I get to England, I'm going to travel through the Lake County." Would we assume that our friend is avoiding using a future tense verb? We would not. A similar situation occurs on the production test, and our interpretation should be equally cautious. One example was seen on page 21 when the child responded *She put it in the water*, instead of *She washed it*. *Put* is a lexical item that does not allow us to tell whether the child is inflecting the verb for past tense. But we do not have to leave it at that. Notice that the tester provided the word *washing* to the child without modeling the past tense. Most of the time the child will then show whether or not he has the past tense—by saying *washed* (as Mark did), the uninflected *wash*, or some other clear variation.

What happens with this probing is similar to what occurs in a clinical interview—we pursue the ambiguous response to determine its meaning. It is necessary to plan ahead of time what will be said, not only for standardization across subjects but also to avoid modeling the structure and to determine what probes are effective. This is exactly the kind of follow-up that does not occur in free speech.

Unfortunately but interestingly, not all "loopholes," as we called them, are closable. The following response to an item that was supposed to elicit the modal auxiliary was a loophole for which an effective probe could not be devised:

> Tester: The dog wanted to go for a walk but Barbara didn't have time to take him, so she asked if Dan _____.
> Child: wanted to (instead of *would*).

This response rarely occurred, but it illustrates the fact that there are almost always acceptable ways to say things differently. For example, in Berko's study, a child could have finished *Here is a wug* (picture). *Here are two others. There are two* _____ by saying *of them* instead of *wugs*. This does not happen often. The "wugs" frame is a highly obvious one, probably because of the child's sensitivity to parallelism, which we discussed earlier. The degree to which unfinished frames are constraining and obvious differs from structure to structure and item to item, but they are never completely so. Even with the use of probes, we cannot always find ways to force the child into giving either a target response or a clear error. However, the incidence of loopholes is sharply reduced by the use of standardized probes.

None of what we have said is meant to argue with the fact that sampling free speech is clearly the way to answer many of the questions we have about child language. But apart from the fact that sampling free speech is not always feasible, speech samples have another limitation for those interested in the acquisition of syntax. Some structures occur commonly, while many others of interest are far less frequent. In contrast, the format of the production technique systematically gave each child occasion to use each of the desired structures, some more than once, within a 10-minute period. When the child's response circumvented the use of the target structure but was correct English, the examiner employed a probe. Probes were not always successful but did reduce the frequency of loopholes. This technique relies on the child's knowledge of patterns of language and communication, and creates a type of interchange that is quite natural for children, while it allows us to tap their production of a wide variety of syntactic structures.

OVERVIEW OF THE BOOK

In this chapter we have given a brief view of the production technique and how it relates to child language. Chapter 2 gives an account of the procedures used in the development of the Potts Language Production Test, from item design and several testings through the final standardization and validation.

Beginning with Chapter 3, we present the results in four groups of structures: noun phrase structures (Chapter 3), verb phrase structures (Chapter 4), propositional structures (Chapter 5), and negative and comparative structures (Chapter 6). Each structure is introduced with a brief discussion of literature in the field that seems directly related. The data are then presented for the middle-class white, lower-class white, and lower-class black children at each age level.

In addition to the acquisition curves, we were of course interested in the variations produced at each age level for each of the groups. Our emphasis is on the empirical data, rather than on hypothesis testing. We summarize the responses of the children of these three samples, with discussion of the strengths and weaknesses of the assessment, as we could identify them. We have tried to avoid linguistic controversies, except where our data seemed able to clarify an issue or vice versa. We have attempted to stay close to the original stimuli—to what the child heard and saw in these particular contexts and to how he or she responded.

The responses are then examined for what they might suggest about the emergence of phonological, syntactic, and semantic structures; about the types of variations that appear in the course of development toward Standard English forms; about dialect patterns that are variant from Standard English; and about points where our data support or fail to support results of other child language research.

Chapters 7 and 8 broaden the viewpoint. In Chapter 7, we look at a number of regularities that emerged in the data as a whole: the overall order of acquisition of structures, the types of social class and racial differences we found, and the interactive and cognitive skills the children brought to bear when faced with unfamiliar structures. In Chapter 8 we examine a number of theoretical notions in developmental psycholinguistics in the light of our data. For example, Brown has suggested that syntactic structures are learned in order of complexity; McNeill has proposed that the scope of a transformation is related to the order of acquisition; Bloom and her associates have discussed the nature of variation in language acquisition; and Bever has proposed the importance of perceptual strategies in language learning. The data provide interesting information on these questions and point to possibilities for further investigation.

Chapter 2
Methodology:
Tapping Syntactic Abilities

So that readers can assess the validity of the data on which this book is based, we present here details of the development and standardization of the production technique. First, we discuss item selection and pilot testing, and what we learned about designing this type of measure for this range of language development. Then, we discuss standardization procedures and present the statistics that emerged from the final measure, including information from the reliability and validity studies. Finally, we outline the statistical procedures used to test the significance of the data on individual structures, and briefly discuss the use and limitations of these data. This outline of instrument development is intended as background information for readers interested in technical research details; it paves the way for discussion of specific structure analyses to follow in Chapters 3, 4, 5, and 6.

ITEM SELECTION AND PILOT TESTING

As we searched the then sparse literature on language acquisition to determine which linguistic structures emerge during the 3- to 6-year-old period (Bellugi and Haas, 1968; Menyuk, 1969), we were especially interested in grammatical forms that might yield information about developmental patterns or that might be produced with variations. From this initial pool of structures, over one hundred stories and pictures were designed and pretested with 120 preschoolers. The original testing sought to determine (a) types of structures that were amenable to testing by this technique; (b) types of items that too often elicited acceptable Standard English responses that circumvented the target syntax; and (c) kinds of modifications necessary, such as the revision, addition, or deletion of specific items. In addition, preliminary tests were run on material and procedural issues that needed clarification, such as interest level, clarity of color versus black-and-white pictures, optimal story length, and suitable thematic content.

Testing revealed no differences, either in attention span or in language responses, between drawings done in color and those done in black and white. The latter were therefore selected as more economical for general use. In testing various story lengths, it was determined that the probability of restricting responses to the target syntax was increased with very brief, constraining story stems; longer stories operated as distractors.

The technique itself did not permit the testing of some structures from our pool, such as relative clauses modifying subjects, conjunctions, question transformations, and so forth. Attempts to elicit these kinds of structures resulted in a high proportion of responses that neither contained the target nor were incorrect, such as the substitution of an indirect question for a direct question. This is the phenomenon of circumvention, or loopholes, discussed in Chapter 1. Considerable effort was directed toward refining the probing procedure, but as we saw in that earlier discussion, some of these loopholes are not closable. In such cases we were forced to drop those structures from further consideration in a standardized technique. But revisions in story content, the use of different pictures, and changes in story stems minimized the incidence of loophole responses on most items.

On the basis of the original testing, items were dropped, revised, or added. We eliminated grammatical forms that were already controlled by all the children. Preposition items that tested for *in* and *on* fell into this category; our lower-class 3-year-olds had no trouble with them. Another example is the participial complement: *I see a man* _____ (*painting*) was responded to correctly by 100 percent of the first sample and therefore was eliminated. The noun plural allomorph /-z/, as in *doggies,* was given by all of these children and was chosen for use as a warm-up item. We learned also that the structures in our original pool did not adequately test the skills of the 5-year-old children. Additional structures were added at this point to include conditionals, nominalizations, and indirect speech.

SECOND TESTING

From the pretested set of items, a test was constructed and administered to determine (a) whether items differentiated among age levels, and (b) whether children's responses would be consistent over time. These issues were investigated for each of the 45 items used in this version of the test.

The sample at this time included 69 middle-class and 46 lower-class children; of the lower-class group, 22 were black. The test was given a second time to 73 of these youngsters, 3 to 4 weeks later. The data showed clear developmental trends and did reflect dialect differences, revealing variable patterns in the emerging language systems of lower-class children.

The second issue, variability of response in individual children, was explored by examining each test item for consistency of performance across the two testings. Consistency meant that a subject responded correctly or incorrectly on both test administrations, even though the particular wording of his responses might vary from one time to the next. For example, one item testing for a nominalization required insertion of the copula and deletion of the past tense marker from the main verb: *Carol got a rag, and what she did next* _____ (*was wipe it up* versus *wiped it up*). On the first testing, one 3-year-old responded *wipe all the paint up.* On the second testing, she said *wash off the sink.* Despite the content change in her answers, the same syntactic error was made both times.

Correct structures also admitted of a wide variety of content. For example, one stem used to test for the counterfactual was: *If this butterfly didn't have wings,* _____. It elicited two different subjunctives from another 3-year-old. On the first testing he said *it would fall down;* on the second he said *it could swim.* Most items showed syntactic consistency levels of 80 percent or better.

In cases of inconsistency, the children usually gave an incorrect response on the first test and a correct one on the retest. Although we would expect that structures which were in the process of emerging would be used correctly and incorrectly at different times, it is unlikely that so many children were acquiring these structures in the short period of a few weeks. It seems possible that familiarity with the entire item context, and greater awareness of the Standard English situation, made processing easier the second time (Potts, 1970). The effect was twice as common in the lower-class sample as in the middle-class sample, and this points to another factor to be considered. Copple (1973) found a similar result in a later study of 5- and 7-year-old black children's processing. In a Standard English context, the children were more likely to give dialect responses on the first testing but Standard English responses to the same items on a second testing. This seems to be evidence of code-switching or style shifting, and the phenomenon probably accounts for the greater proportion of shifts to Standard English in our own lower-class sample.

It seemed critical to determine whether item inconsistency would diminish developmental and social class differentiation, and thus cast doubt on the usefulness of such a test with young children. The percentage of children giving Standard English responses on each item was therefore calculated on the retest of each of the age and class subgroups. Developmental and social class differences were both still apparent. Total test-retest reliability for the sample of 73 was $r = +.96$. No doubt the correlation was inflated by the wide range of age and social class, but it was nevertheless substantial. We decided therefore to make the revisions indicated and to proceed with the final standardization sample.

Test items were retained if they met two criteria: (a) if they differentiated among at least two of the three age levels, and (b) if they demonstrated a consistency level of 70 percent or better. A few items were altered for reasons we discuss in a moment, but the most important change was the inclusion of parallel items. Such items were constructed and tested for two types of structures: (a) those that discriminated most clearly among the three age levels (we hoped thereby to increase the probability of seeing the development of the syntactic structure across the idiosyncrasies of particular items); (b) those structures that showed less than 80 percent consistency from test to retest (the purpose here was to obtain a better sample of typical language performance). Among middle-class children, the odds were that children who did not yet have control of a structure would get both items wrong, that those who had mastered the structure would get both items right, and that children who alternated in free speech might, as a group, fall somewhere in between. In this way we hoped to separate children who consistently used a particular structure from those who used it erratically or very rarely.

Two items on the test were negatively correlated with age, that is, a younger group did better than an older one. One of these items tested for the reflexive form *himself;* it is discussed in Chapter 3, in the section on the reciprocal. The other negative predictor tested for a gerund; 5-year-olds made an error reflecting emergence of a clause structure into the language system. Both items had the effect of penalizing the more advanced speakers and were therefore dropped from the test.

A few items needed revision of story content because of problems with a target word. For instance, a story about horses was designed to elicit the noun plural allomorph /-ɨz/: Many children responded with *horsies* or *ponies*, requiring only the allomorph /-z/. Another item tested for the past tense allomorph /-t/, in *kicked*. This was a poor choice of verb, as the combination of the /-k/ and /-t/ sounds made it difficult to tell from the tapes whether the child had included the ending. Different stories were substituted for the originals in both of these cases.

Items that elicited more than 5 percent loophole responses (i.e., that circumvented the target structure even after probing), were dropped from the test at this point. The instrument as given to the second standardization sample contained 21 syntactic structures, tested across 47 items, and took about 10 minutes to administer.

FINAL TESTING AND STANDARDIZATION

Composition of Sample Groups

The final test was administered to 310 middle-class white children and 163 lower-class children (77 white, 86 black), aged 3, 4, and 5. Each age group was further divided into 6-month subgroups. Male and female subjects were equally represented in the 6-month age groups for each race and social class. Table 1 gives the number of subjects in and the mean chronological age (CA), in months, of each age, social class, and racial group.

Table 1

Composition of sample groups

Age group*	Middle-class white		Lower-class white		Lower-class black	
	N	Mean CA	N	Mean CA	N	Mean CA
Early 3's	41	39.44	6	39.67	8	39.25
Late 3's	65	44.45	20	44.90	15	44.40
Total	106	42.51	26	43.69	23	42.61
Early 4's	45	50.33	9	51.56	12	51.08
Late 4's	55	56.22	15	56.07	24	56.58
Total	100	53.57	24	54.38	36	54.72
Early 5's	49	62.65	14	62.79	15	62.14
Late 5's	55	68.38	13	68.38	12	68.67
Total	104	65.68	27	65.48	27	64.67
Total sample	310	53.85	77	54.66	86	54.61

*Early 3's comprise the range 3:0–3:5, late 3's the range 3:6–3:11; 4's and 5's are similarly divided. CA = chronological age in months.

Social class was determined through school records of parental occupation, with categories 6 and 7 on the Warner scale (Warner, Meeker, and Eells, 1960) defined as lower class. The samples were drawn from nursery schools, day care centers, and Head Start and kindergarten programs in three cities of central New York State: Ithaca, Cortland, and Syracuse. A middle-class black sample of sufficient size for this study was not available within the geographical area.

Criterion Instruments Used

In addition to the Potts Language Production Test, we administered the Bellugi Comprehension Test of Grammatical Structures (Bellugi-Klima 1971) and the Peabody Picture Vocabulary Test (Dunn, 1959). We were particularly interested in looking at the relationship between the comprehension and the production of syntactic structures. The Bellugi Comprehension Test uses three-dimensional materials, such as dolls, blocks, animals, and trucks. Specific toys are set on a table for each item, and the child is asked to move the objects so as to show his understanding of the directions given, for example, Show me—the dog is chased by the cat.

Many of the structures tested by this comprehension test were also tapped by the language production test. In addition, there were structures on each of the measures amenable to testing by one technique and not the other. The production measure had dropped easier structures and added ceiling items on the basis of its previous testing information. In spite of these differences, we were interested in seeing whether any relationship did exist between the two measures. The comprehension test takes 25 minutes to administer, so we decided to give it to only half of our subjects.

The Peabody Picture Vocabulary Test (PPVT) was administered to all subjects. This test was chosen as a brief, standardized instrument that might reflect exposure to the language. We were aware of the cultural bias of this test for use with lower-class children, and data were interpreted accordingly. The PPVT gives estimates of mean mental age (MA) and IQ; our analyses were done on a total raw index of the PPVT, and are reported in Appendix Tables A-1 and A-2.

Procedure

All children were tested individually by one of five white middle-class women, in rooms separate from the regular classrooms. It was not possible to find black examiners to test our black children, and this fact must be kept in mind in interpreting the data for that group. The Peabody Picture Vocabulary Test was administered first, followed by the Potts Language Production Test. One to 3 weeks later, one-half of all subjects were retested on the production test to determine test-retest reliability. The Bellugi Comprehension Test was administered to these children at this time.

Production test protocols of all subjects were taped during administration of the test and transcribed later the same day. Since we intended the measure to be an estimate of language development for middle-class subjects, it was necessary to devise a rating system based on the data to provide a total performance index for each child. To this end, all responses to each item were listed and categorized. A final weighting system (on a scale of 0, 1, 2) was developed, which is sufficiently clear-cut to be used by testers unsophisticated in the theory of language development. Questions of weighting were resolved, as on the pilot test, by reference to the percentage of children at each developmental level who gave the response. Such developmental trends were always checked for replication on our second-testing sample of 115 children. This "performance index," which reflects use of the Standard English forms of the target structures, was used in calculating the statistics given in this chapter.

Final-Test Statistics

Data analyses were done for the three basic 12-month groups—the 3-, 4-, and 5-year-olds—as well as for the 6-month subgroups among the middle-class children.[1] The scatterplot for the performance index of the 310 middle-class children showed a clear linear trend, with variability decreasing with age. The means began to level off at age 5, where those for the 6-month subgroups were not significantly different. At this level, middle-class children began to approach the ceiling of the test; no one, however, reached the total possible weighting of 94.

Regression lines and plotting of means also showed linear trends for both the lower-class samples. However, the scatterplots reflected a marked difference in pattern between the middle-class group and the lower-class groups. While the spread of the middle-class children decreased with age, those of the lower-class groups increased, resulting in clear triangular distributions. This picture represents in part an increasing divergence of linguistic forms with age within each lower-class group—some children using predominantly dialect forms, others incorporating varying amounts of Standard English. It also reflects the extent to which variable rules operate within these dialects for the structures we tested.

The production test differentiated clearly among middle-class 12-month levels but showed less clear developmental gains across the 6-month groups. Middle-class means and standard deviations for total raw scores on the Potts Language Production Test, the Bellugi Comprehension Test, and the Peabody Picture Vocabulary Test are given in Appendix Table A-3.

It cannot be overemphasized that this production technique uses Standard English and therefore does not reflect the level of language maturity of speakers of dialects. It taps their control of those struc-

---

1. Because of the small size of each lower-class sample, data for the lower-class children were not broken down into 6-month subgroups.

tures for which their dialects have the same forms as Standard English, and it reflects Standard English they have learned. In some items, linguistic maturity within their own language systems is working against dialect speakers if one looks only at conformity to Standard English. We questioned the usefulness of developing a total performance index for our lower-class dialect groups, since our major interest was in looking for structural patterns in their own language systems as they emerged in this context. We finally decided to develop a total index to permit assessment of test-retest reliability, internal consistency indices, and concurrent validity coefficients. Appendix Table A-4 reports data on the production, comprehension, and Peabody tests for lower-class black and lower-class white children.

As would be expected, large differences were revealed in the production of Standard English by the lower-class groups on the one hand and the middle-class group on the other. There were much greater differences between middle-class and lower-class white children, in degree of conformity to Standard English, than between lower-class white and black children. Inspection of the lower-class means, however, showed that the two lower-class groups progressively separated from each other with age. The lower-class means for black and white 5-year-olds were substantially further apart than were those for the 3-year-olds of these samples. The effect was just the opposite for the middle-class white/lower-class white comparison. However, the convergence of means with age in the latter groups was at least partly a function of the middle-class children's approaching the ceiling of the test.

Finally, no sex differences emerged in the middle-class data. However, among lower-class whites, girls performed significantly better than boys at the 4-year-old level ($t_{(22)} = 2.37, p < .05$) and at the 5-year-old level ($t_{(25)} = 2.31, p < .05$). And, among lower-class blacks, girls performed better than boys at the 3-year-old level ($t_{(31)} = 2.16, p < .05$).

It is critical to observe at this point that the difference in means between the middle-class group and the two lower-class groups cannot be interpreted as a simple lag in Standard English ability among the lower-class children. Many items showed similar acquisition curves, though at different levels, for middle-class and lower-class white children. But even in these instances, it was only the acquisition curves that were approximately parallel; variation curves of the lower-class and middle-class children were completely different from one another. These data indicate that, for lower-class children, the acquisition of Standard English patterns is not simply a bigger problem but a different kind of problem.

For structures influenced by Black English Vernacular, curves for the black children were quite different from those for the two white groups, and these structures weighed heavily in the increasing differences with age in lower-class black and white performance. Some nontarget responses given by middle-class and lower-class 3-year-olds decreased with age in the two white groups but stayed at the same level or increased with age in the black group. The curves clearly demonstrate that such responses are not errors for these youngsters but part of the well-developed language system of Black English Vernacular.

Another reflection of this difference can be seen in the contrast among the indices of item difficulty across the three samples. For the black children, among the items that seldom elicited a Standard English response were those dealing with the simple present tense marker and the noun plural marker. For the middle-class group, these were among the easiest items, resulting in the Standard English forms in a high proportion of all the age groups. For the lower-class white children, these items fell somewhere in between in eliciting Standard English responses. Again, the extent to which the dialect structures involved have different rules (or variable rules) from their counterparts in Standard English impinges directly on these indices. Item difficulty statistics for all items and all groups are reported in Appendix Table A-5.

Reliability

Several measures of reliability were obtained: test-retest correlations, individual item consistency, and internal consistency coefficients. We were especially interested in retest data to determine whether or not preschool children would give the same types of responses over an interval of one to three weeks. Retest subjects comprised one-half of the original samples and were randomly selected. Reliability was high within all 6- and 12-month age groups and samples, with correlations ranging from +.82 to +.94. Total test-retest correlations were +.92 for 156 middle-class whites, +.94 for 38 lower-class whites, and +.92 for 43 lower-class blacks. These statistics are given in Appendix Tables A-6 and A-7.

Of considerable interest was the extent to which the children's responses to each item were consistent over time. Contingency tables were set up to examine the proportion of subjects who responded similarly to each item on both administrations of the final test. All items were responded to consistently by at least 70 percent of the children; three-fourths of the items by at least 80 percent. This is rather high reliability for individual test items, particularly in light of the variation of correct structure usage in free speech.

To be usable as a language test for middle-class children, this measure had to reflect a child's general level of language development. The particular test items, then, needed to be representative of language performance in general. Internal consistency coefficients were obtained through analysis of variance for the middle-class sample by 6-month groups. Correlations range from +.74 to +.88, indicating that the various items seem to be measuring a common characteristic. Appendix Table A-8 reports these data.

Validity

Three types of validity data were examined: relationship of production to chronological age, concurrent validity of the three instruments used, and relationship to free speech.

Age. Chronological age and test performance correlated +.61 for the middle-class sample, +.68 for lower-class whites, and +.54 for lower-class blacks. Comparisons of mean performance at different ages have already been shown. We were also concerned with the extent to which individual items differentiated among 3-, 4-, and 5-year-olds. Some items discriminated among all three age levels—for example, those for the passive and the relative clause structures. Elements such as subject pronoun and habitual present develop early, and items tapping them differentiated between 3- and 4-year-olds. More difficult structures, such as indirect object, reciprocal, and subjunctive, showed the greatest change between ages 4 and 5.

Concurrent validity. The second index of validity was the relationship among the three tests administered, as an index of concurrent validity. Intercorrelations of raw scores on the Peabody and production test were substantial: +.67 for the middle-class group,

+.65 for lower-class whites, and +.55 for lower-class blacks. Those between the production and comprehension tests varied by social class but were significant for the total groups: +.65 for the middle-class group, +.39 for lower-class whites, and +.43 for lower-class blacks. Within 12-month age groups, all correlations between production and comprehension were significant for middle-class children and nonsignificant for lower-class children. This lack of significance in the lower-class groups may represent, in part, the absence of developmental trends in the comprehension data for these small samples. Appendix Table A-9 reports intercorrelations for the three tests, by 12-month age groups, for middle-class whites, lower-class whites, and lower-class blacks, respectively. The lower total group correlations between comprehension and production performance for the speakers of dialects are interesting and well worth noting. A lower-class black child may leave out a tense marker on the production test because it is deleted in Black English Vernacular. But he may well comprehend that same marker when he hears it in Standard English, and the correlations reflect this fact.

Test/free-speech consistency. The third and most critical measure of validity was the relationship between free speech and performance on the production test. One hundred utterances of free-speech data were gathered from each of 48 new subjects who also took the production test. Because our concern was the validity of the test as a measure of Standard English, all of these subjects were middle-class children. The free-speech sample was composed of 28 4-year-olds, 10 3-year-olds, and 10 5-year-olds, equally distributed by sex within each age group.

For each session, an individual child was taken to a room separate from the regular classroom, where a female examiner encouraged him to play with the toys[2] and engaged him in conversation as he played. The examiner avoided asking questions that could be answered in one word or phrase; she simply tried to keep the subject talking until over 100 utterances had been obtained. All sessions were taped and were transcribed as soon as possible after taping.

In analyzing the data, we began by checking for the occurrence of our target structures in each free-speech protocol. Each child's test was then examined to see whether he had used the structures on the

---

2. The materials were a landscape village (a cloth terrain with wooden cars, buildings, and trees), dolls and animals scaled for use in the village, trucks with movable parts, a boat, two large dolls with removable clothes, and a telephone.

test in the same way. Incorrect usages in free speech were rare: across all subjects, there were only 28 cases where a child made an error on a structure one or more times, and in 6 of these situations the subject also used the structure correctly at least once. In the remaining 22 cases where subjects made free-speech errors, only two of the children were found to have produced the same structure correctly on the test. In other words, when there was a deviation from Standard English in free speech, there was a corresponding deviation (or in a few cases a loophole) on the production test in 90.9 percent of instances. An example of this type of error correspondence is in 4-year-old Samuel's confusion over count and mass nouns and their modifiers. He missed this item on the test, and in free speech he said *not too much schools* at one point and *too much ropes* at another.

Although such examples are gratifying when they occur, it appears that by this age children seldom generate obligatory contexts for structures they cannot handle. In addition to error matching, therefore, it was necessary to examine the appearance versus nonappearance of structures in free speech in relation to test responses. Since our concern was with whether or not a subject used a structure at all, rather than with how often he used it, we recorded a plus for structure usage when the child produced the form at least once correctly and nowhere in his protocol produced it in a way deviating from Standard English. It is preferable to have more than one instance of structure usage as an indication that the child has control of the structure, but the frequency of occurrence of structures is quite variable. As noted in Chapter 1, some structures are produced over and over again and some rarely. So, regardless of how many times a structure was repeated, if it occurred at all, the child received a single plus for that structure. There were 554 such pluses across the 48 subjects. In 91 percent of these cases, the structures had also been produced correctly on the production test.

After finding this high overall correspondence between correct use of a structure in free speech and on the test, we raised two further questions regarding validity: (1) Was test/free-speech consistency as high for the younger subjects as for the older ones? (2) Were there some structures for which the test items did not show correspondence with free speech? Protocols of the 3- and 5-year-olds were compared to answer the first question; the data from all 48 subjects were used to answer the second.

1. *Age and consistency:* Our concern as to the validity of the test for the youngest as well as the oldest subjects stemmed from our asking whether socialization to testing and attentional factors might not be accounting disproportionately for the 3-year-olds' missing of items. In free speech there are, of course, more instances of structure use among the older children. The mean number of structures used correctly both in free speech and on the test was 13.2 for the 5-year-olds and 9.6 for the 3-year-olds; the mean number of structures used correctly in free speech and incorrectly on the test was 1.0 for the 5-year-olds and 1.2 for the 3-year-olds. A chi-square analysis performed on the frequencies of consistent and inconsistent instances among the 3- and 5-year-olds indicated no significant interaction with age, $X^2_{(1)} = 1.17$. For both age groups there were few discrepancies in test/free-speech usage (92.9 percent consistency for those aged 5, 88.8 percent for those aged 3).

2. *Individual structures and consistency:* Thus far we had found high overall consistency of production test responses and free speech and had established that this consistency held even for the younger subjects. There was still the possibility that some of the individual structures (or items) did not relate to what the children produced in free speech. To answer this question, the occurrences of each test structure were tallied separately. As we expected, the free-speech occurrences of some structures were few or nonexistent (e.g., nominalization, use of the reciprocal), and for these structures no validation from free speech was possible. But as noted earlier, there were relatively few cases overall in which test response and free speech did not correspond: in only 52 out of 554 cases where children used structures correctly in free speech, had they missed them on the test; in only 2 out of 22 cases where children made free-speech errors, had they used the structures correctly on the test. The tally of inconsistency according to structure indicated that these 54 inconsistencies were scattered through the structures. There was no single structure for which there were more than 2 cases of test/free-speech inconsistency.

A disparity between a child's performance on the production test and in free speech might result from any of several factors. In free speech there is an infinite variety of outputs, each a little different from every other, whereas the production test is a sample of contexts selected to tap a set of structures. That is, there are idiosyncrasies associated with each eliciting context, and they cannot be identically matched in samples of free-speech occurrences. In some instances, the structural context in free speech and in the test item are very different; for example, the past progressive was required in a subordinate clause on the test: *When Fred came home, he saw that his brother was watching TV*, but it was used without subordination in free speech: *I was watching Batman yesterday.*

Other disparities may be due to wobble in the child's acquisition of a structure. If the element is in the process of emerging, he may use it sometimes correctly and sometimes incorrectly in spontaneous speech, and in a free-speech sample we may or may not pick up instances of both. It has been reported that a child may first learn a subset of the places where a particular structure is required and then gradually acquire further knowledge of where it is needed (Brown, 1973). An example of this partial use of a structure can be seen in the case of the copula in the protocol of Sarah (3:7):

> Sarah: ... And he *is* dead. And the little boy *is* dead. They [ ] all dead. ... [And a little later in the fantasy] Everyone knows *I'm* such a monster. I don't think *you're* such a monster.

Based on a limited protocol we can only guess as to why she uses the copula in some cases and not others. We do not know if it is a competence or a performance question. But this kind of situation, of a child's using a structure both correctly and incorrectly at a given point in time, is fairly common. Some interesting theoretical issues have been raised in connection with this phenomenon (Brown, 1973; Labov, 1973; Bloom, Miller, and Hood, 1975), which we will discuss more fully in Chapter 8. For the present, the fact that a child does not acquire a structure overnight and use it correctly in all contexts from that point on would lead us to expect some inconsistency between test and free-speech performance.

There are yet other possible reasons for lack of a perfect correspondence between free speech and test production. In some cases the test item may require less from the child because he does not have to produce the whole sentence or even the entire structure. For example, in the difficult nominalization structure, the *wh*-nominal clause is provided: *Carol got a rag, and what she did next _____. A* child might be able to get this item right on the test, showing some knowledge of the nominalization structure, although unable to produce the whole structure in free speech.

Another methodological reason for a structure appearing correctly in free speech and incorrectly on the test is the question of modeling. When considering the free-speech samples, perhaps we do not always recall the fact that the child is not simply giving a 100-utterance monologue. He is interacting with someone, in this case an adult. There is no way for the adult to engage in the conversation in even the minimal way needed to sustain the child's talking without using some of the structures on the test. On the production test, we could be sure that the experimenter never modeled a structure in the item where we were testing the child's production of it. In free speech, the adult will use a structure and then the child will, and we cannot tell whether or not this is imitation, as in the following:

Adult: Here's something *that goes with the truck.*
Child: No, not with the truck. That's something *that goes with the car.*

When a child imitated the adult's words exactly, we eliminated the utterance from analysis; but there are many cases, such as the one given here, where the child does not seem to have relied totally on the adult's sentence but may have benefited from it to some degree. Thus, there are uncontrolled opportunities for modeling of structures in free speech, whereas these opportunities have been eliminated in the production test.

A final source of test/free speech discrepancies could lie in differences in the semantic difficulty of the test item and the free-speech context. Either the free-speech context or the test item could be more taxing. This could be simply semantic, involving relative familiarity with the vocabulary used in the sentences; or the difference may be both semantic and syntactic, such as one context having a negative while the other does not.

To sum up, then, several factors contribute to discrepancy of performance on the test and in free speech. In spite of these sources of potential discrepancy, there was a high degree of consistency between test performance and free speech. When there was an error in free speech, there was a corresponding error or loophole on the test in 90.9 percent of the cases. When a structure was used correctly in free speech, it was produced on the test correctly in 91 percent of the cases. We interpret these results as evidence confirming the validity of the methodology.

Data on Individual Structures

As we worked with the data, it seemed that the most interesting questions dealt with the emergence of individual structures and with the types of variations given by the children. A major issue was the problem of identification of developmental versus dialect-associated effects. A particular response, such as the omission of a possessive marker, could be due to immature development of Standard English or could reflect the deletion of that redundant marker characteristic of the adult form of a dialect. Study of the curves for our three samples indicated that the sources of difference of such effects might sometimes be teased out. As mentioned earlier, some variations dropped out with age in our speakers of Standard English but stabilized or increased in our dialect speakers. Such a pattern seemed to indicate that the middle-class 3-year-olds were omitting a feature they had not yet acquired, whereas the black 5-year-olds were deleting the feature in accordance with Black English Vernacular.

Significance of Percentage Differences across Groups

In order to do a detailed analysis of the patterns of variations, as well as of the target response for each structure, it was necessary to estimate the significance of the percentage differences among children who gave a particular response across the different age, social class, and racial groups. The data contained several hundred of these percentages, so we estimated conservative significance levels through chi-square procedures. For example, looking ahead to Table 2, the reader can see that the uninflected count noun *glass* is a variant of the noun + plural item produced by middle-class children at ages 3, 4, and 5 in the following percentages: 16, 17, and 6, respectively. Among lower-class white 3-, 4-, and 5-year-olds, the response had the following percentages: 40, 38, and 33. The problem was to determine significance levels for comparing these percentages in order to assess developmental differences within a class or racial group, or for age comparison across groups. These comparisons were done for all combinations of our various sized samples, and they served as guidelines for estimating the significance or non-significance of an observed difference.

For our middle-class sample, which comprised at least 100 in each age group, the Wilks-Mosteller charts in Cantril (1944) were used to check the significance levels of the differences observed among percentages.[3]

Where one middle-class age group is being compared with another ($N_1 = 100$, $N_2 = 100$), the percentage differences required for significance are 12 percent at the $p < .10$ level, 15 percent at the .05 level (by interpolation), and 19 percent at the .01 level. Where one middle-class age group is compared with both other age groups ($N_1 = 100$, $N_2 = 200$), the required differences are 10 percent at $p < .10$, 13 percent at .05 (by interpolation), and 16 percent at .01.

The differences cited apply to the middle of the distributions; smaller differences would be required for significance at either end of the distribution. The accuracy of these significance levels was confirmed by individual calculation of chi-square values on a sample of eight items.

For the lower-class groups, where age groups ranged from 24 to 36 children, no charts were available. In these cases we calculated trial chi-square values that were considered as screening tests for estimation of the size of the percentage differences required for significance. The calculations were computed on the frequencies of target responses and variations observed in each age group on ten items, and the Yates correction for continuity for one degree of freedom was applied. No attempt was made to formulate percentage difference estimates for situations requiring more than one degree of freedom (e.g., several errors across the various class/race groups). On the basis of these calculations, the differences required for significance at the $p < .05$ level were estimated as follows.

Where one lower-class age group was compared with another, a 30 percent difference was considered as significant at the $p < .05$ level. Where one lower-class age group was compared with the two other lower-class age groups, a 25 percent difference was considered significant. In order to estimate the significance of the difference in the responses of a middle-class versus a lower-class group (e.g.,

3. A complete discussion of the rationale behind these tables is given in Wilks (1940). These particular tables were chosen because of their conservative nature, since these tests were done a posteriori.

$N_1 = 100$, $N_2 = 24$), further calculations were done on our observed frequencies. For these instances, a difference of 20 percent proved to be significant at the $p < .05$ level. Again, the differences apply to the middle of the distributions, and percentage differences at either end are significant at smaller values.

These percentages were a conservative estimate that served as a rule of thumb in studying the hundreds of percentages obtained in the study. Sometimes, however, we found it necessary to discuss a particular issue, and it seemed critical to know whether a difference that fell short of significance using our conservative guidelines might in fact be a real difference. In these cases, individual chi-square values were calculated.

CAVEATS

Lest our readers hope to find here a thorough analysis of all structures used by speakers of English, we need to reiterate that we did not exhaustively test the syntax of Standard English: even preschool children do speak in language other than that encompassed by these 21 structures. Even of those structures included in our measure, only a few aspects were elicited. And these selected aspects of the structures were tested in only one or two particular contexts. The data indicate that these contexts did affect production of the target structures. Our needs demanded a sample of diverse structures that could be tested in a brief period, were positively correlated with age, could be scored easily, and had proved difficult to circumvent in our contexts. Items that violated any one of these requirements were not retained in the final technique. Moreover, the items themselves precluded systematic testing of structures. In one structure, the secondary conjunction, the examiner had to start the structure in order to constrain the situation so that the child would respond appropriately: *This clown laughs all the time and so* _____ (*does this one*). In another structure, the counterfactual, the picture and the story were, of necessity, in contradiction. In some items, the child responded to a question; in most, to a sentence-completion task. Any attempts to compare performance on different structures, therefore, must be cautiously undertaken.

The measure we used focused primarily on the syntactic level.

Yet there were, of necessity, a number of nonsyntactic variables operating. The semantic aspects of language, and cognitive development per se, were factors that of course interacted with syntactic variables in all items. Discourse-level phenomena were more apparent in some items than in others. Moreover, while the measure focused on language production, we need to be clear at all times that comprehension was a prerequisite and that failure to comprehend particular elements was sometimes a factor in variations of production. Where particularly relevant, these variables—the semantics of the context, the cognitive requirements of the task, discourse phenomena, and comprehension of the stem—are discussed in the analyses of the data on each structure. A final concern, that of test sophistication, was discussed earlier, on page 44. As outlined there, interference from factors of attention, socialization, and task comprehension seem to have had a relatively small effect on the results.

We also want to pepper this report with caveats on the interpretation of class/race differences. This measure tested only one dialect, Standard English, and only some of the categorical rules of that dialect. Of necessity, we avoided those structures that admit of variable rules in Standard English. But many of these same structures do have variable rules in nonstandard dialects. One could, alternatively, set out to design a test of Black English Vernacular restricted to categorical rules in that language system. Moreover, the fact that lower-class children were being tested in a Standard English situation makes relevant the literature on style shifting. What we have elicited here is probably an adulterated form of lower-class dialect, rather than a clear reflection of what the children might have said in free speech with their friends or family. Lower-status dialect is known to be contaminated by higher-status dialect (Labov, 1973). The testing situation would have emphasized this effect. There is some risk, too, of regarding the data on our lower-class black children as an index of racial difference. In actuality, these data shed light on dialect differences as associated not only with race but also with class within a race.

There is a different but equally critical issue in studying the data on the lower-class white children. If Black English Vernacular is far from being a monolithic system across regional and other differences, lower-class white language is even more diverse. There is far less literature available for this group than for either middle-class white or lower-class black speakers. What we report here represents data on three language communities that can be presumed to differ from one another; but the reader should also recognize the variation within each sample, particularly in the two lower-class groups.

Summary

The data reported here were gathered during the development of a measure of language production. It was our intention to provide an instrument that could serve a dual purpose—as one criterion measure of control of Standard English, and as a research technique that could quickly gather information on patterns of language acquisition. The technique was pretested, piloted, revised, and standardized. It consistently demonstrated several types of reliability and validity, including a close interrelationship with free speech. As we had hoped, it also provided a large sample of responses on individual structures of potential interest to child language researchers. This report analyzes these responses.

We are keenly aware that these data do not exhaustively assess syntactic structures. Yet the responses of our middle-class children provide checkpoints and hypotheses for researchers who wish to explore the development of particular structures through experimental research. The responses of our lower-class white and lower-class black children reveal aspects of their different language systems, specifically of those structures associated with social class or racial background. We hope that this body of data will be useful to child language researchers and will generate hypotheses for those wishing to test them out experimentally.

Chapter 3
Noun Phrase Structures

NOUN + PLURAL

In English, the regular noun plural morpheme (spelled -(e)s) has three allomorphs: /-s/ after stems ending in most voiceless consonants, such as *cats* /kæts/; /-ɨz/ for stems ending in certain stridents, such as *horses* /hɔrsɨz/; and /-z/ elsewhere, as in *monkeys* /mʌŋkiyz/ or *bags* /bægz/. The same phonetic variants are used for the possessive morpheme and the third singular present tense verb morpheme, as discussed in Chapter 8. Mass nouns, which represent a special case in plural forms, will be dealt with later in this chapter. The several types of irregular plurals, such as *man-men*, will not be treated in this report.

Children seem to be aware of the concept of plurality from an early age, and some are reported to refer to it before any inflections are learned (Miller and Ervin, 1964; Carlson and Anisfeld, 1969). Cazden (1968, 1972) reports that, of the three phonetically identical morphemes (noun plural, noun possessive, and verb third person singular present tense), the noun plural form is used first. Since the phonetic representations are identical, and frequency of occurrence in English does not account for the sequence (McNeill, 1970a; Menyuk, 1971), this difference in acquisition order implies that semantic or syntactic factors play an important role in language acquisition.

Even children who give evidence of controlling the plural inflection, however, acquire the allomorphic variants at different times. Brown (1973) suggests that stems like *horse*, which end in stridents and require the /-ɨz/ variant, are the most specialized and therefore the most difficult category of stems for children to learn to pluralize correctly. Besides the high specificity of the pluralization rule for these stems, it should be noted that the set of final strident sounds in such stems is already similar to the set of sounds added to form the plurals. A word like *glass* already sounds more plural than a word like *cup* (Anisfeld, Barlow, and Frail, 1968). This may be a particular problem for children whose phonological systems are not yet fully differentiated (Locke, 1971). Evidence for the difficulty of these stems may be found in Berko's (1968) morphology test. Nonsense words ending with these sounds were pluralized correctly less often than those requiring other allomorphs. Even the real word *glass* was pluralized correctly by only 75 percent of her 4- to 5-year-old group; ninety-nine percent of her 5:6 to 7:0 group were correct in this pluralization.

We originally tested two noun plural items. One of them, which called for the most frequent allomorph, /-z/, was handled correctly by almost all of the pretest sample. Since this item did not differentiate among ages, it was eliminated from the test itself. However, due to its high success rate, it was retained as a warm-up item. The item was as follows:

> Practice item: This is a story about some children and their pets. Timmy has a turtle. Susan has a kitten. And Bob has two _____ (dogs, puppies).

The second pretest item, using *horse*, proved unsuccessful, as children frequently responded with *horsies*, a plural form that utilizes the easy /-z/ rather than the difficult /-ɨz/ allomorph. The change to an item using a picture of several glasses and the stem *glass* reduced this problem.

The example in the test required of the child only that he pluralize the noun to agree with a sentence in which the verb form was already plural; he did not have to produce an entire clause, but he had to coordinate his response with the given obligatory plural context.

The test item we used was the following:

Item 1a: Lori wanted some water to drink, but she couldn't find a glass. Her mom said, "Look on the table, Lori. There are lots of _____ (glasses)."

The responses of all three samples on the noun + plural item are presented in Table 2.

Table 2

Noun + plural—Percentages of responses on Item 1a*

	Middle-class white			Lower-class white			Lower-class black		
Age:	3	4	5	3	4	5	3	4	5
N:†	106	100	104	25	24	27	23	35	26
There are lots of _____.									
Noun + /-ɨz/ plural									
(*glasses*)	56	59	81	28	29	48	0	20	38
Noun + /-s, -z/ plural									
(*cups*)	13	9	4	24	17	11	9	14	0
Uninflected count									
noun (*glass*)	16	17	6	40	38	33	57	43	31
Mass noun (*water*)	15	15	10	8	17	7	35	23	31

*Because of rounding across many responses, percentages of each group may total above or below 100.

†As explained in Chapter 1, children sometimes gave no response or an irrelevant response. Such instances were dropped from the tabulation of item responses; thus the number in each group (N) may vary from the basic sample sizes of Table 1. The numbers on which response percentages have been based are therefore reported separately for each item throughout the book.

Standard English Acquisition:
Middle-Class White

Target. In the middle-class white sample, the target NOUN + /-ɨz/ PLURAL (*glasses*) was given by slightly more than half of both 3- and 4-year-olds. Another large proportion acquired the target plural between 4 and 5 years; by age 5, 80 percent were producing it. This agrees well with Berko's (1958) report.

Variants. One of the common variants was the UNINFLECTED COUNT NOUN (*glass*), which may be due to the phonological similarity to plural forms noted earlier. With this particular word, it might also be due in part to the fact that *glass* can be a mass noun and occur correctly with *lots of*; however, the child would have to avoid agreement with the verb *are*, as well as use the mass noun in a semantically unusual way, if this were the reason for his response.

As common as the uninflected count noun was the MASS NOUN *water. Water* is a semantically sensible response that fits everything in the story frame except the verb phrase. Completely acceptable substitutions were NOUN + /-s, -z/ PLURAL, such as *cups, drinks*, etc., which fit the syntactic frame perfectly; nevertheless they drop out increasingly with age. The explanation may lie in increasing semantic differentiation of the categories "cups" and "glasses" among the older preschoolers.

Dialect Variation: Lower-Class White

Target. The lower-class white children used the target NOUN + /-iz/ PLURAL *glasses* significantly less than did the middle-class white children at all three ages tested. This lower-class group more often substituted a NOUN + /-s, -z/ PLURAL. Yet combination of the percentages of all plural forms still results in significant differences in plural usage between the lower- and middle-class white 4- and 5-year-olds. Moreover, the increase in target usage with age for the lower-class white children was significantly less than that for the middle-class children.

Variants. The UNINFLECTED COUNT NOUN *glass* was used significantly more often by the lower-class white group than by the middle-class white group. This was not true of the MASS NOUN *water*, where incidence was similar across these two samples.

Dialect Variation: Lower-Class Black

Target. Target NOUN + /-iz/ PLURAL usage in the lower-class black group was significantly lower than in the middle-class white group throughout the age range. At age 3, it was also lower than in the lower-class white group. Usage increased significantly with age, showing a steep and steady curve from zero to 40 percent.

Variants. Among 5-year-old lower-class black children, responses were approximately equal among the three types: the NOUN + /-iz/ PLURAL, the UNINFLECTED COUNT NOUN, and the MASS NOUN. Among the younger children, the most common response was the uninflected form *glass*, given by almost 60 percent of lower-class black 3-year-olds. The mass noun *water* was used steadily by one-fourth to one-third of the group across the age range tested.

Summary

Noun pluralization is learned early by middle-class white children, but the different allomorphs are learned at different rates. The simplest allomorph, /-z/, is controlled by such a high percentage of even 3-year-olds that we were able to use it as a warm-up item. The test allomorph /-ɨz/ is more difficult and is still being acquired over the age range we studied. In the two lower-class groups, some plural marker was used on this item by 60 percent of the lower-class white children at age 5 and by 40 percent of the lower-class black children at age 5. The difficult context requiring /-ɨz/, as it affects use of the plural morpheme, is discussed as a phonological factor in Chapter 7.

NOUN + POSSESSIVE

Linguists describing adult English usually derive possessives from underlying clauses. For example, *John's dog* is sometimes considered as a form that has *John has a dog* as the underlying form. Several alternatives are discussed in Stockwell, Schachter, and Partee (1973: 674–714), including the proposal that some possessives have underlying case relationships. An underlying case structure constitutes a more basic relationship than does a *have* clause. As Brown (1973) points out, structures that are clearly possessive in meaning, such as *Eve lunch*, are among the very earliest of the two-word utterances of a child. *Have* constructions occur much later. We agree with Brown that the possessive relationship is probably as basic as relationships like agentive or dative in child language, and perhaps in adult language as well.

Like the noun plural morpheme, the possessive morpheme (spelled -'s) has three allomorphs: /-s/ after most voiceless consonants, as in *Jack's* /jæks/, *giraffe's* /jɨræfs/; /-ɨz/ after stridents, as in *Gladys's* /glædɨsɨz/, *Mitch's* /mɪčɨz/; and /-z/ elsewhere, as in *monkey's* /mʌŋkiyz/, *John's* /janz/.

According to Cazden (1972), of the three morphemes with the /-s, -ɨz, -z/ set of allomorphic variants, the possessive is the second to be acquired. The full form for expressing possession is noun + possessive inflection + noun: *baby's toy*. There is also an elliptical form, which deletes the final noun: *baby's*. Cazden reports the interesting finding that even though mothers tend most often to use the full form of the possessive, children produce the inflection with the elliptic form much more often than with the full two-noun phrase. The sequence of inflection acquisition seems to be:

1. No inflection: *baby, baby toy*
2. Inflection of elliptic form only: *baby's, baby toy*
3. Inflection of both forms: *baby's, baby's toy*

Berko's data (summarized by Brown, 1973) indicate that with nonsense syllables the 4- to 5-year-old subjects got 68 percent of the regular possessives correct; the 5:6 to 7:0 group got 88 percent. Berko used a *whose* question to elicit the possessive.

There were three items in the language production test that required possessive forms. All required the /-z/ allomorph phonetically. Two nouns ended in vowels (*baby, monkey*) and one in a nasal continuant (*clown*); two frames elicited the possessive with a *whose* question, one elicited it with a contrastive sentence. In addition, previous signaling varied. One item (*monkey*) had a preceding possessive pronoun in the frame. A second item (*baby*) signaled possession through use of the *have* construction in preceding clauses. The third item (*clown*) had no previous possessive in the frame.

The items we used to elicit the noun + possessive inflection were the following:

Item 2a: There's a boy, a girl, and a baby in this family. The boy has a train, the girl has a doll. Whose toy is this? _____ (The baby's [toy]).
Item 2b: A man gave a lion a banana. "Grr," said the lion. "That's not my food. It's the _____ (monkey's [food])."
Item 2c: Here is a little boy and here is a clown. Whose feet are biggest? _____ (The clown's [feet]).

The results obtained on these three items are presented in Table 3.

Standard English Acquisition: Middle-Class White

Target. Among the middle-class white children, the target POSSESSIVE construction appeared early and reached near exclusive usage by 5 years of age. The developmental trend is significant for Items 2a and 2c; in Item 2b, *monkey's* was used by such a large percentage of 3-year-olds that further improvement could not reach

Table 3

Noun + possessive—Percentages of responses on Items
2a, 2b, and 2c

	Middle-class white			Lower-class white			Lower-class black		
Age:	3	4	5	3	4	5	3	4	5
N:	106	100	104	25	24	27	23	36	26
(a) *Whose toy is* *this?* _____.									
Possessive (*baby's*)	75	82	92	54	54	82	44	47	34
Uninflected noun (*baby*)	17	12	4	31	42	15	48	53	59
Possessive pronoun (*his, hers*)	3	2	1	4	4	0	0	0	4
Noun not referring to possessor (*doll*)	4	4	1	8	0	4	0	0	4
Other	2	1	0	4	0	0	9	0	0
(b) *That's not my food.* *It's the* _____.									
Possessive (*monkey's*)	92	93	98	54	67	67	30	17	41
Uninflected noun (*monkey*)	8	7	2	46	33	33	70	83	59
Possessive pronoun (*his*)	0	0	0	0	0	0	0	0	0
Noun not referring to possessor (*food*)	0	0	0	0	0	0	0	0	0
(c) *Whose feet are* *biggest?* _____.									
Possessive (*clown's*)	58	61	88	31	46	61	39	50	46
Uninflected noun (*clown*)	35	37	13	64	54	37	57	50	54
Possessive pronoun (*his*)	6	2	0	4	0	0	4	0	0
Noun not referring to possessor (*feet*)	0	0	0	0	0	0	0	0	0

significance. This item, which elicited the possessive by a contrastive construction, seemed easier for the younger members of the
middle-class group. The *whose* questions were more difficult, especially Item 2c. Several factors may have entered into the added
difficulty of this item. The fact that the word *clown* ends in a consonant, rather than a vowel, may have added to pronunciation

difficulties. The question *Whose feet are biggest?* is also a more complicated question, semantically and syntactically, than *Whose toy is this?*

Variants. An UNINFLECTED NOUN was the most common variant. As we will see in the discussion of nominalizations, it is possible that children interpret difficult constructions with *wh-* words as simpler question constructions. Here, for example, *The clown* would be a correct answer to the question *Who has the biggest feet?*. Similarly, processing *Whose toy is this?* as *Who has this toy?* (on the model of the frame sentence, *The boy has a train, the girl has a doll. . . .*) would lead to such responses as *The baby*. It is interesting that of the three items, the easiest was the one using the possessive pronoun *my* in the frame (*That's not my food*); the second easiest was the one using the *have* form (*The boy has a train*); the most difficult was the one using no previous possessive. As is the case with many of the items in this test, the ability to comprehend the linguistic frames that require a given structure is part of the developing ability that is being tapped.

There was a low incidence of responses with the POSSESSIVE PRONOUN *his* or *hers*—often accompanied by pointing. In most situations this demonstrative use of the pronoun is a valid response, and even on this test it is a syntactically adequate response to the *whose* question. However, since the pictures used were drawn so that pointing would be ambiguous, the response was not satisfactory in terms of communication of meaning. When it did occur, a probe question was used, so the responses remaining represent perseveration. In Item 2b, which furnished a definite article in the frame sentence, the pronominal form, for example: *It's the (his)*, did not occur.

In Item 2a, a very small proportion of younger children labeled the toy with a NOUN NOT REFERRING TO POSSESSOR, answering, for example. *A clown*—perhaps interpreting the frame as *Who (what) is this toy?*

Dialect Variation: Lower-Class White

Target. Lower-class white children showed significantly less use of the target POSSESSIVE forms in every age group and did not demonstrate the marked superiority on the contrastive stress item (Item 2b: *monkey's*) that the middle-class children showed.

Variants. The UNINFLECTED NOUN was much more common among the lower-class white children than among the middle-class children; differences in this response across the groups usually reached statistical significance. The other substitutions (pronominal forms or labeling responses) were as rare as in the middle-class sample.

Dialect Variation: Lower-Class Black

Target. The lower-class black children were more likely to use an uninflected noun than the POSSESSIVE. There was no developmental trend toward inflection, as there was in the other two groups. The inflected form did not typify lower-class black speech at any of the ages tested.

Variants. The persistently high rate of frequency of the UNINFLECTED NOUN among blacks, especially at age 5, seems to indicate that in black speech this form is a viable alternative. Labov (1970) reports that in adult Black English Vernacular, the possessive inflection is omitted in full possessive noun + noun constructions but always occurs in elliptical constructions: *baby toy, baby's*. In our group of 5-year-olds, 17 responses were given in the full form; of these, 7 (or 41 percent) were inflected and 10 (59 percent) uninflected. Of 59 elliptical responses, 24 (again 41 percent) were inflected and 35 (59 percent) uninflected. The adult Black English Vernacular use of the inflection with the elliptical possessive does not appear to be characteristic of children of this age, since there was the same high proportion (60 percent) of uninflected responses in elliptical constructions as in full noun + noun constructions.

Summary

The noun + possessive structure showed consistent development in both white groups, though the level of usage was higher among the middle-class children. In contrast, the lower-class black group tended to prefer the uninflected form at all ages. A large minority of this group, however, used the inflected form as well.

POSSESSIVE PRONOUN

As pointed out in the discussion of noun + possessive, there is some controversy about the linguistic derivation of possessive forms (Stockwell, Schachter, and Partee, 1973). Some linguists derive possessives from underlying *have* clauses; others derive at least some possessives from underlying case relationships. Brown favors the second approach, on the basis of his own data (1973), that of Bloom (1970), and the data of others who have found utterances with possessive meaning very early in child speech. These expressions of possession antedate both full *have* constructions and conventional surface expression of possession, such as noun inflection or possessive pronouns.

Despite the evidence of early command of possessive meaning, the surface structures indicating possession in English are complex and require detailed knowledge of the rules on the part of the speaker. We have already discussed some of the issues in inflection of nouns for the possessive. Another problem for a learner is the alternation between some pronominal forms, where a different form of the pronoun is used when the noun is deleted (*I ate my cake* versus *I ate mine; They took their car* versus *They took theirs*, etc.). A child must learn these alternatives, even though other forms such as *his*, or inflected nouns such as *Jack's*, have the same form whether in the full possessive + noun form or in the elliptical form.

The child's task in our item was to produce a form that was (1) possessive, thus retaining the parallelism of the frame sentence; (2) plural, thus matching the picture; and (3) appropriate for sentence-final position, thus completing the copula clause begun in the frame.

The predicate possessive pronoun was tested with the following item:

Item 3a: These children have lots of pets. The turtle is hers, the bird is his, and the dog is _____ (theirs).

The results on this item are presented in Table 4.

Table 4

Possessive pronoun—Percentages of responses on Item 3a

	Middle-class white			Lower-class white			Lower-class black		
Age:	3	4	5	3	4	5	3	4	5
N:	104	95	104	27	24	26	23	36	23
The turtle is hers, the bird is his, and the dog is _____.									
Possessive plural pronoun (*theirs*)	19	24	43	8	17	30	0	3	0
Several possessive singular pronouns (*his and his and hers*)	6	6	4	0	12	15	22	30	7
Possessive plural noun (*the children's*)	8	4	4	0	4	4	0	0	4
Possessive singular pronoun (*his, hers*)	28	13	8	46	8	4	48	22	19
Noun with possessive omitted (*the children*)	14	13	9	12	13	7	4	0	15
Plural pronoun uninflected for possession (*all of them, those, they, these*)	12	31	26	4	38	30	9	31	37
Incorrect possessive (*all three of them's, him's*)	7	6	6	8	0	11	4	11	11
Other	4	3	1	23	8	0	13	3	7

Standard English Acquisition: Middle-Class White

Target. The target POSSESSIVE PLURAL PRONOUN (*theirs*) evidenced a clear developmental trend among middle-class white children, chiefly after age 4. The response using SEVERAL POSSESSIVE SINGULAR PRONOUNS (*his and his and hers*)—often accompanied by pointing to each of the three pictured children—was far less frequent.

Variants. A few children avoided the target pronominal and substituted a POSSESSIVE PLURAL NOUN, such as *those children's* or
everybody's. A few others gave nouns such as *the kids* which might
or might not have indicated both possession and plurality.

The POSSESSIVE SINGULAR PRONOUN *his* or *hers* was given by
a substantial number of younger children. We thought that perhaps
children giving this response knew the plural possessive but were
interpreting the picture to mean that only one of the children owned
the dog. Therefore a probe question was given. Most of the 4- and 5-
year-olds changed their responses after the probe question; however,
many 3-year-olds perseverated in the response, despite the indication that all three children were owners of the dog.

A fairly stable proportion of the children marked the plurality of
ownership but not the possessive. Some used a NOUN such as *the
children*. The proportion of children giving this response is similar
to the proportions giving uninflected nouns for Items 2a and 2b, two
of the three noun + possessive items. In addition, a few children
gave PLURAL PRONOUNS uninflected for possession, such as *all
three of them* or *these*.

A steady, low percentage of children gave what were probably
INCORRECT POSSESSIVE responses, such as *all three of them's*. Fi-
nally, there were a few syntactically irrelevant responses, such as
Here's a dog.

Dialect Variation: Lower-Class White

Target and variants. In the lower-class white group, target POS-
SESSIVE PLURAL PRONOUN responses (*theirs*) were fewer than in
the middle-class group, but differences did not reach significance.

The proportion of 3-year-olds in this sample who perseverated
with a POSSESSIVE SINGULAR PRONOUN response was larger than
among middle-class children of the same age.

Dialect Variation: Lower-Class Black

Target and variants. The lower-class black group essentially did
not produce the target POSSESSIVE PLURAL PRONOUN (*theirs*)
throughout the age range tested.

Some differences from the other two groups can be seen in the pattern of variations as well. The POSSESSIVE SINGULAR PRONOUN persisted more among these children, and there was also heavy use of SEVERAL POSSESSIVE SINGULAR PRONOUNS (his and his and hers). Of the minority who used nouns rather than pronouns, most in the lower-class black group produced UNINFLECTED NOUNS, as they did on the items testing noun inflections for possessives (2a, 2b, and 2c). Among this group, the response types that increased most with age were the ones marking plurality (but not possession); these remained high or increased for the other two groups as well. Other than indicating a clear difference between lower-class black children and the two other groups in the pattern of usage of this structure, our data do not augment the available literature on possessive structures in the acquisition of Black English Vernacular.

Summary

Middle-class white children were less successful in completing this possessive item, which called for a predicate plural possessive form, than they were in completing the singular noun + possessive items. Most children seemed to understand the meaning and gave responses referring to the possessors, but even at age 5 only about half of them were able to produce the plural possessive. Lower-class white children performed similarly. Among lower-class black children, on the other hand, the rate of usage of the target theirs did not increase with age.

The variations were surprisingly consistent across groups. In all three groups, the favored variation among 3-year-olds referred to possession but not plurality (his). This variation decreased with age, while another—referring to plurality but not possession (all three of them)—increased with age.

SUBJECT PRONOUNS: GENDER

English pronouns are selected according to number, person, and gender (he, she, they, I, we, you, it) and are further inflected for case (he, him, his, etc.). According to Menyuk (1969), the earliest pronoun is it, usually in the predicate (as in Mommy try it). She reports that kindergarten-age children frequently do not observe selectional constraints, such as gender, or animate-inanimate distinctions, (as in their use of *it* to refer to *father*). Later—among first-graders in Menyuk's sample—redundancies are a more frequent variation (as in *He Blacky washed hisself,* using both noun and pronoun). Brown (1973) notes a number of early (2-year-old) segmentation errors with the form *it*; his subject Adam used *its* as a nominative form of the objective *it,* and other children segmented *it* with the verb as in *turniting off.*

Both Brown (1973) and Bloom (1968) report that, in the 2-year-olds they studied, forms such as *I, one,* and *my* all occurred as sentence subjects, with the nominative *I* most frequent. Because of the relatively low frequency of these forms in their samples, it is difficult to tell what features were governing the selection of pronouns in their subjects.

Since there was evidence for fairly early acquisition of person distinctions (*I* versus *it*) and case distinctions (*I* versus *me,* or Adam's overgeneralization of *its* versus *it*), our items focused on the gender distinction that is marked in third person subject pronouns (as well as in possessive and object forms). We were interested in whether or not children would use forms of the wrong gender, case, person, or number on their way to the selection of pronouns in conformity with Standard English.

Subject pronouns were assessed by the following items:

Item 4a: Everyday, when John gets sleepy, _____ (he [goes to bed, etc.]).
Item 4b: Everyday, when Mary gets hungry, _____ (she [eats, etc.]).

The results on these two items are outlined in Table 5.

Standard English Acquisition: Middle-Class White

Target. In the middle-class white group, the target forms appeared fairly early, with about 70 percent of even the 3-year-olds using the SUBJECT PRONOUN (CORRECT GENDER). Development was consistent, and the items were notably parallel.

Variants. OMISSION OF THE PRONOUN was the most common variation. With increasing age, omission declined significantly for the masculine pronoun, but not for the feminine. Frequency of omis-

Table 5

Subject pronouns: gender—Percentages of responses on
Items 4a and 4b

	Middle-class white			Lower-class white			Lower-class black		
Age:	3	4	5	3	4	5	3	4	5
N:	106	100	104	25	24	27	23	35	26
(a) When John gets sleepy, _____.									
Subject pronoun, correct gender (he)	73	86	94	38	63	74	52	61	67
Pronoun omitted	25	14	6	36	33	22	39	34	23
Object pronoun, correct gender (him)	1	1	0	0	4	0	8	0	8
Adjective	1	0	0	16	0	0	0	0	4
Incorrect gender subject pronoun (she)	0	0	0	0	0	0	4	0	0
Other	0	0	0	8	0	4	0	3	0
N:	106	100	104	25	24	27	23	36	27
(b) When Mary gets hungry, _____.									
Subject pronoun, correct gender (she)	65	80	87	36	54	74	26	56	63
Pronoun omitted	19	11	11	16	21	15	52	19	15
Object pronoun, correct gender (her)	5	5	2	20	13	11	13	19	15
Adjective	1	0	0	16	8	0	4	0	4
Incorrect gender subject pronoun (he)	8	3	1	8	4	0	4	3	4
Other	0	0	0	4	0	0	0	3	0

sion did go in the same direction for the feminine pronoun, so this may not be an important difference. However, other variations tended to be concentrated in the feminine form item as well. For example, a small proportion of children used the incorrect case form, that is, the OBJECT PRONOUN (her), or the incorrect GENDER (he), for the feminine pronoun. Menyuk's claim that gender distinctions are often not observed is supported slightly, but only for the feminine item. We had no instances of a child ignoring the animate-inanimate distinction by using it for either item.

It appears that most middle-class children, even at 3, control the use of pronouns of different gender for the subject position, but that the feminine pronoun may be acquired slightly later than the masculine.

Dialect Variation: Lower-Class White

Target. Target usage of the CORRECT GENDER SUBJECT PRO-NOUN was lower, usually significantly so, in the lower-class white group than in the middle-class group. However, by age 5, 75 percent of this group had attained the target for both masculine and feminine forms.

Variants. There were more substitutions of OBJECT PRONOUN for the feminine than for the masculine frame. Responding with an ADJECTIVE, usually from the story frame, probably indicated inability to interpret the frame sentence.

Dialect Variation: Lower-Class Black

Target. In the lower-class black groups, developmental use of the CORRECT GENDER SUBJECT PRONOUN paralleled that of the lower-class white group, except for a trend showing earlier emergence of the masculine than of the feminine form in the black children. The masculine target was given by 50 percent of black 3-year-olds, the feminine target by only 25 percent of them.

Variants. There were no significant racial variations. The lower-class black children also showed the tendency found in the lower-class white children to substitute an OBJECT PRONOUN in the subject position. About 15 percent of both lower-class groups gave this response.

Summary

In general, we can conclude that most middle-class children control the use of pronouns of different genders for the subject position by the age of 3. Over half of the lower-class children control them by the age of 4. The most frequent variation, omission, tends to drop out with age. There are no significant lower-class white versus lower-class black differences, but there is a tendency in both groups to use the form *her* as the feminine subject pronoun—around 15 percent of the time. This variation is used by a lower percentage of middle-class children.

Several differences were noted between the masculine and feminine items: greater frequency of substitution of *her* for *she* than of *him* for *he*; slightly lower levels of target acquisition in the case of *she* than of *he*; and slightly greater frequency of other variations for the feminine pronoun, including substitution of the masculine form *he*. We see, then, several indications that the masculine pronoun is acquired somewhat before the feminine pronoun by some children in all groups.

DETERMINER + COUNT NOUN
OR MASS NOUN

Two classes of nouns in English require rather different syntactic agreements. Count nouns, such as *toy*, can be inflected for plural, can occur with numerals, and can occur with plural verb forms, as in *Three toys are in the sandbox*. Mass nouns, such as *attention* or *water*, often refer to concepts of indefinite extension; they occur with a different set of determiners (*some, much* instead of *a, many*), do not inflect for the plural form, and do not occur with numerals: *Some sand is in the sandbox*. There are also variable nouns, which occur with either set of forms according to whether units or indefinite amounts are the focus: *Do you want some beer?* versus *Do you want a beer?* or *Do you want two beers?*

The "units" versus "indefinite amount" distinction cannot be taken as an ironclad rule, however. Many pairs exist which demonstrate that the boundaries are rather vague; *some peas* (count) versus *some corn* (mass), *a pile of logs* (count) versus *a pile of wood* (mass). [Note also that languages do not always agree; compare English *some grapes* (count) with French *du raisin* (mass)]. A child learning this distinction thus can note the correlation but must learn many usages individually. Cognitively, it is a classification skill that he must learn, with classes based partly on semantic criteria and partly on linguistic convention.

In order to test acquisition of the distinction between mass and count nouns, the language production test utilized the determiners *much* (which occurs with mass nouns) and *many* (which occurs with plural count nouns). The development of the noun phrase into "determiner + noun" has been discussed by Brown (1973) and by Menyuk (1969). Each reports use of both the definite article (the) and the indefinite article (a.); demonstrative this, that; and quantifiers some and more before the age of 3. We expected the children to know the general meaning of much and many by the age of 3; the test assessed their ability to select the right kind of noun, count or mass, for the given linguistic frame. The item used [with two appropriate pictures, (1) and (2)] was the following:

Item 5a:
(1) Look at this sandbox. There's lots of sand and lots of toys in it. Joe said, "There's no room for me in my sandbox. There's so many _____ (toys, things). And there's so much _____ (sand, junk).
(2) Now Joe can get into his sandbox. There's not so much _____ (sand) and not so many _____ (toys).

In this item, the child is provided with possible nouns, sand (mass noun) and toys (count noun inflected for plural), in the frame story. The child's task is to choose a count noun or mass noun to go with the given determiner, much or many.

During the pretesting phase, this item was presented in a slightly different form, so that the correct sequence was count-mass-count-mass. Many children said toys first and sand second, then repeated the same order for the second picture. We were concerned that some of them might each time be responding first to the most salient element in the picture, the toys. Then they might keep the same order (toys-sand), on the model of a regularity in English discourse—which is that when items are repeated, they are repeated in the same order. This regularity is a very common convention in children's stories; for example, in The Three Bears, the order is almost always Papa Bear, then Mama Bear, and finally Baby Bear. A child who happened to say toys first and then followed this regularity could get all four items correct without knowing anything about selecting count versus mass nouns. We decided, therefore, to reverse one pair and to give the child credit for knowing the structure only if he employed the correct type of noun in all four responses.

Another problem with this item involved the verb agreement. We had two options. We could keep the form there's even when a count noun followed, as in there's so many toys, which is acceptable in many dialects of English. This would force the child to attend to the quantifier *much* or *many* and would avoid the additional cue of the plural verb form (*are*). We could change to *there're* for the count noun, as in *there're so many toys*, which is preferred in some dialects. The extra cue, however, would blur the question; the child might be responding to the plural verb rather than to the restrictions imposed by the quantifier. We chose the first option so that a correct response would clearly indicate agreement with the quantifier. However, the reader should keep in mind that children who speak dialects favoring *there're* for count nouns might be receiving conflicting cues for the first of the four responses. A correct answer is therefore interpretable as supporting quantifier comprehension. But an incorrect one does not necessarily mean that the child did not understand the quantifier.

The responses of the three samples to the determiner + count noun or mass noun item are summarized in Table 6.

Standard English Acquisition: Middle-Class White

Target. The middle-class group showed a significant development toward the target QUANTIFIER AGREEMENT *many toys, much sand; much sand, many toys.* Even at age 5, however, fewer than 40 percent of the group were giving correct responses.

Variants. One variant pattern was used at least as frequently as the target and increased through age 5. This was the pattern of repeating the SAME ORDER. We looked at several hypotheses to explain this middle-class increase in repeating the same order. One possibility was that the toys were mentioned first for both pictures because of their salience. In other items, however, dependence on the picture was found to decrease rather than increase with age. For example, responses like *ears* to the picture of the elephant on Item 6b or *He does have wings* to the counterfactual Item 13c were less common among the older children. For this reason we think that a conflicting rule may be a more likely explanation for the *toys-sand-toys-sand pattern.* These middle-class children may be acquiring the discourse pattern described earlier, along with their other language knowledge, and at these ages it may be just as powerful as the quantifier agreement rule.

Table 6

Determiner + count noun or mass noun—Percentages of
responses on Item 5a

	Middle-class white			Lower-class white			Lower-class black		
Age:	3	4	5	3	4	5	3	4	5
N:	106	100	104	22	24	27	22	34	25
There's so many _____. And there's so much _____. Now . . . there's not so much _____ and not so many _____.									
Quantifier agreement correct	17	31	37	0	8	70	4	21	48
Count nouns only or mass nouns only	15	11	4	41	50	0	55	26	16
Same order both pictures	15	36	42	4	8	11	9	18	8
Unsystematic combination	52	22	17	55	32	19	32	35	28

We thought that one of the reasons for using an alternative rule
might lie in the conflict between *is* and *many* in *there's so many*
(toys) in the first item, and that switching to *there are so many* might
have avoided a cue conflict for some children. Our Item 10a, which
required the plural of the copula *be*, was correctly completed by over
60 percent of the middle-class 3-year-olds and over 80 percent of the
5-year-olds, so we knew that this group controlled number in the *be*
forms. The best comparison with our middle-class sample in these
tests was the group of middle-class white New Zealand children
tested by Potts and Lewthwaite (forthcoming), as part of a larger
study of language development in various New Zealand ethnic
groups. In that study, this item was administered in the form *There's*
no room for me in my sandbox because of so many–(toys) etc.
Twenty-five children at each of the ages, 4, 5, and 6, were tested. The
results are summarized in Table 7.

It is clear that avoiding the cue conflict of *is* + *many* does not aid
the target at all; in fact, the New Zealand sample used the same order
to an even greater extent than the United States sample, and there
was no reduction in the incidence of this response at age 6. The

Table 7

Determiner + count noun or mass noun—A comparison
of middle-class white children's responses: United States
and New Zealand

		United States		
	Age:	3	4	5
	N:	106	100	104
There's so many _____. And there's so much _____. Now . . . there's not so much _____. and not so many _____.*				
Quantifier agreement correct		17	31	37
Count nouns only or mass nouns only		15	11	4
Same order both pictures		15	36	42
Unsystematic combinations		52	22	17

		New Zealand		
	Age:	4	5	6
	N:	25	25	25
There's no room . . . because of so many _____ and so much _____. Now . . . because of so much _____ and so many _____.†				
Quantifier agreement correct		4	12	20
Count nouns only or mass nouns only		16	4	16
Same order both pictures		56	60	60
Unsystematic combinations		24	24	4

*Item 5a.
†Modified version of Item 5a.

same-order rule is followed with or without conflicting agreement in the stem. Further research is necessary to discover whether the children are being guided by discourse regularity; also, to discover the age at which the quantifier agreement rule is given higher priority by most middle-class children.

The pattern given by over half of the middle-class 3-year-olds was UNSYSTEMATIC COMBINATION—a response that drops sharply with age. It was given by about one-quarter of middle-class 4-year-olds and continued to decrease at age 5. A decrease with age is also apparent for the response giving COUNT NOUNS ONLY or MASS NOUNS ONLY.

Dialect Variation: Lower-Class White

Target. A very rapid development of the target QUANTIFIER AGREEMENT response between ages 4 and 5 characterized the lower-class white sample; by age 5, it was nearly twice as common as in the middle-class group at age 5. A possible explanation is that the alternate rule we have postulated, the discourse regularity that leads to keeping the same order, is not part of this group's language experience. Perhaps lower-class children are exposed to fewer stories than are middle-class children. Thus, acquisition of the quantifier agreement rule would be the only factor influencing noun selection for these lower-class children.

Our other hypothesis, that the middle-class children were responding to the perceptual salience of the toys in each picture, is more difficult to adapt to these lower-class curves. It is possible that there are differences in cognitive strategies between the two groups, but there is no reason to predict it in this case. Lack of exposure to same-order regularity seems more likely.

Variants. The most common variant among lower-class white 3-year-olds, as among middle class 3-year-olds, was UNSYSTEMATIC COMBINATION. The response declined sharply with age, as it did in the middle-class group. Use of COUNT NOUNS ONLY or MASS NOUNS ONLY was significantly more common among lower-class white 3- and 4-year-olds than among their middle-class counterparts. This type of response plummeted with age: it was given by half of the 4-year-olds, none of the 5-year-olds. The SAME-ORDER response, so common in the middle-class children, was given by only 10 percent of lower-class white 5-year-olds, the majority of whom preferred the target form.

Dialect Variation: Lower-Class Black

Target. Among the lower-class black children we again found a strong developmental trend in acquisition of the QUANTIFIER AGREEMENT response, with a 5-year-old level equal to or better than that of the middle-class sample.

Variants. UNSYSTEMATIC COMBINATION was a less common variant at age 3 than in the other groups but did not decline so rapidly with age. As was the case with the lower-class white children,

COUNT NOUNS ONLY or MASS NOUNS ONLY variants were used by over half of the black 3-year-olds but decreased with age. SAME-ORDER responses were given by a relatively small percentage of this group.

Summary

In general, we may say that the selection of count or mass nouns to agree with *much* or *many* was infrequent among 3-year-olds, emerged at 4, and developed more slowly thereafter in the middle-class white and lower-class black groups than in the lower-class white group. Using the same type of noun (count or mass) through-out was common among 3- and 4-year-olds but was less frequent at age 5; the same was true of unsystematic variations. The increase of same-order responses (*many* [*toys*], *much* [*sand*]; *much* [*toys*], *many* [*sand*]) in middle-class children, not shared by the lower-class groups, suggests the possibility that a same-order convention in stories had been learned by the middle-class children and that this regularity conflicted with the determiner agreement rule in this particular story frame.

DIRECT AND INDIRECT OBJECTS

An English sentence such as *Dad gave a balloon to Dick* involves an agent (Dad), an object (*balloon*), and a recipient or dative (*Dick*). Traditionally, in surface structure, the object has been called direct object and the recipient indirect object. We will continue to use this terminology here. Our assumption is that objective relationships are understood early (Brown, 1973); datives are rarer in early production, but begin to emerge after the basic verb relations (Bloom, Lightbown, and Hood, 1975). Our concern here is with the expression in the surface form.

There is an alternative form for expressing the relationships listed above, as in *Dad gave Dick a balloon*. Most linguists have tended to produce descriptions of this structure that are derivationally more complex than the first (Stockwell, Schachter, and Partee, 1973). The derivation involves inverting the positions of the direct and indirect objects and deleting the preposition associated with the indirect object.

A problem with constructing items to tap the child's command of direct and indirect objects is that they are optional, not obligatory, for most English verbs. Even *give*, which requires both objects in most contexts, occasionally occurs in contexts where one or the other can be deleted: *He gave to the church, He gave ten dollars, He gave ten dollars to the church.* In our pilot work we found that some items were unsuitable for the test because such a large proportion of children responded as though such deletion were always acceptable. For example, in the pilot item *Yesterday was Dick's birthday, so Dad gave a balloon _____,* most adults feel that a recipient such as *to him* should follow. Among the children, however, the most common pilot response was simply a murmur of agreement, "mm-hmm." Apparently the necessity for expressing the surface indirect object, which is felt strongly by most adults in this context, develops later. In this story context, the recipient may be so self-evident and semantically unnecessary that the children do not add it. Altering the stem slightly, however, resulted in Item 6c (discussed later) which elicited both objects from over 50 percent of the standardization group 3-year-olds.

We were able to construct four items that elicited the object forms fairly consistently. In two, the direct object was supplied in the frame and the child was required to add *to* + indirect object noun phrase. In the other two, the child had to supply both the direct and the indirect objects.

INDIRECT OBJECT: *TO* + NOUN PHRASE

The child's ability to produce the preposition + noun phrase form of the indirect object, considered by most analyses to be derivationally simpler than the inverted form, was assessed with the following items:

Item 6a: Bill found a bird's nest outside in a tree. He showed it _____ (to his friends).

Item 6b: Sue went to see an elephant in the zoo. She got some peanuts and gave them _____ (to him).

The responses of the children on these items are summarized in Table 8.

Table 8

Indirect object: *to* + noun phrase—Percentages of
responses on Items 6a and 6b

	Middle-class white			Lower-class white			Lower-class black		
Age:	3	4	5	3	4	5	3	4	5
N:	106	100	104	26	24	27	23	36	26

(a) *He showed it* _____.
  Indirect object:
    to + noun phrase (*to
    the boys, to him, for
    the boys*)

to + noun phrase	56	73	92	15	42	48	26	58	48
Noun not referring to recipient (eggs, nest)	10	4	0	12	17	4	9	3	0
Preposition omitted (boys, him)	8	5	2	27	13	15	17	11	11
Inappropriate prepositional phrase (in a boy, to the eggs, from the nest)	5	2	4	0	4	4	0	6	4
New clause or sentence (and there were eggs, yes)	11	6	2	27	25	7	17	17	15
Omission of indirect object (he showed a tree, he showed it)	8	8	0	19	0	15	30	0	19
Alternate form of indirect object (he showed them the eggs)	1	0	0	0	0	7	0	0	4
Other	2	0	0	0	0	0	0	4	0

(b) *She got some peanuts
and gave them* _____.
  Indirect object:

to + noun phrase (to the elephant, for the elephant)	57	75	75	12	42	70	57	47	52
Noun not referring to recipient (peanuts)	17	12	13	23	33	7	17	17	26
Preposition omitted (elephant, him)	12	9	2	15	8	4	4	3	4
Inappropriate prepositional phrase (in the mouth, in there)	3	1	1	4	4	7	0	6	11

Table 8—continued

	Middle-class white			Lower-class white			Lower-class black		
Age:	3	4	5	3	4	5	3	4	5
N:	106	100	104	26	24	27	23	36	26
New clause or sentence (and the elephant he opened his mouth)	1	0	1	8	0	0	0	0	0
Omission of indirect object (gave the peanuts)	0	0	1	15	4	0	4	0	0
Alternate form of indirect object (him the peanuts)	7	3	8	19	8	11	17	27	4
Other	4	0	0	4	0	0	0	0	4

Standard English Acquisition: Middle-Class White

Target. In the middle-class white group, the curves for acquisition of the INDIRECT OBJECT were different on the two items, perhaps because of the very different semantic contexts and the difficulty of interpreting the referent in Item 6b. Item 6a was easier for the middle-class group at age 5; Item 6b, although equally well controlled at 3 and 4, did not show any further improvement among the 5-year-olds.

Variants. *Preference for inverted form:* Children who did not give the target response were apparently interpreting the frame in a variety of ways. A fairly large proportion (10–17 percent) of 3-year-olds, and some 4- and 5-year-olds, completed the sentences with a NOUN NOT REFERRING TO THE RECIPIENT, such as He showed it (the nest) or She gave them (the peanuts). This may have been a redundant response, like an adult appositive with two expressions of the direct object. Alternatively, it may have been the result of interpreting the stem pronoun as an indirect object, and adding the direct object. This interpretation of the pronoun would not be compatible with the context pictures. Bill's friends in the picture are clearly human and plural, and should not be referred to with an inanimate singular pronoun; in the other item there is only one elephant in the picture and story. Similar gender or number errors did not occur in the simpler subject pronoun items. This response may indicate that, at least for the young children in the middle-class group, the supposedly more complex inverted form (*showed his friends a nest, gave him some peanuts*) was easier than the form with a prepositional phrase. On Item 6b, a few children used a similar strategy but restated the stem so they could give the ALTERNATE FORM OF THE INDIRECT OBJECT correctly, as in *She got some peanuts and gave them* (*gave him peanuts*) or . . . *gave them* (*him a peanut*). Again, this seems to indicate a preference for the inverted form. This finding substantiates a trend in Roeper's data (1973) on German-speaking children. Over one-third of his subjects, on a repetition task consisting of *give* + direct object + indirect object, placed the indirect object before the direct.

Other variants: Some children OMITTED THE PREPOSITION, responding *boys* or *his brothers*, etc. Others substituted an INAPPROPRIATE PREPOSITIONAL PHRASE such as *in the nose* or *from the bird's next.* Finally, there were children who began a NEW CLAUSE without first completing the frame, as in *He showed it* (*and there were eggs*).

Differences between give *and* show: The middle-class white group, unlike the other groups, did not demonstrate different interpretations of the syntactic requirements of *give* and *show*. The target, as noted earlier, was better for *show* than for *give* among 5-year-olds, and most variants occurred at similar rates for the two items. The data suggest that for this group *give* and *show* are parallel in their syntactic requirements.

Dialect Variation: Lower-Class White

Target. Although the 3- and 4-year-olds in the lower-class white group did not use the target INDIRECT OBJECT form as frequently as did their middle-class counterparts, by age 5 the proportions of the various responses were quite similar across classes for Item 6b, the *give* item. In contrast, Item 6a, the *show* item, did not elicit as many target responses from 5-year-olds.

Variants. *Preference for inverted form:* Again, a number of children used a NOUN NOT REFERRING TO THE RECIPIENT, or gave an ALTERNATE FORM OF THE INDIRECT OBJECT, especially on Item

6b. Like the middle-class children, those in this group also appear to prefer the inverted form.

Other variants: The only other common variant in this group was OMITTING THE PREPOSITION.

Differences between give *and* show: On Item 6a, the *show* item, common variants at age 5 were to OMIT THE INDIRECT OBJECT completely, or to start a NEW CLAUSE OR SENTENCE without referring to the recipients. These variants suggest that some children were interpreting *he showed it* as a complete sentence. It may be that in the form of English these children were learning, *show* does not require both objects in the surface form. *Give* apparently does require both, since so few of these 5-year-olds interpreted *and gave them* as complete in Item 6b. The hypothesis that the difference is probably due to the difference in verbs was supported by the results on the two remaining object items, 6c and 6d, to be reported later.

Dialect Variation: Lower-Class Black

Target. There was no clear developmental trend toward use of the target INDIRECT OBJECT structure in the lower-class black group as there was in the other two groups. Except for 3-year-olds on Item 6a, about half of the black children used the target structure at all ages for both items.

On Item 6b, the lower-class black 3-year-olds used target forms more than children of the same age in the lower-class white group; there were no other significant differences.

Variants. *Preference for inverted form:* On Item 6b, the lower-class black children, like the other two groups, produced evidence suggesting that the inverted order, indirect object + direct object, was preferred. A NOUN NOT REFERRING TO THE RECIPIENT and an ALTERNATE FORM OF THE INDIRECT OBJECT were again the most frequent variants for the *give* (but not the *show*) item.

Other variants: The PREPOSITION WAS OMITTED on the *show* item by over 10 percent of these children at all ages. On the same item, nearly one-third of the 3-year-olds OMITTED THE INDIRECT OBJECT, as in (*He showed it*).

Differences between give *and* show: As in the case of the lower-class white group, the most frequent variants on Item 6a, the *show* item, were OMISSION OF THE INDIRECT OBJECT or starting a NEW CLAUSE OR SENTENCE without mentioning the recipient. These responses again were rare on the give item and suggest that show may not require both objects in the dialect these children are learning.

INDIRECT OBJECT + DIRECT OBJECT

Two items were constructed to assess the child's ability to produce both the direct and the indirect object. We hoped they would offer a high probability of drawing responses that would invert the direct and the indirect object and consequently delete the preposition to. As already noted, most linguists suggest that this inversion and deletion results in a more complicated structure than the alternative form discussed in the preceding subsection. The items were the following:

Item 6c: Yesterday was Dick's birthday. Dad gave_____ (him a balloon).
Item 6d: Ann was very cold, so Mother gave _____ (her a sweater).

The responses of the children to these items are summarized in Table 9.

Standard English Acquisition: Middle-Class White

Target. The ability to use the INDIRECT OBJECT + DIRECT OBJECT in inverted form had been developed by over half of the 3- and 4-year-olds and 70–80 percent of the 5-year-olds in the middle-class white sample. Another Standard English form, the basic uninverted DIRECT OBJECT + to + INDIRECT OBJECT form, was used by less than 12 percent of the children.

Variants. The most common variation was OMISSION OF THE INDIRECT OBJECT, resulting in such responses as Dad gave (a balloon). As noted above, the majority of English verbs (including give in some circumstances) do not require two objects, so the prevalence of this omission at the young ages was not surprising.

A very few children used a SUBJECT FORM OF THE INDIRECT OBJECT, such as he a balloon, and a few others began a NEW SENTENCE on Item 6d. An interesting but very rare response was a

Table 9

Indirect object + direct object—Percentages of responses
on Items 6c and 6d

		Middle-class white			Lower-class white			Lower-class black		
	Age:	3	4	5	3	4	5	3	4	5
	N:	103	99	104	24	24	27	23	36	27
(c) *Dad gave* _____.										
Indirect object + direct object (*him a balloon, Dick a balloon*)		58	58	70	54	54	78	30	53	44
Direct object + *to* + indirect object (*a balloon to him*)		7	8	12	4	4	11	0	3	4
Omission of indirect object (*a balloon*)		31	31	17	37	42	11	61	31	41
Subject form of indirect object (*he a balloon*)		2	1	1	4	0	0	9	14	11
New sentence		0	0	0	0	0	0	0	0	0
Wrong preposition or words inverted		0	0	0	0	0	0	0	0	0
	N:	103	100	104	25	24	27	23	36	26
(d) *Mother gave* _____.										
Indirect object + direct object (*her a sweater, Ann a sweater*)		66	70	79	28	75	85	43	75	78
Direct object + *to* + indirect object (*a sweater to her*)		3	2	7	0	0	0	0	0	0
Omission of indirect object (*a sweater*)		29	24	13	48	25	11	52	25	11
Subject form of indirect object (*she a sweater*)		0	1	0	4	0	0	0	0	2
New sentence		1	1	1	16	0	4	4	0	8
Wrong preposition or words inverted		1	2	0	4	0	0	0	0	0

sweater her. This might be either a re-inversion of the inverted *her a sweater* form or deletion of the preposition without inversion, depending on which indirect object construction was intended. Sometimes the WRONG PREPOSITION was used, as in *a sweater for her.*

Dialect Variation: Lower-Class White

Target. Acquisition curves were steeper for the lower-class white group than for the middle-class white group, since fewer 3-year-olds used the target INDIRECT OBJECT + DIRECT OBJECT forms and more 5-year-olds used them, though only the 3-year-old result on 6d was significant.

Variants. There were no significant differences between this group and the middle-class white group, except that 3-year-olds OMITTED THE INDIRECT OBJECT more often on Item 6d.

Dialect Variation: Lower-Class Black

Target. Fewer black than white 5-year-olds gave the target INDIRECT OBJECT + DIRECT OBJECT response on Item 6c. But the acquisition curve for 6d was similar to that of the white groups.

Variants. On Item 6c, about 10 percent of the black children gave the response *he a balloon*, using the SUBJECT FORM OF THE INDIRECT OBJECT. Indeed, the black 5-year-olds OMITTED THE INDIRECT OBJECT significantly more often on the balloon item (6c) than they themselves did on the sweater item (6d). Otherwise, the general pattern of results was similar to the pattern of the lower-class white group.

Summary

Linguists working with adult English usually posit somewhat different derivations for the two surface orders of indirect and direct object sentences. Descriptively, the simplest surface order is subject–verb–direct object–indirect object; a more complex derivation is generally provided for the inverted subject–verb–indirect object–direct object order. If this inverted order is psychologically more complex for children, we would expect it to be learned later.

This result was found only for the *show* item for middle-class white children. Holding the verb constant as *give*, we found no support for this hypothesis. The indirect object *give* item and the two indirect object + direct object *give* items were produced correctly by similar proportions of children at each age. If anything, there was a tendency for children to prefer the inverted form with indirect object first, since, in the indirect object items, a number of them interpreted the direct object pronoun given by the examiner as indirect object, and others restated the stem. The indirect object + direct object items offered the child much more freedom; the item could be completed either with inverted indirect object + direct object, as *Dad gave (him a balloon)* or direct object + indirect object, as *Dad gave (a balloon to him)*. In fact, the second option was taken by only a few children. We must conclude that, at least in these *give* contexts, the supposedly more complex form is more frequently used.

The most common variation across all four items was the omission of the indirect object. As pointed out, the model for this overgeneralization could lie in the fact that the majority of verbs in English do not require two objects.

RECIPROCAL

In addition to structures that indicate action affecting someone other than the self, such as *We entertained them*, two structures in English indicate specific types of involvement of the participants themselves. For example, the reciprocal *We entertained each other* means that each person involved entertained the others but did not entertain himself. On the other hand, the reflexive *We entertained ourselves* means that each person entertained himself but did not necessarily entertain anyone else (although this possibility is not excluded).

Reciprocal pronouns are a special case of linguistic transformation deriving from the pronominalization transformation. In the pronominalization transformation, the referential index of the noun phrase must be taken into account. For the reciprocal, the noun phrase is replaced with a pronoun that is coreferential with a noun phrase in the same clause. Similarly, the reflexive form adds the reflexive transformation to the pronoun that is coreferential with the noun phrase in the same clause (Langendoen, 1969).

Originally we had hoped to include both reflexive and reciprocal structures, since we thought there might be some interesting over-generalizations of one form to the other. Unfortunately, the reflexive item we tested, which required *himself*, had to be dropped from the test because it turned out to be useless as a developmental index. The source of its poor predictive power may in itself be interesting developmentally, however. The problem was that middle-class 3-year-olds on the pilot test tended to use the correct *himself* in the frame *He can dress*_____ (*himself*) as often as did the 5-year-olds. In between, however, the 4-year-olds were using it *less* than were the 3-year-olds. The reason appeared to be that the form *hisself* was increasing at this age (and still occurred frequently among 5-year-olds). This finding, if replicated, suggests that some 3-year-olds may be imitating a lexical item *himself*, which they have heard as an individual word, but that the older children are integrating it into a reflexive pronoun system. The first and second person reflexive pronouns, *myself* (*ourselves*) and *yourself* (*yourselves*), have the surface form possessive pronoun + *self* (*selves*). The third person *itself* and *herself* are ambiguous—they could be possessive pronoun + *self* (*its* + *self*, *her* + *self*) or object pronoun + *self* (*it* + *self*, *her* + *self*). However, the forms *himself* and *themselves* have to be object pronoun + *self* (*selves*). If possessive pronoun forms are used instead, we get *hisself* and *theirselves*—and these are just the forms our 4- and 5-year-old pilot subjects gave most frequently. Menyuk (1969) also reports that these forms occurred frequently in her sample. Although we had to drop the reflexive item from our test, we hope that others will be able to follow up this interesting problem.

The reciprocal item was more successful, in terms of both consistency and developmental trend. The item we used to test for the reciprocal structure was the following:

Item 7a: Sometimes when dogs see other dogs, they bark. These dogs are barking at _____ (each other).

The results on this item are presented in Table 10.

Table 10

Reciprocal—Percentages of responses on Item 7a

	Middle-class white			Lower-class white			Lower-class black		
Age:	3	4	5	3	4	5	3	4	5
N:	98	97	104	19	24	27	21	34	26
These dogs are barking at _____.									
Reciprocal (*each other*)	25	37	63	4	8	37	0	20	31
Singular noun or pronoun (*that dog, him*)	53	33	26	37	54	41	24	47	19
Verb phrase or clause (*playing, they playing*)	15	10	3	47	29	15	62	30	23
Dual pronoun or phrase (*both*)	3	12	4	5	4	4	0	0	11
Separate reference to both agents (*that dog and that dog*)	2	3	1	0	0	4	10	3	11
Reflexive pronoun (*themselves*)	2	4	3	5	4	0	4	0	4

Standard English Acquisition: Middle-Class White

Target. The trends for the RECIPROCAL structure were clearly developmental for the middle-class group. These children attained control in a pattern that started with one-fourth of the 3-year-olds, moved to one-third of the 4-year-olds, and then spurted to two-thirds of the 5-year-olds.

Variants. The most common deviation was the substitution of a SINGULAR NOUN OR PRONOUN referring to only one of the agents, such as *that dog* or *him*. Half of the 3-year-olds gave this response, but the incidence dropped to only one-fourth of the 5-year-olds. For this reason we feel supported in our judgment that the best interpretation of the picture was that both animals were barking, not just one, and that the single-agent response probably reflects a lack of linguistic resources rather than an alternative interpretation of an ambiguous picture. These children were able to supply an object for *barking at* but not the more complex reciprocal.

What seems to be an even more primitive response—a VERB PHRASE OR CLAUSE, such as *playing* or *they playing*—also tended to decline with age. This response seems to indicate a complete inability to stay within the original frame, even to the extent of supplying an object.

The last three responses listed in Table 10, although relatively low in frequency, did not decrease across the range tested. The fact that they did not simply drop out with age indicates that they are perhaps more "advanced" variations on the way to development of the Standard English form *each other*. The DUAL PRONOUN OR PHRASE (*both*) and SEPARATE REFERENCE TO BOTH AGENTS (*that dog and that dog*) indicate an effort by the child specifically to include the two agents in the picture. *Both*, which includes the two agents in a single lexical item, may be the more advanced response of the two.

Very few children gave a REFLEXIVE PRONOUN response (*themselves*). The majority of children did not confuse the self-included versus self-excluded dimension.

Dialect Variation: Lower-Class White

Target and variants. Significantly fewer lower-class white children than middle-class children used the target RECIPROCAL structure across all ages tested. Instead, more of the lower-class children used a VERB PHRASE OR CLAUSE, though the response decreased at ages 4 and 5. The 4- and 5-year-olds in this group used SINGULAR NOUN objects to a greater extent than did their middle-class counterparts.

Dialect Variation: Lower-Class Black

Target and variants. No significant race variations were found. In gereral, the results for the lower-class black group echoed those for the lower-class white group. There was an increase in the target RECIPROCAL (*each other*), from no usage by the 3-year-olds to usage by one-third of the 5-year-olds.

The lower-class black children showed steady or increasing proportions of such "advanced" errors as the DUAL PRONOUN OR

PHRASE (*both*), and decreasing proportions of the more primitive responses of a new clause or a noun referring to only one agent.

Summary

The reciprocal construction showed increasing use with development in all of our groups. The younger children frequently gave a response referring to only one of the two agents; some children in each group gave more advanced responses referring to both agents. In the white groups, the greatest developmental increment occurred between 4 and 5. The lower-class groups used the form only about half as often as the middle-class group; this structure is therefore discussed further in Chapter 7.

Chapter 4

Verb Phrase Structures

Habitual Present Tense

Despite its label, the simple present tense in English only occasionally refers to things happening only at the present moment. The most frequent use is probably to express general truths (H_2O means water) or tell about customary actions (He swims every day, She teaches science), where past, present, and future are all implied but not necessarily the present moment. The present progressive tense (He is swimming) is more often used for ongoing present-moment activity; but even this tense may imply past, present, and future (He is studying chemistry). The regular allomorphs of the present indicative are the same as those of the regular plural and regular possessive forms: /-s/ after voiceless stops, /-ɨz/ after stridents, and /-z/ elsewhere. (The relative difficulty of these three allomorphs has been discussed in the sections on noun + possessive and noun + plural in Chapter 3.) Brown (1973) reports that the third person regular is learned later than the simple progressive -ing (without auxiliary) and past tense forms, both regular and irregular; it is also acquired later than plurals and possessives, despite the identical phonological representations of these three morphemes. Menyuk (1969) agrees that the third person regular is the last of the three to be acquired.

Our items focused on the customary action meaning of the present indicative, and we constructed one item to elicit the common /-z/ allomorph and another to elicit the least frequent and apparently more difficult /-ɨz/ allomorph. (A separate item, to be discussed in a later section of this chapter, focused on the present tense of the copula.)

The items we used to test the third person indicative were the following:

Item 8a: Every day, when this baby is tired and hungry, he_____ (cries).
Item 8b: These boys and their dad are playing ball. Every time the boys throw the ball, Dad _____ (catches it).

The responses of the children to these items are summarized in Table 11.

Standard English Acquisition: Middle-Class White

Target. Among the middle-class white group, Item 8a, which tested for the /-z/ ALLOMORPH (cries), showed higher rates of usage at all ages than Item 8b, which tested for the /-ɨz/ ALLOMORPH (catches). The latter was complicated by the fact that a large proportion of the younger children used *throw* instead of *catch* as the stem. Although this response was probed (the tester said: *This is catching. Every time the boys throw the ball, Dad _____.*), many younger children persisted in this choice. Older children, on the other hand, clearly preferred *catch*. The concept of "taking turns" was apparently clear to the younger children, but the more refined analysis of the action into the reciprocal "throwing" and "catching" components was not common until a later age. This is an interesting example of semantic development.

Variants. The UNINFLECTED VERB (cry, catch) occurred in decreasing proportions of the children. As would be predicted by the phonological form, the verb ending in a strident (catch) was more likely to be left uninflected than the verb ending in a vowel. A few children used PAST TENSE forms on both items, and a few used the PRESENT PROGRESSIVE on Item 8a; but these variations were not common. They may indicate that children knew an inflection was needed but did not know which one, or they may indicate in-

Table 11

Habitual present tense—Percentages of responses on
Items 8a and 8b

	Middle-class white			Lower-class white			Lower-class black		
Age:	3	4	5	3	4	5	3	4	5
N:	106	100	104	26	24	27	23	36	27
(a) When this baby is tired and hungry, he _____.									
/-z/ allomorph (cries)	76	92	100	46	50	70	13	31	22
Uninflected verb (cry)	7	3	0	23	38	15	57	58	63
Past tense (cried)	7	2	0	4	8	0	4	0	0
Verb phrase substitution (crying)	8	2	0	20	4	15	21	11	8
Other	3	0	0	8	0	0	4	0	4
N:	106	100	104	26	24	27	23	36	27
(b) Every time the boys throw the ball, Dad _____.									
/-ɨz/ allomorph (catches)	32	45	80	4	17	7	4	0	11
/-z/ allomorph (throws)	42	34	10	15	21	44	4	11	3
Uninflected verb (catch)	14	13	6	58	50	30	61	81	74
Past tense (catched, caught)	8	8	5	4	8	19	13	6	11
Verb phrase substitution	2	0	0	4	4	0	9	3	0
Other	0	0	0	12	0	0	9	0	0

attention or misinterpretation of the frame story. The present progressive might have been a labeling response.

Dialect Variation: Lower-Class White

Target. Higher target performance on the /-z/ ALLOMORPH item
(8a) than on the /-ɨz/ ALLOMORPH item (8b) characterized the lower-
class white group; both items showed developmental gains. *Throws*
was more common than *catches* even among the older children in
this group.

Variants. A nonsignificant decline in use of an UNINFLECTED VERB occurred between the ages of 3 and 5. The increase in use of PAST TENSE forms on Item 8b may indicate either an attempt to inflect or a misinterpretation of *throw* in the stem as a past tense. Other variants occurred at relatively low rates.

Dialect Variation: Lower-Class Black

Target. The target forms, /-z/ ALLOMORPH on Item 8a and /-ɨz/ ALLOMORPH on Item 8b, never became the preferred forms for the lower-class black group; there were no significant developmental trends in the proportions of children using the target at different ages. We suggest that the uninflected variant may be the true target form for this dialect.

Variants. The UNINFLECTED VERB *cry* or *catch* occurred in well over half of the children tested. Although the developmental increase in the use of the uninflected forms did not reach significance, the high rates were increasingly and significantly different from the rates of use in the other two groups. Labov reports that in his two groups of black adolescent boys, "the 3rd person singular marker /-s/ does not exist in the particular grammar being used here. . . . A striking fact about this situation is that the older group has gained in several respects as far as approximation to standard English forms is concerned, but their development has not affected the grammatical status of the 3rd person singular marker" [1972a: 33]. Our group of lower-class black children were clearly learning a similar grammar, rather than one that marks the third person singular present indicative.

Other than the uninflected verb, the variations produced on these items by the lower-class black children did not differ significantly from those of the lower-class white group. These variations (i.e., PAST TENSE, PROGRESSIVE, VERB PHRASE SUBSTITUTION, and other forms) tended to decrease with age in both groups.

Summary

A steady developmental trend for two allomorphs of the third person singular present indicative was shown by the middle-class children. The most common allomorph, /-z/, was demonstrated by nearly all of the 5-year-olds. The least common, /-ɨz/, occurred at lower rates and was sometimes replaced by an uninflected form of the verb ending in a strident or by another verb—one that took the /-z/ allomorph instead. The lower-class groups used the uninflected form more frequently, although it dropped out by age 5 in the lower-class white group. The lower-class black group, on the other hand, used the uninflected form at a high rate at all ages tested. This trend is consistent with the analysis of the grammar of Black English Vernacular, which indicates that there is no special marker for the third person singular present.

PAST TENSE

The past tense in English expresses two different meanings: first, what Roger Brown (1973) calls "earlierness" or occurrence anterior to the expression itself; and, second, hypothetical status (as in *If I were you*. . .). The items discussed here refer to earlierness. A hypothetical past, the counterfactual, is reported on in the section on modal auxiliaries later in this chapter. Brown reports no example of the past tense used for hypothetical status in his 2- and 3-year-old subjects; however, "earlierness" is semantically very well controlled from an early age.

One of the most important aspects of early development is the child's freeing himself from the constraints of the immediate situation in terms of time, space, and action. This acquisition of freedom is construed as a gaining of "distance" by Werner and Kaplan (1963), and they suggest that this "distancing principle" leads to symbolic and representational behavior. That is, the child comes to represent time, space, and action dimensions of his life space through a vehicle such as a distancing principle. Sigel (1972) has suggested that lower-class children do not experience interactions with adults that focus upon the anticipation and recollection of experiences, and hence these children lag behind their middle-class counterparts in their representations of time and space.

Menyuk (1971), on the basis of Cazden's (1968) work, concludes that the development of verb inflections seems to progress in the following sequence:

1. Progressive (-ing)
2. Past (-ed, etc.)
3. Third singular present (-s)

She suggests that ongoing time and past markers refer to clear attributes of the state of activity, but that the present tense marker of habitual action does not clearly refer to a particular time.

In the past tense, regular verbs in English undergo no internal change; they form their past tense by addition of the suffix -(e)d.

Both regular and irregular formations of the past tense are frequent in English. The regular past is formed by adding /-t/ to verb stems that end in voiceless consonants, by adding /-ɨd/ to stems that end in dental /-t/ or /-d/, and by adding /-d/ to all other stems: *washed* /wašt/, *kicked* /kɪkt/, *melted* /mɛltɨd/, *combed* /koʷmd/, etc. Irregular past tenses characterized many frequent verbs: *catch-caught, can-could,* etc. Brown notes that the (theoretical) transformational complexity of past tense forms is not predictive of how soon they are acquired. The irregular past involves an additional transformation not required by regular verbs, and yet many irregular past tenses precede the regular in order of acquisition.

Brown further notes that events of very short duration, which are likely to terminate just before an utterance, carry the first past tenses. Examples are *fell, dropped, slipped, crashed,* and *broke.* He suggests that the child probably hears these verbs in the past tense from the mother. Later, the past tense is used productively to refer to events increasingly remote in past time, and to agree with linguistic context such as the question *What happened?* Our items deliberately tested for agreement with the linguistic context of the past tense. (The pictures could as easily have been described in the present tense.)

We tested two regular verbs for the past tense. One item was designed to elicit a form that required /-t/; the other, one that required /-d/. The items we used were the following:

> Item 9a: This morning mother woke Tom up and gave him breakfast.
> Then she _____ (combed his hair).
> Item 9b: Donna was trying to get her doll's dress clean. What did she do
> to it? _____ (She washed it).

The children's responses to these items are summarized in Table 12.

Table 12

Past tense—Percentages of responses on Items 9a and 9b

	Middle-class white			Lower-class white			Lower-class black		
Age:	3	4	5	3	4	5	3	4	5
N:	106	100	104	26	24	27	23	36	26
(a) *Mother woke Tom up*									
... Then she _____.									
Verb + past (*combed*)	89	96	99	50	58	81	8	30	33
Uninflected verb									
(*comb*)	6	3	1	35	38	18	78	69	59
Present tense (*combs*)	3	0	0	4	4	0	4	0	4
Progressive (*is/was*									
combing)	1	0	0	8	0	0	8	0	4
Other	0	0	0	0	0	0	4	0	0
N:	106	100	104	26	25	27	23	36	26
(b) *What did she do to*									
it? _____.									
Verb + past (*washed*)	66	66	78	31	52	67	13	36	58
Substitution of									
irregular verb (*put*)	2	4	6	15	4	0	9	6	0
Uninflected verb (*she*									
wash it)	15	21	16	31	32	30	65	47	38
Present tense (*washes*)	7	3	0	0	0	0	0	0	0
Progressive (*she is/was*									
washing)	10	4	1	15	8	4	13	8	4
Other (*dirty*)	1	3	0	7	4	0	0	3	0

Standard English Acquisition:
Middle-Class White

Target. Apparently the target VERB + PAST response on Item 9a (*combed*) was easier than on Item 9b (*washed*) at all age levels for the middle-class white children. It may be that phonologically the /-š/ ending of the Item 9b verb stem was more difficult to manage than the /-m/ of Item 9a; or it may be that 9a, which contained two (irregular) simple past tense forms in the frame, was a less ambiguous past environment for the response than the combination of past progressive and *did-do* past resulting from the question transformation in the frame of 9b. Questions tended to present difficulties on other items as well, for example, Item 2a. On Item 9b, a few children gave a "correct" past tense response that nevertheless presents problems of interpretation, as in the SUBSTITUTION OF AN IRREGULAR VERB: *She put it in the water.*

Variants. The most prevalent variant was use of an UNINFLECTED VERB: it occurred more often on Item 9b. There was no decrease with age.

Another small proportion of children used a PRESENT TENSE rather than past tense inflection (*combs, washes*). Finally, a few children used the PROGRESSIVE *-ing* inflection, possibly intending a description. The *-ing* form of verbs is acquired early (see "Progressives: Present and Past," later in this chapter) and was part of the frame. Therefore, children who could not handle the tense information in the question in Item 9b might have been giving forms to agree with the progressive *-ing* form in the story frame. No other variants were frequent in the middle-class group.

Dialect Variation: Lower-Class White

Target. Again, with the lower-class white children, Item 9a was somewhat more successful in eliciting the target VERB + PAST. Fewer of these children used the past tense compared to the middle-class group, but the increase among the lower-class children is steeper and reaches the two-thirds level by age 5.

Variants. Use of an UNINFLECTED VERB form was a stable response in the lower-class white group, being given by about one-third of the children at all ages. We do not know whether past tense endings can be deleted frequently in this group's dialect, as they can be in Black English Vernacular.

Other variants were seldom used, except that about 10 percent of the 3-year-olds used a PROGRESSIVE *-ing* inflection on both items, a finding that relates to Brown's and Menyuk's discussions of the sequence of tense marker acquisition. It may also be related to Werner and Kaplan's discussion of the representation of time as contemporaneous in lower-class groups. (The responses of the lower-class black group, discussed next, may support their suggestion also.) Our data give only fragmentary evidence, in view of the different stem structures, the phonological characteristics of the items, and possible dialect differences.

Dialect Variation: Lower-Class Black

Target. A lower proportion of black children than white used the target VERB + PAST at all ages, although there is a strong developmental trend toward its increased use. The uninflected form is apparently also a correct form for this group.

Variants. A large proportion of the lower-class black children used an UNINFLECTED VERB (*comb* or *wash*), even at age 5. Labov (1972b) points out that the regular past tense inflection is a marginal form in Black English Vernacular. The past tense morpheme is definitely part of the grammar, since such irregular forms as *ran* or *told* are used consistently, just as in Standard English. However, due to a phonological rule that variably deletes final /-t/ or /-d/ after another consonant, the regular past tense marker is frequently not present in Black English Vernacular speech; instead, most regular verbs are treated like Standard English *put* or *hit*, with no change of form even when the past tense meaning is intended. Labov's preadolescent group deleted the past tense marker 74 percent of the time before a consonant and 24 percent of the time before a vowel (in careful speech). Part of the difference between the black children's responses on Items 9a and 9b may be due to the phoneme that follows. *Combed his hair*, a probable response for Item 9a, puts the past tense marker before a consonant; whereas *She washed it*, in Item 9b, puts it before a vowel. In the latter instance, the marker is less likely to be deleted. In fact, black 5-year-olds did include the past tense marker more often on Item 9b. This reversal of the pattern found in the two white groups supports our hypothesis that the black 5-year-olds' production of -ed may be partly conditioned by the following vowel or consonant. Some children, of course, gave responses, such as *washed the dress*, that did not follow the suggested pattern of preconsonantal past tense on Item 9a and prevocalic past tense on Item 9b.

Labov reports further that, even though 90 percent of his adolescent readers picked up the past tense meaning from adverbials such as *last month*, less than 50 percent picked it up from the -ed spelling of the written past tense marker. He concludes, "the -ed cannot function as an effective marker of the past tense for many children" (1972a:32). The status of this marker in spoken Black English Vernacular also remains murky. Our figures suggest a definite developmental acquisition of the form by increasing proportions of children, but the omission or deletion of the past tense marker continued at a much higher rate in this group than in the white groups. While our results tend to support Labov's, they do not clarify the uncertain status of the regular past tense marker.

We should note here that black children supplied the irregular past tense *could* or *did* on Item 13b, which requires a past tense modal, in higher proportions than they supplied the /-t/ or /-d/ in these items. This also agrees with Labov's findings.

The PROGRESSIVE -*ing* form was given by a large proportion (39 percent) of black 3-year-olds on Item 9b. As suggested earlier, the frame included the form *was trying*; younger children who could not fully handle the *did-do* question form in Standard English might be likely to give the progressive form to agree with the first verb form.

Summary

Despite the differences between the two items used to assess the regular past tense, we can conclude that there is a consistent developmental trend for the target structure /-t, -d/, and considerable consistency in the alternative forms given. High proportions of middle-class white children controlled the past tense marker in these environments even at age 3; lower-class white and black children also showed developmental increases in use of the forms, although deletion of final /-t, -d/ is common in Black English Vernacular and complicates the picture for the black children.

SUBJECT-COPULA AGREEMENT:
PRESENT TENSE

The verb *be* is one of the most frequently occurring verbs in English. It is also one of the most complicated. It has three forms in the present indicative: *am* for the first person singular, *is* for third person singular, and *are* for all others. None of these forms is phonetically similar either to the uninflected *be* or to each other. In addition to this complexity, the forms are used both as copulas (main verbs of a sentence) and as auxiliaries of main verbs, as in the progressive. Finally, Labov (1972b) has pointed out the importance of contractibility of these forms. There are various environments in which *be* forms are never contracted, such as sentence-final position (*How beautiful you are*, not **How beautiful you're*). Labov relates the constraints on contraction to stress assignment and vowel reduction rules, as delineated by Chomsky and Halle (1968). These assign primary stress to the last lexical item in each underlying phrase marker, operating cyclically from smaller to larger phrase units in a sentence, and eventually allow deletion of unstressed schwas. Brown (1973) reports that Labov's analysis clarifies many phenomena in the acquisition of *be* forms by his subjects. In his data, the uncontractible copula was learned first, uncontractible auxiliary next, and contractible copula and auxiliary last. Brown points out that the uncontracted forms are phonologically simpler, in that fewer rules have operated upon them. It should also be pointed out that they are perceptually more salient, since they contain vowels as well as consonants and are surrounded by forms with less stress or even by pauses.

The item we used required the third person plural form *are*. The context allowed contraction, but the other contractible copulas in the frame were given in their full forms. In any event, contraction would not be expected in the first word the child said, even if the total sentence allowed it.

The item in the test was the following:

> Item 10a: This is Maria's room. Her dress is on the bed, her doll is on the chair, and her shoes _____ (are on the floor).

The responses of the children to this item are summarized in Table 13.

Standard English Acquisition: Middle-Class White

Target. The target THIRD PERSON PLURAL COPULA (*are*) was used in this context by over half of the middle-class white 3-year-olds, with continuing gains each year. No attempt was made to separate contracted from uncontracted forms, because the response required the child to begin with the copula, and beginning with a con-

Table 13

Subject-copula agreement: present tense—Percentages of
responses on Item 10a

	Middle-class white			Lower-class white			Lower-class black		
Age:	3	4	5	3	4	5	3	4	5
N:	106	100	104	24	24	27	22	34	27
Her doll is on the chair, and her shoes _____. 3rd person plural copula (are on the floor)	66	75	82	17	54	63	14	9	15
Omission of copula (on the floor)	25	16	13	63	38	15	68	56	56
Singular copula (is on the floor)	8	8	5	17	8	22	5	35	30
Other (down floor)	1	1	0	4	0	0	14	0	0

tracted copula would not be expected even though it was
permissible.

Variants. The most common variant was OMISSION OF THE
COPULA; there was a nonsignificant decline in this response from
age 3 to 5. There are three possible reasons for the omission. First,
the child may not use copulas in any context. Second, as Brown suggests, he may use them only in uncontractible environments; this
may imply the existence of an underlying form, which is deleted before it reaches the surface. Third, despite the best efforts of the testers to indicate both shoes in the picture, the younger children may
have interpreted the frame as referring to only one shoe, and the resulting form on the floor would be syntactically correct, though semantically dubious. That is, the child may have thought the frame
ending was . . . and her shoe's (shoe is) _____. All of these hypotheses would predict increasing conformity to adult English usage
with age, so the direction of the trend is not helpful.

Less than 10 percent of the children used the SINGULAR COP-
ULA, is on the floor. This suggests the existence of an underlying
copula without full adult specification of the number agreement
forms. Is is probably the most frequently occurring form of the copula in English.

A small proportion of children gave such forms as down floor.
These may have been a variant of the omission of the copula.

Dialect Variation: Lower-Class White

Target. Significant development of the target THIRD PERSON PLURAL COPULA (are) occurred between ages 3 and 4 in the lower-class white group, and the trend continued upward. Only at age 3 were the proportions of these children using the target form significantly lower than those of the middle-class white group.

Variants. The OMISSION OF COPULA variant (on the floor) declined steadily from over 50 percent at age 3 to 15 percent at age 5, which is comparable to the 13 percent of the middle-class group.

Up to one-fifth of the children substituted the SINGULAR COPULA, is, for are. Again, it is clear that in the speech of these children the copula is required, but the particular form of it is the more frequent is. Some of these responses may have been modeled on the occurrences of is in the frame sentence. The frequency of the is response did not decline between ages 3 and 5.

Dialect Variation: Lower-Class Black

Target. The pattern of results for the black group is strikingly different from that of the two white groups. The target THIRD PERSON PLURAL COPULA (are) was used by only 10–15 percent of the children, regardless of age, whereas it was used by over half of the white 4- and 5-year-olds. On the other hand, variants were used by high proportions of black children through age 5.

Variants. OMISSION (or deletion) OF THE COPULA was characteristic of over half the children at all ages. The omission or deletion frequencies are not surprising in view of Labov's work (Labov, Cohen, Robins, and Lewis, 1968), where he presents evidence that in Black English Vernacular copulas are commonly deleted in the same environments that allow speakers of Standard English to contract them. As we have pointed out, the structure with which this item is usually completed does permit contraction, even if speakers did not happen to contract. It is difficult to predict the fine details of Black English Vernacular performance from Labov's work. For example, in this item shoes ends in a sibilant, and the form are is required. Labov states that there is less deletion after sibilants, but he also reports that are is deleted more often than is (Labov et al., 1968:52). In this item, then, there are some variables with which we would expect deletion and others with which we would expect nondeletion.

Labov's data would not lead us to predict, however, the occurrence of the SINGULAR COPULA (*is*) in one-third of the 4- and 5-
year-olds—a significant increase over its occurrence in the 3-year-
olds. He states that person-number disagreement is very rare in adult
Black English Vernacular. Apparently when disagreement does occur, *is* tends to be used in contexts calling for *are*, as in this item

Our suggestion is that structures involving the copula pose quite
a different problem to children learning Black English Vernacular
than to those learning Standard English. To begin with, there is the
high incidence of deletion of the forms reported by Labov. It is reasonable to suppose that if contractibility increases the time required
to acquire forms, as Brown suggests, deletability should increase it
even further. This may account for the occurrence of *is* in a third of
the 4- and 5-year-olds. These children may be at the beginning
stages of copula acquisition, and since *is* is less often deleted in the
speech around them (and is modeled twice in the frame, besides), it
may represent an early undifferentiated form of the copula. A second
factor that may be at work is one that Labov (1972a) has observed in
his work and in that of Torrey (1972)—a possible inverted U shape in
the developmental trends for copula deletion. Preadolescents and
adolescents delete more often than either 6-year-olds or adults. It is
possible that among the more advanced 4- and 5-year-olds in our
sample, the response we call omission of the copula is actually deletion of an underlying copula. The children may be learning that
the copula should often be deleted in Black English. The resulting
response would look the same as the more primitive stage where the
copula is not yet used at all.

Summary

As Brown and Labov have shown, the English copula is subject to
change by a wide variety of grammatical and phonological environments. The groups in this sample displayed predictable trends in
their use of the target *are* + locative. Both white groups steadily increased their use of it, while the black group maintained a stable low
rate of usage. The most common variation, omission of the copula,
dropped out in the white groups but remained characteristic of black
speech. Although it is difficult to come to hard conclusions at this
point, we suggest that this variation reflects at least two kinds of response: (1) omission by children who do not use it because the cop-

ula is not yet in their internalized rule system, and (2) among the older black groups, deletion by children who have acquired not only the copula but also the rule for deleting it in this type of environment.

PROGRESSIVES: PRESENT AND PAST

The progressive tenses in English involve the use of an appropriate form of *be* + verb stem + *-ing* (*He is eating, He was eating*). Not all verb stems can occur in progressive forms; most progressives involve actions (*He is falling*) or voluntary temporary states (*I am being good*, but not *I am liking it*).

Cazden (1968) and Brown (1973), among others, report early acquisition of the *-ing* inflection; it is frequently the first inflection learned and is normally used in situations that suggest ongoing action, like the later full present progressive. However, the *be* forms used in the full adult present progressive are acquired much later. Of the 14 morphemes Brown studied, both uncontractible (*was*, etc.) and contractible (*-'s*, etc.) auxiliaries were among the very last to be acquired. Interestingly, the same *be* forms are used much earlier as copulas. The auxiliary uses emerge later.

Labov (1972a) comes up with a set of "parallel but distinct rules of the phonological component" to account for the contraction of *be* forms and their deletion in dialects where this is an option. Some grammatical environments, such as occurrence after pronouns or verbs, operate to favor contraction or deletion. On the other hand, phonetic environments often have different effects. Occurrence after vowels tends to favor contraction, occurrence after consonants tends to favor deletion. In short, the progressive forms—like most other linguistic structures—are subject to a wide variety of influences. Obviously a much fuller test than this one is required to capture fully the acquisition of these structures in all their varying environments.

In addition to variations discussed by Labov and Brown, there is a tense difference between present and past progressive forms. Present ongoing activity and past activity often occur at the time something else is happening or happened. The second of these forms is somewhat more complex, since it involves marking the past tense as well as the ongoing activity.

Our items differed on a final, grammatical, dimension. While we put both of the progressive structures into subordinate clauses, the present progressive item was subordinated by *because*, whereas the past progressive item was in a nominal *that* clause. The first item is probably a more familiar structure to children. Another difference between the items was that we found it necessary to model the present progressive in the frame story, contrary to our usual practice. Originally, the item was phrased: *One day, Willie asked if Sam could come out and play. "Not now," said Sam's mother, "because* _____ *(he's eating)."* However, a large proportion (20 percent) of the older children responded *he was eating.* This response is correct if the interpretation is that the *because* clause is not said by Sam's mother but is explaining her refusal (*"Not now," said Sam's mother, because he was eating*). In order to reduce these responses, the frame was changed to the present tense: *Willie is asking if Sam can come out and play.*

Because of the differences between the two items, we will present the findings for them separately.

PRESENT PROGRESSIVE

The item we used to test the present progressive was the following:

Item 11a: Willie is asking if Sam can come out and play. "Not now," says Sam's mother, "because _____ (he's eating)."

The responses of the children are summarized in Table 14.

Standard English Acquisition:
Middle-Class White

Target. The target PRESENT PROGRESSIVE structure was used by a steady 70 percent of the middle-class white sample, at all age levels. Another correct completion, a *have to* PHRASE, was used by up to 14 percent of 5-year-olds.

Variants. About 10 percent or so at each age level used one of the less complete -ing forms, some with OMISSION OF THE AUXILIARY (*he eating*) some with OMISSION OF THE AUXILIARY AND A PRONOUN ERROR (*him eating*) and some with OMISSION OF AUXIL-

Table 14

Progressives: present and past—Percentages of responses
on Items 11a and 11b

	Middle-class white			Lower-class white			Lower-class black		
Age:	3	4	5	3	4	5	3	4	5
N:	101	100	104	23	23	27	22	36	27

(a) *"Not now," says*
Sam's mother,
"because _____."

Present progressive, full or contracted (he is eating, he's eating, it's raining)	73	70	70	26	43	67	9	8	22
Have to phrase (he has to eat)	4	8	14	9	9	0	0	6	11
Omission of auxiliary (he eating)	4	1	1	26	22	15	36	50	52
Omission of auxiliary and pronoun error (him eating)	0	3	3	4	4	3	0	0	0
Omission of auxiliary and pronoun (eating)	7	8	5	12	8	4	32	25	7
Other verb forms (he eat, he got eat)	7	8	3	22	13	7	14	8	7
Noun phrases (food, he supper)	6	2	3	0	0	4	9	3	0
N:	106	100	104	26	24	27	23	36	26

(b) When Fred came
home, he saw that his
brother _____.

Past progressive (was watching TV)	40	49	72	4	29	44	13	3	30
Omission of auxiliary (watching TV)	23	29	15	31	33	33	39	58	33
Uninflected verb (watch TV)	6	1	0	27	25	7	30	31	19
Past tense inflection (watched TV)	25	19	11	12	13	11	4	6	11
Other (TV, in there)	8	2	2	24	0	4	13	3	7

IARY AND PRONOUN (*eating*). This is consistent with Brown's report that the -*ing* form is acquired earlier than the auxiliary forms required by the complete progressive forms. The last two variants listed for Item 11a—OTHER VERB FORMS and NOUN PHRASES—are never used by large proportions of this group.

Dialect Variation: Lower-Class White

Target. The target PRESENT PROGRESSIVE -*ing* form with *be* auxiliary was acquired with a clear and significant developmental trend by the lower-class white sample.

Variants. The variants involving OMISSION OF THE AUXILIARY (*he eating, him eating, eating*), which, combined, were given by over 40 percent of the 3-year-olds, tended to drop out slowly as the auxiliary forms were acquired. OTHER VERB FORM responses also dropped out with age, but they were never common.

Dialect Variation: Lower-class Black

Target. In the lower-class black sample, we again see that the -*ing* forms in this context were used by a high percentage of all age groups. Although the full or contracted PRESENT PROGRESSIVE and *have to* PHRASES were used by increasing proportions of the lower-class black children, even at age 5, only one-third of these children used the target forms appropriate to Standard English.

Variants. The use of the pronoun + -*ing* form, with OMISSION OF THE AUXILIARY, also increased with age. It is unusual to have both target and variant responses increasing with age to this extent, and we view the finding as support for Labov's contention that auxiliary deletion is a variable rule in Black English Vernacular. Probably, in the older children, both *he's eating* and *he eating* responses reflect the same underlying structure with an auxiliary that is optionally deleted. This may not be true in the younger children. As in the case of the copula, we should distinguish deletion of an underlying form from simple omission of a form that is not in the child's linguistic system at all. Our 5-year-old black children seemed to be following deletion rules in similar ways to Labov's preadolescent group: Our sample included the auxiliary 33 percent of the time and deleted it 52 percent of the time, while Labov's preadolescents included it 34 percent of the time and deleted it 66 percent of the time. Data beyond the age range tested here are required to enable us to be sure of what is happening, but it looks as though these black children are demonstrating acquisition of the linguistic system of their own vernacular just as clearly as the white groups are demonstrating acquition of theirs. Other variants tended to decrease with age.

PAST PROGRESSIVE

The item used to assess the past progressive was the following:

Item 11b: Yesterday when Fred came home, he saw that his brother _____ (was watching TV).

As pointed out, this item varied in several respects from the present progressive item: The auxiliary *was* is not contractible, the structure occurs in a *that* clause rather than a *because* clause, and the form is not modeled in the frame sentence.

The responses on this item are summarized in Table 14.

Standard English Acquisition:
Middle-Class White

Target.   The middle-class white children show a significant rise in their use of the target PAST PROGRESSIVE between ages 4 and 5.

Variants.   About one-fourth of the two younger groups OMITTED THE AUXILIARY. Perhaps, as in the present progressive, the -ing form alone is acquired first and the auxiliary later; this may be the beginning of the use of the past progressive for situations where one activity is going on when another occurs. Another possibility is that the children cannot yet handle *that* clauses. In this case, the frame: He *saw that his brother* _____ might be interpreted as: He *saw his brother* (*watching TV*), with the -ing phrase functioning as a modifier.

Few children used an UNINFLECTED VERB. About one-fourth of the 3-year-olds, and somewhat fewer 4- and 5-year-olds, used a verb with PAST TENSE INFLECTION, such as He *saw that his brother* (*watched TV*). It might be possible for an adult to complete the item in this way, meaning He *made sure that his brother watched TV.* However, this response is syntactically more sophisticated, and semantically less likely, than the target progressive. Since the response becomes less frequent with increasing age, we tend toward a simpler explanation. We feel that the children giving this response have picked up the constraints calling for past tense in the frame, but have not yet acquired the rule that puts ongoing action into the past progressive tense in the context of another event.

Dialect Variation: Lower-Class White

Target. In the lower-class white groups, the target PAST PROGRESSIVE (*was watching*) increased from a very low proportion among 3-year-olds to nearly half of the 5-year-olds.

Variants. About one-third of the children at all age levels OMITTED THE AUXILIARY. As in the case of the middle-class children, this omission could be due to a primitive form of the rule that requires a progressive for the ongoing action when two events co-occur or it could be inability to interpret a *that* clause.

About one-fourth of the 3- and 4-year-olds used an UNINFLECTED VERB. This usage may have been a labeling response, which names the action but does not attempt to complete the syntactic frame, or an attempt to complete the frame with an uninflected present tense. Smaller proportions of children responded to the PAST TENSE constraints but did not use the progressive.

Dialect Variation: Lower-Class Black

Target. The full PAST PROGRESSIVE form was used by up to 30 percent of black lower-class 5-year-olds; this percentage is about the same as the percentage using the full present progressive form on Item 11a.

Variants. In this group, the pattern for the past progressive tends to be different from the pattern for the present progressive. There was a steady increase in the use of -*ing* forms, as before, but inclusion or OMISSION OF THE AUXILIARY fluctuated. On the basis of this admittedly inadequate evidence, we would like to suggest that the proportions may show support for the acquisition of a variable deletion rule, as in the case of the present progressive. On both items, there was a low percentage of auxiliary use at ages 3 and 4, followed by an increase to almost one-third at age 5. On both items, use of the -*ing* form *without* auxiliary increased between 3 and 4. At this point, however, the patterns diverged. For 5-year-olds, the present progressive structure continued to elicit a high proportion of deleted auxiliary responses, the past progressive did not. This pattern contrasts with the steady or declining rate of auxiliary omission for the two white groups on both items. While this contrast could be due to the selective effect on black children of item differences, such as having to furnish the pronoun in the present progressive, it could also be due to the effect of an adult variable rule. The auxiliary in the present progressive item is contractible and therefore deletable in Black English Vernacular; the auxiliary in the past progressive item is not contractible. It is possible, therefore, that the more mature black children may be furnishing the auxiliary in the context where it is uncontractible and deleting it in the contractible environment of our present progressive item.

As in the case of the two white groups, the past progressive appeared to be more difficult generally than the present progressive. About one-third of the black children at all ages gave nonprogressive responses, with PAST TENSE INFLECTIONS gaining slightly at the expense of UNINFLECTED VERB forms.

Summary

Despite a number of differences in the frame stories, our data on the present and past progressive structures show interesting developmental trends. In contexts that require progressive forms, every group on both items showed a steady increase in the use of -ing forms at the expense of other verb forms. However, an interesting racial dialect difference emerges when we look at use of the auxiliary. In the white groups, use of the auxiliary increased with age, and omission of the auxiliary generally decreased. In the black group *both* responses increased on the present progressive item, with auxiliary omission favored somewhat. Omission on the past progressive item also increased to age 4 but then dropped sharply. This contrast between the present and past progressive seems to be related to the difference between the auxiliary *is,* which is deletable in Black English Vernacular, and the auxiliary *was,* which is not. We suggest that the data are consistent with the acquisition of a variable rule by the black children.

PASSIVE

The passive construction is generally used in English when there is a reason to begin a clause with its grammatical object. Typical situations occur when the recipient of an action is the topic of discussion (*This tricycle was dented by some big boys*) or when the agent is unknown, unspecified, or unimportant (*The passive construction is generally used . . .*).

Fraser, Bellugi, and Brown (1963) found that very few 3-year-olds responded correctly to passive voice stimulus items on comprehension and production tasks, and, in terms of rank order of difficulty of their ten structures, the passive ranked ninth. Brown (1973) reported that the passive was almost never produced by his subjects even at Stage V, when mean length of utterance was 4.0. However, Menyuk (1963a) reported that, by nursery school age, all of the children in her group could correctly repeat the passive when it was modeled for them, and 5 of the 14 were observed to use the form productively. Thus, we can expect some of our sample children to control passive structures, although later than the active equivalents.

Work by Slobin (1966), Turner and Rommetveit (1967), and Bever (1970) has pointed out an important semantic feature relevant to passive sentences. Slobin calls this feature "semantic reversibility." Briefly, a reversible sentence is one in which the actor and the acted-upon can reasonably change places with respect to that action. Thus, *The boy is chasing the girl* is a semantically reasonable sentence, and it can be reversed to *The girl is chasing the boy* and remain semantically reasonable. On the other hand, nonreversible sentences refer to one-way actions. *The girl is riding the pony* is reasonable; *The pony is riding the girl* is anomalous. Slobin found that in the age range of 5 to 11 years, verification time to nonreversible passive sentences like *The pony is ridden by the girl* was faster than to reversible passives like *The girl is chased by the boy*. Bever, Mehler, and Valian, working with 2- to 5-year-olds, found an interesting interaction. The younger children did about equally well with actives and passives. Performance with actives improved slowly and steadily with age. With reversible passives, however, there was a tendency to improve only slightly until 3½ to 4 years of age, then to deteriorate sharply at about 4 to 4½, when a rapid improvement brought the rate of success up to the level of the active sentence at age 5. This experiment, together with others using various kinds of sentences, led Bever to suggest that perceptual strategies change as children get older. The youngest children do not have enough knowledge of the world to depend heavily on semantic constraints; this ability develops during the third year, leading to improvement on nonreversible sentences. At about 4 years, however, another language comprehension strategy takes over when semantic constraints are absent, as in reversible sentences. This strategy interprets the first noun-verb-noun sequence as actor-action-object. Thus, reversible passive sentences are systematically misunderstood (not just randomly, as earlier) and performance on comprehension tasks drops; nonreversible passives continue to improve.

We included only nonreversible situations in our items and thus avoided possible interference from this comprehension strategy characterizing 4-year-olds. This allows us to follow the development of passive constructions without confounding them with perceptual strategies. However, Turner and Rommetveit (1967) have reported that 4- to 9-year-olds who comprehend nonreversible sentences may still produce erroneous forms as descriptions, such as *The tractor drives the farmer*. Thus, the perceptual strategies described by Bever may not be relevant to the language production of children, except indirectly.

A difficulty not noted at the time is that one item has an ambiguity in the frame. The sentence *Some children were drawing pictures but they weren't quite finished* can mean that the children were not finished, or that the pictures were not finished. If the second interpretation is chosen, we find that a passive structure has been modeled in the frame. However, the form required in the response is not modeled.

Both items in the test occurred with modal *have to*, because we encountered difficulty in constructing reliable items with passive main verbs. The specialized meaning of the items, however, does not change the object-verb-(subject) relation characteristic of the main verb passive.

The items we used to elicit the passive after *have to* were the following:

Item 12a: Some children were drawing pictures but they weren't quite

Table 15

Passive—Percentages of responses on Items 12a and 12b

		Middle-class white			Lower-class white			Lower-class black		
Age:		3	4	5	3	4	5	3	4	5
N:		106	100	104	23	24	26	23	36	27
(a) "Those pictures have to _____."										
Be passive (be finished/done)		33	55	86	4	33	58	0	25	48
Get passive (get finished/done)		3	8	2	4	13	8	0	8	7
Appropriate active (drip)		14	7	5	0	8	8	9	11	4
Auxiliary + uninflected verb (be/get finish)		0	0	0	0	0	0	0	3	0
Adjective (wet)		1	2	0	4	4	4	13	3	7
Uninflected verb (finish)		43	26	6	74	38	15	78	47	33
Other		5	2	0	17	4	8	0	0	0
N:		106	100	104	26	24	27	23	36	26
(b) "Take off your dress, Nancy, it has to _____."										
Be passive (be washed)		38	47	79	8	13	48	9	19	33
Get passive (get washed)		10	12	13	0	17	15	4	25	11
Appropriate active (dry)		0	0	0	4	0	0	0	0	4
Auxiliary + uninflected verb (be/get wash)		4	6	1	0	13	0	4	4	7
Adjective (dirty, many)		4	7	3	15	0	4	22	17	11
Uninflected verb (wash, clean)		43	28	5	73	58	33	61	32	33
Other		1	0	0	0	0	0	0	0	0

finished and it was time to go outside. The teacher said, "In 5 minutes those pictures have to _____ (be finished, get done)."

Item 12b: Nancy got her dress dirty, so her mother wanted to wash it. She said, "Take off your dress, Nancy, it has to _____ (be washed, get washed)."

The children's response to these items are summarized in Table 15.

Standard English Acquisition:
Middle-Class White

Target. An increasing developmental use of the target PASSIVE construction characterized both items in the middle-class white group, to a high 90 percent level at age 5. Menyuk (1969) noted that 64 percent of the children in her study were using the passive, and that the most frequent form was get + participle. This was not so on our items. On Item 12a, for example, only 3 percent of 3-year-olds, 8 percent of 4-year-olds, and 2 percent of 5-year-olds (out of a combined total 36, 63, and 88 percent used get instead of be. Perhaps the stylistic context tended to favor the be forms; Menyuk's data were not constrained in this way.

A few children at each age gave an APPROPRIATE ACTIVE FORM, such as *Those picture have to (drip)*.

The infinitive complement items requiring active completions (discussed in greater detail in the first section of Chapter 5) were acquired at a higher rate than the passive form: approximating 80 percent at 3 years, 85 percent at 4 years, and 95 percent at 5 years. Acquisition of modal items (discussed in the final section in this chapter)—in which the target required the child to produce the modal as well as an active verb—was also higher: roughly 65 percent at age 3, 80 percent at age 4, and 90 percent at age 5. It seems reasonable to suggest that some of the children who succeeded in completing those somewhat similar active items were not able to manage the passive form, at least not in structures of this complexity.

Variants. Over 40 percent of the youngest children gave an UN-INFLECTED VERB form that did not seem to be an appropriate active, such as *Those pictures have to (finish)* or *It has to (wash)* or *It has to (go to bed)*. The last of these seemed to involve an interpretation with Nancy as subject of the verb. The other responses were more difficult to interpret; they also may have involved assignment of verb subject to animate characters in the stories.

Other forms did not occur frequently as responses in the middle-class white group. It should be noted that we trained administrators to say the colloquial *hafta* and *hasta*, rather than a too careful pronunciation of *have to* and *has to*, in order to avoid such interpretations as *It [the dress] has too (much dirt)* or *It [the dress] is too (dirty)*. Therefore, very few of the ADJECTIVE responses can be assigned to administrator pronunciation.

Dialect Variation: Lower-Class White

Target. The lower-class white group also showed a steady developmental trend of PASSIVE acquisition, parallel to but lower than that of the middle-class group.

Variants. Again, an UNINFLECTED VERB was the most common variant, whether due to assignment of a different (animate) subject, to inability to express an intended passive meaning, or to frequency of auxiliary *be* deletion in the adult dialect. Some "uninflected" forms on Item 12b may be APPROPRIATE ACTIVES for this lower-class white group. Some dialects of English use *wash* in an active construction with clothes, etc., as subject. Possibly this construction was characteristic of the dialects of some of these children.

As in the other two groups, there were a few ADJECTIVE responses. As explained in discussing Black English Vernacular variants on these items, some American dialects have characteristic auxiliary deletion and so-called "double modal" forms that may favor this response.

Other forms occurred only erratically and at low frequencies in this group, except for an incidence of 17 percent for 3-year-olds on Item 12a.

Dialect Variation: Lower-Class Black

Target. The same general pattern—increase in the use of a PASSIVE construction and decrease in the use of uninflected forms—characterized the lower-class black group. The general level of passive use was somewhat lower than in the lower-class white group. The reason may involve alternative correct constructions in Black English Vernacular, as emerges in the ensuing discussion of variants.

Variants. The most common variant given by the black children was an UNINFLECTED VERB. It is possible that both lower-class groups, and particularly the black group, were hindered in their acquisition of the passive by the high rate of deletion of the inflected auxiliary *be* in their dialects. *The picture is finished* might normally appear as *The picture finish(ed)* in Black English Vernacular, so there would be fewer *be* + participle forms heard by the children in their everyday life. However, Labov notes that *be* occurs in Black

English Vernacular without exception where Standard English has it in the infinitive form, so children should supply it in our items as soon as they have a *be* passive in their systems. If this were the whole story, one could claim that black children are later than whites in acquiring the passive. However, the situation is further complicated by another feature of Black English Vernacular, and we cannot assume that our figures reflect passive acquisition unequivocally. Labov (1972b:58) notes the existence of a number of "double modal" sentences, such as *"In deep water, I might can get hurt, . . . they must don't have too much in they wardrobe, . . . people useta would ask us to sing."* He suggests that only the second "modal" is a true modal. The first so-called modal in these sentences actually has adverbial status in Black English Vernacular; *hafta* is among the words with this status. Thus, some children in our black sample may have been hearing a frame with an adverb; *Those pictures hafta . . .* would be similar in structure to *Those pictures certainly. . . .* If the child deletes an auxiliary inflected *be* form, or assumes that the administrator has deleted one, a wide variety of ADJECTIVE or UNINFLECTED VERB completions are satisfactory. *Those pictures (are) certainly wet* and *those pictures (are) certainly finish (ed)* would be structural equivalents of *Those pictures (are) hafta wet* and *Those pictures (are) hafta finish(ed)* (although obviously the Black English Vernacular adverb *hafta* and the adverb *certainly* differ in meaning). Note that the auxiliary *be* is in a deletable inflected form in this interpretation. Thus, as was often the case, we found that for this group our test items raised more questions than they answered. Some of the children who gave variations from the *be* + participle target probably could not handle the frame syntax in any acceptable way. Others might have interpreted the frame *have to* as an adverb and thus supplied adjectival or participial completions. Finally, we had the group of children who gave target responses, interpreting *have to* as a verb form that requires the passive *be* + participle. In fact, this was clearly the most mature response for this sample, since it was the only one that increased rather than decreased with age. It is apparently the favored response in Black English Vernacular, even though the others may be acceptable if the above interpretations hold true. No other variants were common in this group.

Summary

All of our groups showed a fairly steady developmental acquisition of the passive complement construction required by these items. The two lower-class groups appeared to be learning it just as rapidly as, although possibly at a later time than, the middle-class group. We suggest that this may be due in part to a higher rate of deletion of the inflected forms of the auxiliary *be* in passive constructions in their dialects, thus giving the children fewer models of the auxiliary + participle form of the passive. A complicating factor in Black English Vernacular is the possible status of *hafta* as an adverb rather than a verb.

All three groups supplied uninflected forms as the most common variation; this response dropped out rapidly with age. It can be interpreted as the omission of *be* from an attempted passive, as the reassignment of the subject from the inanimate *pictures* or *dress* to the animate participants in the stories, or (in Black English Vernacular) as the result of interpreting the *have to* in the frame as adverb rather than verb, together with deletion of the participial ending.

MODAL AUXILIARIES

English modal verbs, such as *can, could, will,* etc. have many important functions. As the first members of verb phrases, they carry tense and sometimes negation information: *He can't swim, He couldn't understand, He could have been found,* etc.

Modals are used in a variety of semantic contexts in English (Quirk, Greenbaum, Leech, and Svartvik, 1972: 82–103). Some are fairly straightforward, with meanings like ability (*He can reach the cookies*) or future prediction (*He will arrive tomorrow*). Somewhat more complicated situations involve *if* clauses and main clause modals in conditional sentences, such as *If they fall, they can (will, might) get hurt.* Counterfactual sentences are similar in form, as in *If this butterfly didn't have wings, it couldn't fly.* Another use is in indirect questions, such as *She asked if he could do it.*

Most grammarians introduce modality or auxiliary information at a basic level of the grammar, although details of transformations or realization rules vary somewhat from one linguist to another. We have grouped together a rather disparate group of items on the basis of the target modal forms in surface structure. Although we do not want to make any claims about underlying identity of process, the similarity of the acquisition curves motivated our decision to discuss these items together.

An interesting pattern in the development of auxiliaries, including modals, is reported by Bellugi (1967). The earliest forms, *don't* and *can't*, are negatives. Bellugi suggests that these forms are unanalyzed negative elements for the child at this point. Later on, *do* and *can* begin to appear in other contexts; a general proliferation of auxiliary forms occurs at the same time. According to this analysis, a form such as *can't* is thus produced by two totally different rules at different points in linguistic development: first as a negative lexical unit, and later as the product of modal + negative rules.

We included five items to test modal auxiliaries. One tested a future or conditional clause after an *if* clause; one tested *can* + past tense + negation; one tested a counterfactual clause after an *if* clause; and two tested indirect questions in an *if* clause. On the basis of the target curves, the first three items are discussed together, then the last two.

FUTURE-CONDITIONAL, NEGATIVE MODAL, AND COUNTERFACTUAL

The items we used to test for our first three uses of the modal auxiliary were the following:

Item 13a (future-conditional):
Rose and Sarah climbed way up into this tree. If they fall out of the tree now, _____ (they'll get hurt, they might get hurt, they're going to get hurt).

Item13b (modal + negative):
James wanted to get some cookies from the table. So he stood on his tip-toes and he stretched and he stretched but _____ (he couldn't get them, he didn't get them).

Item13c (counterfactual):
If this butterfly didn't have wings, _____ (it couldn't fly).

Our results on these items are summarized in Table 16.

Table 16

Modal auxiliaries: future-conditional, modal + negative, and counterfactual—Percentages of responses on Items 13a, 13b, and 13c

	Middle-class white			Lower-class white			Lower-class black		
Age:	3	4	5	3	4	5	3	4	5
N:	105	100	103	25	24	27	23	35	27
(a) (future-conditional): *If they fall out of the tree now _____.*									
Modal + verb (they will get hurt, they might get hurt)	69	85	88	20	71	56	13	37	44
Premodal *be going to* + verb (they're going to get hurt, they're gonna get hurt)	4	5	1	24	0	11	9	0	0
Omission of modal (they get hurt)	15	2	5	24	8	7	22	6	30
Omission of *be* (they going to get hurt, they gonna get hurt)	3	0	1	12	4	7	35	40	11
Double modal (they might could get hurt)	0	1	1	8	0	0	4	3	0
Other clause or verb phrase	9	7	3	12	17	19	17	14	15
N:	105	99	102	23	24	27	21	36	26
(b) (modal + negative): *He stretched and stretched but _____.*									
Modal + past + negative (he couldn't get them)	58	73	87	9	13	63	10	53	46
Do + past + negative (he didn't get them)	7	7	6	9	42	11	0	8	8
Omission of modal (he not get cookies)	4	5	1	35	8	11	14	6	12
Omission of past tense (he can't get them)	25	12	3	39	33	15	42	28	27
Omission of negative (he got them)	5	2	0	4	0	0	33	0	8
Other clause	1	0	1	4	4	0	0	6	0

Table 16—continued

	Middle-class white			Lower-class white			Lower-class black		
Age:	3	4	5	3	4	5	3	4	5
N:	105	99	104	24	24	27	23	36	27
(c) (counterfactual): *If this butterfly didn't have wings.* _____.									
Modal + past + verb (*could, couldn't, would, wouldn't*)	64	73	91	21	33	52	0	47	41
Omission of modal	13	4	2	17	21	11	30	14	4
Omission of past tense (*can, will, can't, won't*)	13	21	7	4	33	33	13	22	37
Substitution of *do* (*didn't, don't*)	3	2	0	4	0	0	4	3	4
Other clause	8	1	0	54	13	4	52	14	15

Standard English Acquisition: Middle-Class White

Target. There were no significant differences in target MODAL acquisition on the three items at any age for middle-class white children. There was a tendency, however, for the target forms to be given at a slightly higher rate at age 3 and especially at age 4 on the future conditional item (13a).

On the negative item (13b), we see that as on such other items as the secondary conjunction, the addition of negation may have increased the difficulty of items for children who have only tenuous control of the structure. For the modals, however, this may not hold at the youngest age; recall Bellugi's report that *can't, don't,* etc. appear very early as undifferentiated negative elements. We investigated Bellugi's hypothesis by comparing Items 13a (conditional) and 13b (negative). (We temporarily ignored Item 13c because either affirmative or negative forms could be given.) On the two items being compared, we added together all modal responses, including those that had incorrect tenses. We found no differences at ages 4 and 5; at these ages, 90 percent or more of the children supplied some sort of modal for both items. At age 3, however, 76 percent supplied a modal on the conditional item, and 90 percent on the negative item! This unexpectedly high performance at age 3 suggests to us that some of our 3-year-olds were at the more primitive stage reported by Bellugi, where the earliest *can't* or *don't* utterances are actually still undifferentiated negative elements. Support is given by the fact that on this item fully one-fourth of the 3-year-olds gave *can't* rather than *couldn't*. Bellugi reports that *can't* is one of the early undifferentiated negative elements; *couldn't* is learned later.

Another explanation of the high percentage of *can't* in this group is that the meaning of ability may be easier than the meanings carried by the future or conditional modals. If this is true, the 3-year-olds might supply the semantically simpler *can*, even in a negative context, more often than *might*, *will*, etc.

Item 13c, the counterfactual, also appeared to be slightly more difficult than the future-conditional, although not significantly so. There are two features of the item that might contribute to its difficulty. First, we should note that this is the only item on the test in which the picture gives clues conflicting with the linguistic context, rather than supporting and clarifying it. This was shown clearly by some of the 3-year-olds, who responded: *He does have wings!* Second, the stem included a negative hypothetical: *If this butterfly didn't have wings, _____* as opposed to a positive hypothetical: *If they fall out of the tree now, _____.* Despite these potential sources of difficulty, and surprisingly in view of Brown's (1973) report of no instances of the past tense for hypothetical status among his 2- and 3-year-old subjects, this item has a high success rate even for the youngest subjects. Our results indicate that nearly two-thirds of the middle-class 3-year-olds used the target MODAL + PAST + VERB on the counterfactual item. It would seem that the counterfactual is a structure that emerges relatively seldom in free speech but is nonetheless controlled rather early.

Variants. The MODAL WAS OMITTED by about 15 percent of the 3-year-olds on both the conditional and the counterfactual items but by only 4 percent on the negative. This is probably due to the same situation discussed earlier—that some 3-year-olds may have learned *can* but not the more conditional *will*, *might*, etc.; or they may be furnishing *can't* as an undifferentiated negative element, as Bellugi suggests.

Use of the modal with PAST TENSE OMITTED was a variant given by up to one-quarter of the younger children. A few children at each age

SUBSTITUTED do or PREMODALS, such as He didn't get them, or They're going to get hurt on these structures. These responses, though uncommon in our sample, are acceptable Standard English.

Dialect Variation: Lower-Class White

Target. In the lower-class white group, the level of target MOD-AL use is not as high or as clear-cut as in the middle-class group, but the pattern of acquisition is similar to that of the middle-class children on each item, with the target forms for the future conditional item (13a) tending to be given at higher rates than for the other items, especially at ages 3 and 4.

Turning to the negative item (13b), it will be recalled that in the middle-class group, a high incidence of can't at age 3 was part of a higher total of auxiliaries supplied on the negative than on the affirmative item. We did a similar computation of categories in this lower-class group, to arrive at total auxiliaries supplied regardless of correct tense inflection. The total percentages of subjects providing auxiliaries were statistically equivalent across items, and if anything, it was the affirmative item that was favored at age 3. We do not know if Bellugi's account is expected to apply across social class boundaries. Our data neither support nor refute her hypothesis for this group.

As in the middle-class group, the counterfactual item (13c) tended to be more difficult than the others, though not significantly so.

Variants. Higher proportions of lower-class white children than middle-class white children OMITTED THE MODAL in all three items. It is possible that this group is acquiring a dialect in which these forms are supplied variably rather than categorically (Labov, 1972a). If so, Bellugi's observation about the early status of modals as negative elements would have to be modified according to the obligatory contexts in adult speech.

On Item 13b, the OTHER AUXILIARY do + PAST + NEGATIVE response, didn't, rose at age 4, then declined again at age 5 as the MODAL + PAST + NEGATIVE response, couldn't, became more common. Neither of the other two groups showed this pattern. While the lower-class subjects at age 4 gave many didn't responses, the lower-class black and the middle-class white children preferred couldn't in this context. We know of no dialect feature that would explain this difference.

Among these lower-class white children, PAST TENSE OMISSION occurred among one-third of the 3- and 4-year-olds on the negative item, and among one-third of the 4- and 5-year-olds on the counterfactual item. OTHER CLAUSE responses were somewhat more common among these children than in the other groups, particularly on the counterfactual item, where half of the 3-year-olds gave such responses.

Dialect Variation: Lower-Class Black

Target. Again, the MODAL acquisition curves are not as clear for the lower-class black group as for the middle-class group. A closer look at Black English Vernacular suggests some reasons.

The future-conditional item (13a) did not seem to be favored to the same extent by the black children as by children in the other groups. In the other groups, the target forms on this item were supplied by up to one-third more 3- and 4-year-olds than were the targets of the other items. Labov's work suggests that among adolescent speakers of Black English Vernacular, two dialect rules are relevant to the responses on Item 13a. He notes, first, that deletion of *be* forms before the verb *gonna* is practically categorical—it is almost never realized in the surface forms. *They gonna get hurt* is thus a good form in Black English Vernacular. Second, he reports that in Northern black dialects, final /-l/ is frequently not present. He states, "The loss of final /-l/ has a serious effect on the realization of future forms:

> you'll = you   he'll = he
>
> they'll = they   she'll = she

In many cases, therefore, the colloquial future is identical with the colloquial present" [Labov, 1972b:24].

Thus, a variety of forms are generated for Item 13a by the rules for Black English Vernacular: *They will get hurt, They get hurt, They gonna get hurt, They might could get hurt,* etc. Four categories for Item 13a in Table 16 (modal + verb, omission of modal, omission of *be*, double modal) are all acceptable in Black English Vernacular.

The percentage of black children using one of these acceptable forms rises slightly from 79 percent of 3-year-olds and 81 percent of 4-year-olds to 85 percent of 5-year-olds. This variety of acceptable forms makes it difficult to compare across items or across groups. Among the acceptable Black English Vernacular forms on this item, there was a shift of preference. The favored response at ages 3 and 4 is *they gonna* with OMISSION OF *be*; at age 5 it is the target MOD-AL + VERB forms, *they will*, etc. (Note that 5 percent or less of the middle-class white 3- and 4-year-olds used *going to* on this item, whereas 70–85 percent used modals.) Thus, the decline in our category OMISSION OF *be* is not due to its status as an error, since it is acceptable in Black English Vernacular. Rather, it is due to the 5-year-olds making less use of the premodal *gonna* as they shift to modal forms.

The negative item (13b), which required MODAL + PAST + NEGATIVE, elicited as many target responses as did the future-conditional item (13a); none of the variations on 13b is acceptable in Black English Vernacular.

As in the case of the lower-class white children, the Bellugi hypothesis regarding the negative is neither supported nor refuted for the lower-class black group. Modals or premodals were supplied at a greater rate for the affirmative than for the negative item at age 3; at ages 4 and 5, more modals or premodals were supplied for the negative than for the affirmative item. However, if all correct Black English Vernacular forms are counted, the affirmative item (13a) is ahead (81 percent versus 61 percent). In short, the data give no clear-cut answers about the genesis of modals for this group.

On the counterfactual item (13c) the black group shows an abrupt increase in the target MODAL + PAST + VERB response, from no instances at age 3 to 40–50 percent at ages 4 and 5.

Variants. As explained in the discussion of the target, OMISSION OF THE MODAL is an acceptable Black English Vernacular completion of Item 13a. The other two items had relatively low or declining percentages of this variation.

OMISSION OF THE PAST TENSE was the most common variation in this group, ranging from about 40 percent of the 3-year-olds to about 25 percent of the 4- and 5-year-olds. This response may be consistent with the less frequent marking of the past tense in Black English Vernacular, since the regular final /-t/ or /-d/ is often deleted by phonological rules. Irregular verbs, however, normally are marked for past (*tell-tol'*). Note that more of the black 4- and 5-year-old children marked the past in the irregular forms (*could, did*) on this item than on items 9a and 9b, where fewer than half included the /-d/ or /-t/ in the regular verbs *comb* and *wash*. On Item 13c, OMISSION OF THE PAST TENSE, as in *It can swim* or *It will fall*, increased to reach 37 percent at age 5. As in the future-conditional item, the *if* seemed to be a clear signal to the children that a modal was required. It is more difficult to explain the increase in present tense modals in the context of *didn't*; possibly older children would use more tense concord, although the leveling off of the target curve did not look especially promising.

The only other variation that occurred to any extent was OMISSION OF THE NEGATIVE (*and got cookies*) by 30 percent of the 3-year-olds. Possibly these children did not comprehend the constraints imposed by *but*. Very few older children gave this response.

INDIRECT QUESTION

The items we used to test the modal auxiliary in an indirect question were the following:

Item 13d: The dog wanted to go for a walk but Barbara didn't have time to take him, so she asked if Dan _____ (would take him).

Item 13e: Eddie didn't know how to tie his shoes, so he asked if his mother _____ (would tie them).

Our results on these items are summarized in Table 17.

Standard English Acquisition: Middle-Class White

Target. The two indirect question items were clearly more difficult for the middle-class white group, than were the other three modal items—significantly so at every age. Again, they yielded similar curves, which go from about one-third at age 3 to two-thirds at age 5. In contrast, close to 90 percent of the middle-class white 5-year-olds responded correctly to the other modal items.

It is obvious from the striking parallelism of these two items, in contrast to the other three, that those children who controlled modals in such structures as the conditional did not acquire the indirect

Table 17

Modal auxiliaries: indirect question—Percentages of
responses on Items 13d and 13e

	Middle-class white			Lower-class white			Lower-class black		
Age:	3	4	5	3	4	5	3	4	5
N:	99	99	103	21	24	26	22	31	27
(d) She asked if Dan _____.									
Modal + past (could/ would take him)	33	40	61	8	33	22	0	33	33
Past tense (did, wanted to)	7	7	1	4	0	0	3	3	0
Omission of modal (take him)	15	15	1	15	33	37	35	33	32
Omission of past (can/ will take him)	12	14	9	4	12	26	0	7	12
Infinitive (to take him)	3	4	2	4	8	7	18	19	8
New clause (and he took him)	28	19	23	31	8	7	20	7	15
Other	0	0	0	35	4	4	22	0	0
N:	100	98	103	23	24	27	23	35	27
(e) He asked if his mother _____.									
Modal + past (could/ would tie them)	35	45	64	4	46	33	4	28	19
Omission of modal (tie them)	19	13	7	43	38	26	74	33	44
Omission of past (can/ will tie them)	7	14	8	11	12	15	0	0	15
Infinitive (to tie them)	21	8	10	4	0	26	12	30	19
New clause (and she tied them)	18	20	11	26	4	0	9	6	4
Other	0	0	0	11	0	0	4	4	0

speech structure until somewhat later. The complexity of the response itself is not a problem. For example, the response *He couldn't
reach it* on Item 13b involves supplying subject and negative elements as well as the modal, past, verb, and object. In Item 13e, subject and negative are not required, and verb and object are optional,
in the response *would (tie them)*. Only the MODAL + PAST is needed.
The difference, therefore, must lie in the complexity of the total
structure. We suggest that the clauses involving the indirect ques-

tion response are more deeply embedded syntactically than are those in the other items. The modal + negative item is simply conjoined with *but;* the future-conditional and counterfactual items both involve *if-then* constructions with no further subordination. Here, in the indirect question items, we have an *if* clause (*if Dan would take him*) within another clause (*she asked* . . .), which in turn is subordinated by *so* after a main clause involving a negative (*Barbara didn't have time to take him, so* . . .). Further work on modals should include a less embedded indirect question or a more deeply embedded conditional item, to permit more accurate comparison of the structures.

Variants. The most common variations on the indirect question items suggest that the children were disregarding the *if* in the story stem, although the testers were compulsively careful to articulate it clearly. This interpretation of the stem led to such responses as a NEW CLAUSE: *She asked [if] Dan (and he took him)* and *He asked [if] his mother (and she tied them)*; or an INFINITIVE: *He asked [if] his mother (to tie them)*.

Similarly, about 15 percent of the children OMITTED THE MODAL at ages 3 and 4; this response did not drop out until age 5. In contrast, modal omission dropped out at age 4 on the first three items.

Dialect Variation: Lower-Class White

Target. With the lower-class white children, as in the case of the middle-class children, the two indirect question items lagged behind the other three modal items. The proportion of target MODAL + PAST responses climbed sharply between ages 3 and 4, then dropped slightly at age 5, but there were never more than half using the target forms.

Variants. The variations were not consistent, which may indicate that children who did not yet control the target structure were responding to idiosyncratic semantic aspects of the individual items. On Item 13d, OMISSION OF THE MODAL: *She asked if Dan (take him)* and OMISSION OF PAST: *She asked if Dan (can)* increased nonsignificantly with age; on Item 13e, omission of the modal remained high, as in 13d, but there was also an increase in INFINITIVE responses: *He asked if his mother (to tie them)*.

Dialect Variation: Lower-Class Black

Target. Again, with the lower-class black children, the two indirect question items lagged behind the other modal items in rate of acquisition; use of the target MODAL + PAST increased between ages 3 and 4, then leveled off or dropped slightly at age 5, just as in the lower-class white group.

It should be noted that if these items were to appear in Black English Vernacular, or in informal Southern speech, they might well be expressed as *She asked Dan would he take him* and *He asked his mother would she tie them.* Labov (1972b) found that 80 percent of the preadolescent boys in his study produced such forms, preserving the order of the yes-no question and embedding it without a complementizer. An imitation task indicated to Labov that the boys had no difficulty understanding the Standard English *if* form, since they quickly translated it into their own preferred form. Although our subjects were younger and might have experienced some trouble understanding the items, the Labov finding and the semantically reasonable nature of the children's responses seem to indicate that our sentence frames did not completely confuse the children. What is more likely is that these children had heard relatively few Standard English indirect questions; they were learning a different form and thus did not produce the target form as early as did the middle-class children. To the extent that the lower-class white group may experience the influence of Southern dialects, they could be expected to show a similar lag. It is interesting that only a few of our subjects converted the word order in their responses to correspond to the preferred Black English Vernacular form, which required them to overlook the *if* and respond *She asked [if] Dan (would he take him)* or *He asked [if] his mother (would she tie them).*

The situation in the lower-class groups is complicated by the fact that modals are deleted more often in adult lower-class dialects than in middle-class speech, and by the fact that—in Black English Vernacular especially—alternative forms are frequently permissible on some items.

Variants. The same variants (OMISSION OF MODAL, NEW CLAUSE) seemed to be favored by the black children as by the white, although at somewhat different levels than in the white groups; for example, three-fourths of the 3-year-olds in this group omitted the modal on Item 13e. INFINITIVE responses were also common on both

items in this group, with about 15 percent giving infinitive structures, as opposed to 4 percent of the lower-class whites.

Summary

Despite class and race differences, the use of the particular target
modals we were testing tended to increase with age in all groups.
The middle-class white group, for whom the test was designed, were
using the target responses over half the time at age 3 and around 90
percent of the time at age 5 on the future-conditional, negative, and
counterfactual items; on the two indirect question items, they were
using target responses one-third of the time at age 3 and two-thirds
of the time at age 5.

Several conclusions may be drawn from the responses to these
five items. First, in all groups, the indirect question structure tends
to lag behind the other modal structures, as may be seen by comparing percentages of target responses. Since the surface responses
were not more complicated than on the other modal auxiliary items,
we assume that the indirect speech items were more difficult for
these groups to comprehend, perhaps because of deep embedding in
the sentences of the story frames.

Middle-class white 3-year-olds show support for Bellugi's suggestion that modals originate in such undifferentiated negative
forms as *can't*, since more 3-year-olds gave modals on the negative
item than on the positive one. However, the two lower-class groups
do not show a similar pattern.

Chapter 5

Propositional Structures

INFINITIVE COMPLEMENT

The infinitive complement structures we tested were of the type that involve transformed sentences as objects of the verb. Chomsky (1965) and Stockwell, Schachter, and Partee (1973) have distinguished between verbs of the *expect* type and verbs of the *persuade* type. In the first type, the entire complement is object: *They expected the doctor to examine John* is equivalent to *They expected John to be examined by the doctor*. With verbs of the *persuade* type, however, *They persuaded the doctor to examine John* is not the same as *They persuaded John to be examined by the doctor*. We tested only the first type of structure, using the verb *want* in two items. The *persuade* type of verb might give different results.

Want, expect, and similar verbs can occur with either the same or a different noun phrase as subject of the complement sentence. If the same noun phrase is underlying subject, it is deleted in the surface structure: *John wants (Bill leave)* becomes *John wants Bill to leave,* but *John wants (John leave)* becomes *John wants to leave*. Again, the first type of sentence can be postulated to be less complex transformationally, since the second noun phrase is not deleted. This simpler type was used in both items to ensure parallelism.

The items used to assess the infinitive complement were the following:

Item 14a: These boys took out too many toys to play with. Mother said, "Boys, I want you _____ (to clean up, to put them away)."
Item 14b: Doug's wagon broke—the wheel came off. He wants his brother _____ (to fix it).

The responses on these items are summarized in Table 18.

Standard English Acquisition: Middle-Class White

Target. Within the middle-class white sample, the target IN-FINITIVE COMPLEMENT, *to* + verb, occurred at a high frequency even among the 3-year-olds (81–88 percent) and continued to increase at ages 4 and 5, though the level was too close to ceiling to attain significance.

Variants. The only variant of any frequency was the OMISSION OF *to*. The children did not appear to have difficulty with the mean-

Table 18
Infinitive complement—Percentages of responses on Items 14a and 14b

		Middle-class white			Lower-class white			Lower-class black		
Age:		3	4	5	3	4	5	3	4	5
N:		102	99	102	25	24	27	23	36	27
(a) "I want you _____."										
Infinitive complement (to clean up)		81	84	90	28	38	56	39	67	67
Omission of *to* (clean up)		19	16	10	72	63	44	61	33	33
N:		104	100	104	25	24	26	23	35	27
(b) He wants his brother _____.										
Infinitive complement (to fix it)		88	89	98	28	54	77	35	86	74
Omission of *to* (fix it)		13	11	2	72	46	23	65	14	26

ing involved. They seemed to know that a proposition such as *You (clean it)* or *his brother (fix it)* was the reasonable completion of the story. One possible reason for the omission of *to* is that it normally occurs with weak stress. Some children may not differentiate the obligatory *to* from the rest of the speech stream until a later age. On Item 14a, another interpretation is possible. A few children may have been giving a command form, as in *Mother said, "Boys, I want you. (Clean up!)"* This interpretation is not possible for Item 14b. The higher frequency of *to* omission on Item 14a than on Item 14b among most groups may be because children were using this interpretation on Item 14a.

Dialect Variation: Lower-Class White

Target and variants.   While the pattern of acquisition was roughly similar to that of the middle-class white children, the lower-class white children used the target INFINITIVE COMPLEMENT far less frequently. At age 3, they lagged behind the middle-class group by 50–60 percentage points; at age 5, the gap, though narrowing, is still 20–30 percentage points. Although there is a possibility that the dialect of this group deletes unstressed syllables more frequently than does the middle-class dialect, the difference would seem to be quantitative rather than qualitative. The data indicate that including the *to* is the more mature form in both dialects.

Dialect Variation: Lower-Class Black

Target and variants.   The lower-class black group also seems to be headed for a usage of the INFINITIVE COMPLEMENT similar to that of Standard English; two-thirds to three-fourths of the black 5-year-olds used the form. These children began at a low level (35–40 percent at age 3); but they acquired the form very rapidly between ages 3 and 4, then held steady. This contrasts with the somewhat more even rate of increase shown by the white groups, as can be seen in the tables.

Summary

On these two infinitive complement items, all three groups seemed to be acquiring a similar favored structure. Another similarity across the three groups was the lack of variants other than the omission of *to*. The middle-class white children began with a high rate of usage of the infinitive complement and increased to around 90 percent by age 5. The two lower-class groups began at a much lower rate but increased even more rapidly, to a 5-year level of 55–75 percent. The lower-class black group showed a very rapid increase in percentage of target usage between ages 3 and 4, whereas the proportions of target usage by the white groups increased at steadier rates.

RELATIVE CLAUSE

When a whole clause becomes a constituent of another clause in English, there are various signals of this embedding. One type of embedding is the relative clause. The embedded clause modifies a noun phrase in the main clause by addition of the appropriate relative pronoun [usually considered to be the realization of the features (+WH) and (+pronoun)], and by deletion of the original noun. For example, if one wishes to say that *Sophomores love beer* and also that *Sophomores are pudgy*, one clause can be embedded in the other by relativization: *Sophomores, who love beer, are pudgy*. A logically different meaning is expressed in the restrictive relative clause. This type of relative clause limits the applicability of the main clause assertion to the particular members of subgroups specified by the embedded clause. For example, the foregoing sentence asserts that all sophomores are pudgy; but one can limit the assertion by using a restrictive relative instead: *Sophomores who love beer are pudgy*, or even *The sophomore who loves beer is pudgy*—which imply that all the other sophomores are *not* necessarily pudgy.

Deletion of the relative pronoun in these clauses occurs in rather restricted environments in Standard English (although it is common in Southern dialects such as Black English Vernacular). These environments are specified in the relative clause reduction transformation rule (Jacobs and Rosenbaum, 1968). This rule states that the pronoun subject of a relative clause may be deleted if it precedes a segment with the features (+copula) and (+present); the copula is deleted also. For example, we can optionally delete the relative pronoun to yield semantically equivalent sentences such as *The soph-*

omores *who are drinking beer are pudgy* and *The sophomores drinking beer are pudgy.*

Although the relative pronoun subject may be deleted only in these restricted environments in Standard English, the relative pronoun object can always be optionally deleted. For example, if the two clauses involved are *The beer is delicious* and *Sophomores love the beer,* a restrictive relative construction could be *The beer that sophomores love is delicious* or, alternatively, *The beer sophomores love is delicious.* Similarly, *He lives in the house* and *This is the house* can yield *This is the house (that) he lives in,* or *This is the house where he lives.*

We tested relative clauses with three items that could be completed with restrictive relatives. In two, the usual way of completing the item would be with the relative pronoun subject of the embedded clause. These items required obligatory use of the relative unless the reduction transformation yielding the -ing form was applied. Therefore, each could be completed either by adding an embedded clause with habitual present tense verb and obligatory relative pronoun or by using a present progressive and optional relative pronoun. Both of these items involved human referents for the pronouns, allowing *who* or *that* to be used.

The third item involved a relative pronoun (*which* or *that*, in the usual completion) that was object of its clause and could be deleted; it referred to an inanimate object or location. Another possible completion used the relative *where.* This pronoun includes prepositional information relating to location and therefore cannot be deleted: *This is the street that he lives on, This is the street he lives on,* but *This is the street where he lives, *This is the street he lives.*

The items we used to test restrictive relative clause structures were the following:

> Item 15a: Some children walk to school and some children ride the bus. These are the children _____ (who ride the bus, that ride).
> Item 15b: Some mothers go to work and some mothers stay home. These are the mothers _____ (who stay at home, that stay home).
> Item 15c: This is a street in our city. Jack lives in one of these houses. This is the house_____ (where he lives, he lives in, that he lives in).

Two comments on scoring are necessary here. First, errors of verb agreement were not scored separately; for example, *that he live in* would be counted as a target response. Second, we had hoped to have a separate category for *what* relatives, as in *These are the children (what ride the bus)*. Only one child uttered an unmistakable *what*, however; on most protocols the pronoun was transcribed /ʌt/, which did not allow us to differentiate between *what* and *that*.

The responses of the three samples on these items are summarized in Table 19.

Table 19

Relative clause—Percentages of responses on Items 15a, 15b, and 15c.

	Middle-class white			Lower-class white			Lower-class black		
Age:	3	4	5	3	4	5	3	4	5
N:	102	100	102	26	24	27	21	34	25
(a) *These are the children* _____.									
Relative clause (*who ride the bus*)	64	79	91	23	58	67	28	24	36
Reduced relative: progressive (*riding the bus*)	3	1	0	4	4	4	0	24	11
Omission of relative pronoun (*ride the bus*)	26	13	7	58	25	19	52	32	40
Another type of clause	5	1	0	12	8	4	5	5	5
Other (*bus*)	1	6	0	4	4	7	15	13	7
N:	106	100	104	25	23	27	23	35	27
(b) *These are the mothers* _____.									
Relative clause (*who stay at home*)	72	80	88	16	34	56	3	23	56
Reduced relative: progressive (*staying at home*)	1	0	1	0	14	11	8	23	0
Omission of relative pronoun (*stay at home*)	25	17	10	40	39	30	22	40	33
Another type of clause	1	2	1	16	9	0	17	11	4
Babies	2	2	1	28	4	4	52	3	7
Other	0	0	0	0	0	0	0	0	0

Table 19—continued

	Middle-class white			Lower-class white			Lower-class black		
Age:	3	4	5	3	4	5	3	4	5
N:	99	97	100	26	24	27	23	36	26
(c) *This is the house* _____.									
Relative clause (*where he lives, that he lives in, he lives in*)	54	73	65	24	46	74	27	55	41
Faulty relative clause (*he lives, what he lives in, where he lives at, as he lives in*)	16	10	8	4	0	7	0	4	15
Another type of clause	8	10	15	24	25	0	23	20	7
Noun (*roof*), irrelevant prepositional phrase, or repeated phrase	19	4	7	48	25	11	50	20	37
Relevant prepositional phrase (*of Jack, for Jack*)	0	3	3	0	4	7	0	0	0

Standard English Acquisition Middle-Class White

Relative Pronoun as Subject—Items 15a and 15b

Target. The data show that roughly two-thirds of the middle-class children had command of the RELATIVE CLAUSE by the age of 3. Control of the structure developed steadily, so that 80 percent of the 4-year-olds and 90 percent of the 5-year-olds used it correctly.

Very few children in the middle-class white group chose the option of using the REDUCED RELATIVE (present progressive with deleted relative pronoun and auxiliary): *These are the children (riding the bus)*.

Variants. The most common variation was OMISSION OF THE RELATIVE PRONOUN where it was required; the proportions giving this response decline with age, from 25 percent to 10 percent. A few children gave ANOTHER TYPE OF CLAUSE that did not seem to be an attempt at a relative clause, such as *These are the mothers (and these are the babies)*. These responses were probed with a further attempt to elicit the relative clause. Only responses of the children who perseverated in this completion after the probe are categorized as such in the table.

Relative Pronoun as Object—Item 15c

Target. On item 15c, in which the relative pronoun was object of the target RELATIVE CLAUSE, the pattern of results is not as clear-cut as that on the first type of clause. About half of the 3-year-olds and three-fourths of the 4-year-olds handled the structure correctly. No further progress was made by the 5-year-olds, whose target usage showed a nonsignificant decline.

Variants. A fairly large proportion of children (declining with age from 16 percent to 8 percent) gave FAULTY RELATIVE CLAUSE responses that showed an attempt to form a relative clause without being able to handle the locational verb *live in* and the locational relative *where.* For example, a child might respond *where he lives at* instead of *where he lives,* adding a preposition that adults omit in the context of *where;* or he might respond *(that) he lives,* omitting a preposition that adults add when *where* is not the relative pronoun (Quirk et al., 1972: 866). Another subgroup of these children had difficulty with the form of the relative pronoun, giving responses like *as he lives in.* These children apparently had the basic relative clause structure but were still on their way to fully acceptable forms of this rather specialized type.

More children gave responses that were ANOTHER TYPE OF CLAUSE on Item 15c (such as *and this is the sidewalk* or *mm-hmm*) than on the other items. Item 15c also elicited more REPEATED PHRASES or NOUNS (*the house*) than did the other items. It is clear that, combining these categories, about one-fifth of these children did not feel constrained to use a relative clause on this item even after probing; less than 5 percent failed to give relative clauses on the other items. We have no way of knowing whether on Item 15c the large proportion of responses other than relative clauses was due to the overall semantics of this story or to difficulty with the relative clause structure itself. In this item, the relative pronoun is object of an embedded clause, may include locational information, and can be deleted. Any or all of these factors may have contributed to the lower proportions of target responses.

Dialect Variations: Lower-Class White

Relative Pronoun as Subject—Items 15a and 15b

Target. On the two items with the relative pronoun as subjects of the clause, 15–25 percent of the lower-class white 3-year-olds had mastered the Standard English form of the RELATIVE CLAUSE or REDUCED RELATIVE. This mastery escalated rapidly, so that 50–60 percent at age 4 and about 70 percent at age 5 used one of the two target structures.

Variants. Again, the most common variation on these two items was OMISSION OF THE RELATIVE PRONOUN. By age 5, this variation had declined to 20 percent on Item 15a and 30 percent on Item 15b. Southern dialects allow more deletion of relative pronouns, according to Labov (1972a). We do not know the linguistic background of the lower-class white group in our Northern cities, but it is interesting to see the high proportions of older children who omitted or deleted the relative pronoun in this group.

Relative Pronoun as Object—Item 15c

Target. On the item that required a relative pronoun in the object slot of the target RELATIVE CLAUSE, the lower-class white group showed steady development, with one-fourth of the 3-year-olds, one-half of the 4-year-olds, and three-fourths of the 5-year-olds handling the pattern correctly in Standard English.

Variants. Few FAULTY RELATIVE CLAUSE responses were given. As in the case of the middle-class white children, larger percentages (than on 15a and 15b) gave responses that were neither relative clauses nor attempts at relative clauses. Again, it is not possible to determine whether this was due to less constraint in the item or to avoidance of a more difficult structure by the children.

Dialect Variations: Lower-Class Black

Relative Pronoun as Subject—Items 15a and 15b

Target. Combined target RELATIVE CLAUSE or REDUCED RELATIVE responses increased from 28 percent to 48 percent on Item 15a, and from 11 percent to 56 percent on Item 15b. The latter item was more difficult for the 3- and 4-year-olds of this group, as it was for the lower-class white children. Although the curves for the two groups are not completely parallel, it is clear that the restrictive relative forms are increasingly favored in this group. Up to one-fifth of the children at age 4 used the reduced relative (progressive) form (*riding the bus*), which is a greater proportion than in either of the other groups.

Variants. As mentioned previously, Labov (1970: 189) notes that deletion of *that* is common in many Southern dialects, including Black English Vernacular. The steady high percentages of children OMITTING THE RELATIVE PRONOUN in such responses as *These are the children (go on the bus)* may reflect this option of Black English Vernacular. As in other items (such as those involving *be*), the younger children may have been omitting a form because they had not acquired it; the older children may have been sometimes supplying the form and sometimes deleting it in accordance with Black English Vernacular rules.

Over half of the 3-year-olds gave the response *babies* on Item 15b, apparently reflecting an interpretation of the plural *mothers* as possessive *mothers'*. This response dropped out abruptly at age 4.

Relative Pronoun as Object—Item 15c

Target and variants. On Item 15c, there does not seem to be the consistent lag in the use of the target RELATIVE CLAUSE that we noted in the white groups, although the curves are only roughly parallel. The deletion of the relative pronoun, which was discussed in relation to Items 15a and 15b, may account for some of the similarity, since such responses would be target responses on this supposedly more difficult item but not on the first two. Rather larger proportions of 4- and 5-year-olds gave NOUN or PREPOSITIONAL PHRASE responses on this item than on the other two; we find again that it was less successful as an item in constraining possible types of responses.

Summary

All three groups showed strong developmental trends favoring the target forms of the restrictive relative clause in which the relative pronoun is subject of the embedded clause and cannot ordinarily be deleted in Standard English. The most common variation was omission or deletion of the relative pronoun, particularly by the lower-class groups. This response may be related to the tendency in certain dialects, including Black English Vernacular, to delete relative pronouns more often than does Standard English. Item 15c, which was designed to assess the restrictive relative (in which the relative pronoun is object of the embedded clause), elicited more responses, compared to 15a and 15b, that were unsuccessful attempts to give a relative clause. However, there were also more responses of other types, which suggests that 15c may have been less constraining than the other two. Therefore, the conclusion that this type of relative clause is more difficult must remain tentative.

SECONDARY CONJUNCTION

English, like other languages, has a variety of devices for shortening reference to elements of the message that the hearer or reader already knows. Some of these devices involve rather complicated linguistic descriptions and could be expected to be relatively late in acquisition. One of these structures is the secondary conjunction, as in the sentence *John was eating and so was Bill*. The second of the two conjoined clauses means *Bill was eating too*; however, since the predicate is identical to that of the first clause, a complicated set of predicate transformations can yield *so was Bill*. The set includes the following: (1) predicate truncation deletes the predicate except for the first member of the auxiliary; (2) if there is no auxiliary (such as *have* or *be* or a modal), *do* insertion adds the pro-form *do* to carry the tense and other verb information; (3) auxiliary shift places the auxiliary or *do* in front of the nominal. In addition to these predicate transformations, the obligatory subject noun phrase may be pronominalized optionally. The forms must be in the appropriate tense, number, and so forth. *So* has been treated in different ways. Stockwell, Schachter, and Partee (1973) suggest that *too* and *so* can be viewed as conditioned alternates, *so* occurring at the beginning of the conjoined sentence, *too* at the end of it.

If the sentences being conjoined are negative, further operations are involved. *Too* is transformed to the indeterminate *either*, and the negative element is attracted to this first indeterminate in the clause. Thus, from *John was not eating* and *Bill was not eating (too)* we can derive *John was not eating, and neither was Bill*. While there are problems with the derivation of these structures, discussed at length by Stockwell, et al. (1973: 269–273), the picture that emerges is one of complex structures likely to be fairly late in the acquisition process.

We tested four variations of this structure. Two items were affirmative: one with a simple habitual present tense that required *do* insertion in the second clause, the other with the auxiliary *be* in the present progressive. The other two items were negative: one used the modal *can*; the other used auxiliary *be* in the present progressive, to permit direct comparison with the affirmative *be* form. All of our items, positive and negative, required the same form of response from the children: *so* or *neither* was given in the stem, and the child was required to furnish the truncated predicate (with verbs *do* or *be* or a modal) in the appropriate form, to shift the auxiliary to the front of the nominal, and to furnish an appropriate noun phrase. The effects of negation and of individual verbs could be examined separately, since the response forms were the same.

There was a possibility that *and so* in the story stems would be interpreted *and therefore*, which of course would lead to a different type of response. The type of structure desired was therefore presented to the children in advance—two examples before the affirmative items and one before the negative items.

Following are the set items and test items for the secondary conjunction. All seven were presented in succession, so that the set to complete the items in the required way would remain relatively constant, but care was taken not to model the precise verb forms required by the test items.

> Set item: This girl ate some ice cream and so did this girl.
> Set item: This dog was barking and so was this dog.
> Item 16a: This clown laughs all the time and so _____ (does this clown).
> Item 16b: This girl is running and so _____ (is this one).
> Set item: This baby didn't finish her soup and neither did this baby.
> Item 16c: This baby can't walk and neither _____ (can this one).
> Item 16d: This baby isn't eating a cookie and neither _____ (is this boy).

The responses on the four test items are given in Table 20.

Table 20

Secondary conjunction—Percentages of responses on
Items 16a, 16b, 16c, and 16d

	Middle-class white			Lower-class white			Lower-class black		
Age:	3	4	5	3	4	5	3	4	5
N:	106	100	104	26	24	27	23	36	26
(a) (Affirmative) *This clown laughs all the time and so _____.*									
3rd person singular present tense form of verb *do* (*does that one/he*)	49	71	81	4	12	41	4	6	4
Uninflected form of verb *do* (*do that one/ he*)	0	0	0	0	19	7	0	22	22
3rd person singular form of *do* + negative (*doesn't that one/he*)	0	1	1	0	0	7	0	0	0
No auxiliary (*that one/ he*)	23	13	7	65	42	11	43	14	15
Clause that repeats verb (*that one [is] laughing*)	8	2	1	12	8	11	26	28	15
Wrong auxiliary (*is, can*)	9	4	3	4	16	11	7	0	0
Wrong tense (*did that one*)	2	3	3	0	0	15	0	6	19
Wrong order; right auxiliary and tense (*that one does, do*)	4	1	3	4	0	0	0	17	12
Primitive negative (*no, not*)	0	0	0	0	0	0	0	0	4
Other	2	2	0	12	0	0	17	8	11
(b) (Affirmative) *This girl is running and so _____.*									
3rd person singular present tense form of verb *be* (*is that one/ she*)	50	72	84	8	58	52	9	25	37
Uninflected form of verb *be* (*be that one*)	0	0	0	0	0	0	0	0	4

140

Table 20—continued

	Middle-class white			Lower-class white			Lower-class black		
Age:	3	4	5	3	4	5	3	4	5
N:	106	100	104	26	24	27	23	36	26
3rd person singular form of *be* + negative (*isn't that one/she*)	0	2	0	4	0	0	0	0	0
No auxiliary (*that one/ she*)	21	8	3	31	12	7	13	8	15
Clause that repeats verb (*that one [is] running*)	5	2	1	12	21	7	52	28	18
Wrong auxiliary (*can/ does/would*)	8	7	1	4	4	11	8	14	4
Wrong tense (*was*)	1	1	4	0	0	7	0	0	4
Wrong order; right auxiliary and tense (*that one is/isn't*)	14	8	7	19	4	8	9	17	4
Primitive negative (*no, not*)	0	0	0	0	0	0	0	0	0
Other	2	0	1	23	0	4	8	8	15
(c) (Negative) *This baby can't walk and neither* _____ .									
3rd person singular present tense form of verb *can* (*can that one/she*)	21	37	80	4	17	48	0	0	11
No auxiliary (*that one/ she*)	52	46	12	19	42	22	30	42	44
Clause that repeats the verb (*that one [is] walking*)	0	0	0	8	8	0	0	0	0
Wrong auxiliary (*does/ is*)	6	4	4	4	4	4	0	6	11
Wrong tense (*could*)	1	1	0	0	0	4	0	0	4
Wrong order; right auxiliary & tense (*that one can*)	0	1	1	4	4	0	4	6	4
Double negative with auxiliary (*that one can't*)	15	9	2	54	21	22	56	44	22
Primitive negative (*no, not, not walk*)	3	2	1	8	4	0	8	0	0
Other	3	1	0	0	0	0	0	3	4

Table 20—continued

	Middle-class white			Lower-class white			Lower-class black		
Age:	3	4	5	3	4	5	3	4	5
N:	106	100	104	26	24	27	23	36	26
(d) (Negative) *This boy isn't eating a cookie and neither* _____.									
3rd person singular present tense form of verb be (*is that one/he*)	24	43	80	0	33	48	4	14	22
No auxiliary (*that one/he*)	48	47	10	35	42	37	17	47	41
Clause that repeats the verb (*that one/he* [*is*] *eating*)	2	0	0	0	8	0	4	3	4
Wrong auxiliary (*does/can*)	2	4	4	8	0	8	4	0	4
Wrong tense (*was*)	0	0	0	0	0	0	0	0	0
Wrong order; right auxiliary and tense (*that one is*)	0	0	0	0	0	0	0	3	0
Double negative with auxiliary (*isn't, ain't*)	16	5	2	16	8	0	26	22	4
Primitive negative (*no, not, not eat*)	6	2	0	27	4	4	34	6	19
Other	0	1	1	12	4	4	9	6	7

Standard English Acquisition: Middle-Class White

Target. *Differences among auxiliaries:* In the middle-class white group, there were no differences in target attainment with THIRD PERSON SINGULAR PRESENT TENSE FORM OF VERB among items with different auxiliaries.

Affirmative-negative differences: The middle-class children were unusually consistent in target structure attainment with THIRD PERSON SINGULAR PRESENT TENSE FORM OF VERB and in sequence and rate of variation for the four items. On the two affirmative items, the target responses were given by almost identical proportions of the group—half of the 3-year-olds, 70 percent of the 4-year-olds, and 80 percent of the 5-year-olds. Development was steady and substantial through the ages studied. In contrast, the structures that combine negation with the secondary conjunction appeared later and were slower to develop; but again, the acquisition curves show close parallelism across the two negative items. The target responses, *can this one* for Item 16c and *is this boy* for Item 16d, were given by less than 25 percent of the 3-year-olds and 40 percent of the 4-year-olds, showing a considerable lag in control of the negative operation. Only about half of the 3- and 4-year-olds who had managed the affirmative item with *be* gave the corresponding response after *neither*, even though the required response was identical in form; 5-year-olds, however, performed at approximately the same target level (80 percent) on both constructions.

Variants. The most common variation on all four items was a response with NO AUXILIARY, resulting in such responses as *this clown* or *that one*. Such responses may reflect an appreciation of the semantic omission in the story stem—a second character had not been mentioned—without a corresponding ability to complete the syntactic structure. They may also reflect an overgeneralization of the deletion and truncation that occurs in this type of conjoining. This kind of response was far more common on the negative items; approximately half of the middle-class 3- and 4-year-olds omitted the auxiliary on Items 16c and 16d, but only 10 percent did so at age 5. On the affirmative items, 16a and 16b, incidence of the NO AUXILIARY variant was lower: 20 percent at age 3, 10 percent at age 4, and 5 percent at age 5.

Less than 10 percent of the middle-class children used the WRONG AUXILIARY even at age 3. A few used the WRONG ORDER, responding *that one is*, instead of *is that one*, especially on Item 16b. The only other common variation was the use of a DOUBLE NEGATIVE—a second negative after *neither* in the negative items—such as *This baby can't walk and neither (that one can't)* or, an even more PRIMITIVE NEGATIVE, *This boy isn't eating a cookie and neither (he not)*. This type of response was given by 15–20 percent of the 3-year-olds, but it dropped off sharply. These children may have had difficulty with the word *neither*; the response appeared to be a new sentence rather than an attempted completion.

Dialect Variation: Lower-Class White

Target. *Differences among auxiliaries:* On Item 16a, the lower-class white group, like the lower-class black group, showed a higher incidence of uninflected *do* at age 4; however, *do* was dropping out in favor of *does* by the age of 5. One of the more interesting findings on the secondary conjunction set was the lack of parallelism across items in the lower-class groups, which probably reflects in part the difference in the attainment of *do*, required by 16a, and *be*, required by 16b. In the lower-class white group, only one-third of the 4-year-olds and one-half of the 5-year-olds correctly used the negative *be* pattern. There were parallel differences in the performance of 3- and 4-year-olds on the negative items, where *can* was clearly more difficult than *be*.

The pattern of the four items shows that at age 4, the affirmative *be* form (*is*) was used by nearly 60 percent, the negative *be* (*is*) form by 33 percent, the affirmative *do* forms (*does* or *do*) by 31 percent, and the negative *can* (*can*) form by less than 20 percent.

These findings were somewhat puzzling at first, since these lower-class white children supplied *do* and *can* and negatives at a much higher rate in some of our other items. These children also deleted the affirmative auxiliary *is* about half the time in our present progressive item, where many dialects allow deletion. The clue may reside in relative ease of comprehension. Cazden (1968), working with middle-class children, found that the present progressive is used before the third person singular present tense marker. Brown (1973) reports that the progressive -*ing* is learned early, the third singular present later, and the progressive auxiliary *be* form later still. For the youngest lower-class white children, Item 16b may therefore have been easier to comprehend, contributing to the difference in response on these items. Another possibility is that the *is* form was modeled by the examiner in the first clause; *do* was not modeled, and its insertion probably involved added processing.

Affirmative-negative differences: As with the middle class group, only about half of the lower-class white children who gave the THIRD PERSON SINGULAR PRESENT TENSE FORM OF THE VERB *be* in the affirmative did so in the negative, indicating that extra comprehension processes are probably needed for the latter.

If we compare the verbs in secondary conjunction items with items testing simpler constructions, we find that the simpler constructions were completed correctly more often than the complicated secondary conjunction constructions. We may have in these items an example of the same sort of phenomenon observed by Bloom in younger children who "reduced" (deleted) certain constituents when they were producing complex structures. She notes that one of the main factors influencing which constituents were deleted was "the relative recency of the appearance of the category components that dominated the deleted or retained constituents in the phrase structures" (1968:168). We know that Brown's (1973) subjects acquired both the auxiliary *be* and the copular *be* before *do* or modals. If Bloom's observation is applicable to these older children, we could predict that increasing complexity of structure (by addition of negation or secondary conjunction operations) would affect the later acquired *do* and modals more than the *be* forms. Presumably the middle-class children have learned *be*, *do*, and modals thoroughly by this age, so the effect of negation is more even.

To summarize lower-class white target acquisition, 3-year-olds rarely used any form of the secondary conjunction; 4-year-olds supplied affirmatives with *be* over half the time, but extra operations like *do* insertion or negation depressed the proportion of target responses to about one-third; and negation with a modal verb rather than the auxiliary *be* was more difficult still. By age 5, however, half of the children completed the items successfully regardless of their form.

Variants. As in the case of the middle-class children, a response with NO AUXILIARY was a common lower-class white variation, particularly among the 3- and 4-year-olds. Significantly more subjects omitted it on the *do* item than on the *be* item, and on the negative items than on the affirmative items. Three-year-olds also gave a DOUBLE NEGATIVE variation, such as *that one can't* or *he ain't*, on the negative items. These forms dropped out on the item with *be* but were given by over 20 percent of even the 5-year-olds on the difficult negative modal item.

On the affirmative items, a number of children gave a CLAUSE THAT REPEATED THE VERB, rather than using the auxiliary or *do* substitute, giving such sentences as *This clown laughs all the time and so (this clown laughs)*. This may have indicated an interpretation of *so* in its "therefore" meaning, despite the set items; or it may simply have been a new sentence given with no attempt to finish the examiner's sentence; or it may indicate the child has not yet learned to use the pro-form.

About 10 percent of the lower-class white children used the WRONG AUXILIARY on the positive items (e.g., *can* where *do* was called for). These items also elicited responses in the WRONG TENSE from some children, the highest incidence being at age 5, at which age 7 percent responded in a wrong tense on the *be* item and 15 percent did so on the *do* item. Although a number of other variations appeared, none occurred in large enough percentages to warrant discussion for this group.

Dialect Variation: Lower-Class Black

Target. *Differences among auxiliaries:* The lower-class black children showed patterns of development roughly similar to those of the lower-class white group. Again, on both the affirmative and the negative items, we see a tendency to use the THIRD PERSON SINGULAR PRESENT TENSE FORM OF THE VERB more often with *be* than with *do* or *can.* The black children showed much more gradual gains in the use of *be* in this secondary conjunction context, remained at the 25 percent level through age 5 in combined *do* or *does* usage, and began to use the modal *can* at 5.

Affirmative-negative differences: As in the other groups, target responses with the THIRD PERSON SINGULAR PRESENT TENSE FORM OF THE VERB were not given as often on the negative items as on the affirmative ones.

Variants. Consistent with the other two groups, the most common variation given by the black children was a response with NO AUXILIARY. Omission of the auxiliary in the negative contexts tended to increase with age on both items, instead of declining as it did for the affirmative items. The response seemed to be increasing at the expense of DOUBLE NEGATIVE responses, which were most common among the youngest children.

The second most common variant on the affirmative items was giving a CLAUSE THAT REPEATED THE VERB rather than substituting the auxiliary or pro-form. This response, used by up to 20 percent of the lower-class white groups, was used by up to half of the black children. It was most frequent on Item 16b, *This girl is running, and so* _____ , where possibly the action picture and progressive tense made ongoing action more salient.

Over half of the lower-class black 3-year-olds supplied a DOUBLE NEGATIVE—that is, they included negative elements in their responses—after *neither: that one can't* on Item 16c and *he ain't* or *not eat* on Item 16d. The proportions decreased over age, more rapidly on the *be* item. Labov (1972b) notes that in Black English Vernacular, negation applies to various elements of a sentence with different frequencies. Negation applies almost always to indeterminates within a clause. However, it applies only half or less than half of the time to the verb, and less than one-third of the time to indeterminates outside the clause. Labov furnishes no figures on the particular type of reduced clause we are dealing with here. Our guess is that *neither* would elicit a relatively low rate of negative concord in the following clause in adult speakers of Black English Vernacular, and that the falling developmental curves may be indicative of increasing mastery of the Black English Vernacular negative concord rules, as well as of the secondary conjunction rules.

As in the other two samples, responses with the WRONG ORDER, such as *this one is,* occurred occasionally in the lower-class black group, especially on Item 16b. What might have been happening in these responses is a failure to shift the auxiliary to the front of the noun phrase. If so, the result is surprising, since lower-class dialect provides for much practice in auxiliary shift. For example, in embedded questions, when the Standard English form is *I asked her what I should do,* in Black Vernacular and Southern dialect the auxiliary is shifted; *I asked her what should I do,* as an indirect question (Jacobs, personal communication, 1974). On the other hand, the response may reflect a strategy of starting a new sentence without trying to complete the old one.

A few children also used the WRONG AUXILIARY on the affirmative items (e.g., *can* where *do* was called for). Responses that were correct except for having the WRONG TENSE increased with age in this group. This is a "good" mistake; children who gave such responses were probably close to acquiring the standard form. As in the other two groups, a variety of other responses occurred, but not frequently.

Summary

These four items make it possible to look separately at the effects of negation and of different auxiliaries on these truncated conjoined clauses. The responses of all three groups show the effects of negation, the affirmative context being easier in all instances. This is most clearly seen in the use of *be* in the affirmative versus the negative contexts.

The middle-class white responses do not show effects of different auxiliaries; response patterns are similar for the two affirmative items, as they are for the two negative items. We assume this lack of auxiliary effects among these children to be due to their high level of mastery of all of the different auxiliaries used in these items. Data from both lower-class samples suggested, however, that the *be* auxiliary was easier to handle in this context than either the *do* substitute or the modal *can*. This trend was consistent: in the acquisition curves, in the differential omission of the auxiliaries, and in the percentages of inappropriate use of the auxiliaries when they did enter into the responses. We suggest that the complete process of producing these reduced secondary conjunction clauses, particularly when a negative element must be kept in mind as well, affects the different verbs to different degrees. *Can* and *do* are more affected by the added complexity than is *be*, which is acquired earlier.

The lower-class groups used the target structures at lower rates than the middle-class group on all four items. Auxiliary omission, both on the affirmative and on the negative items, and supplying a negative element in the responses to the two *neither* items are the most common variations in all groups. These responses are later superseded by more advanced variations. Repetition of the original verb on the affirmative items is common among lower-class children. Use of an inappropriate auxiliary seems to be a more mature response; it shows that the child knows a pro-form is required. An even more sophisticated variation, which increased with age in both lower-class groups, was use of the required auxiliary in an inappropriate tense. This response involves the operations of truncation and inversion, and only the requirement that the tense agree with the first clause is not met.

In addition to the trends shown in these responses, there were alternative forms elicited by the secondary conjunction items that did not fall into a clear pattern, as is shown in Table 20. Children did not seem to work consistently within the syntactic constraints until they actually acquired the structure; until then, they responded chiefly to the semantic task demand to mention the character not yet mentioned.

NOMINALIZATION

Sometimes, in conversation or writing, it is necessary to focus upon a particular part of the communication as the important new information being conveyed. For example, A might say: *I really need some money*, and B might reply: *What you really need is a good rest*. B's statement is a pseudo-cleft sentence, one of the techniques of focusing on new information in English. In this structure, the given or shared information is nominalized in a *wh*-nominal clause (*what you really need . . .*), a copula is added in the appropriate tense, and then a noun phrase, adjective, or uninflected verb form is added as a complement (in the given example it is the noun phrase *a good rest*) (Stockwell, Schacter, and Partee, 1973). In situations calling for special focus on the *new* part of a communication, the pseudo-cleft construction beginning with a *wh*-nominal clause is a common device in Standard English.

The word *do* in the *wh*-nominal clause of pseudo-cleft sentences may have one of two functions. It may be a normal verb, parallel to *need* in our first example, as in: *What he did was a crime, What he did was nice*. Or, when the verb phrase is itself the new information focused on, it may be a pro-verb, as in: *What she did next was clean the table*. In this example, *did* is considered to be a substitute for *cleaned* and carries the tense information in the first half of the pseudo-cleft.

Not all *wh*-nominal clauses occur in pseudo-cleft sentences. Another structure relevant to the items we gave is the subject-verb (as opposed to subject-copula-complement) construction. The same type of *wh*-nominal clause is subject, but a main verb is used rather than copula + complement: *What he did next ruined the table, What I did next exhausted me*. While this structure did not occur in our data, its consideration is necessary to our discussion of some of the responses we collected.

The items involving nominalization turned out to be the most difficult on the language production test. The child was given a story, a nominalization frame, such as *What she did next . . .* , and a picture of an appropriate action. The target pseudo-cleft completion required (1) a copula inflected for third person singular, to agree with the subject clause, and for past tense, to agree with the verb in the clause; and (2) an adjective, noun, or uninflected verb form such as *nice, fun,* or *wipe it up*.

The items we used to test this structure were the following:

Item 17a: Jerry spilled some paint. Carol got a rag, and what she did next _____ (was clean it up, was nice).

Item 17b: It was hot out, so Doug put on his bathing suit. What he did then _____ (was go swimming, was fun).

The responses of the three samples on these items are summarized in Table 21.

Table 21

Nominalization—Percentages of responses on Items 17a and 17b

	Middle-class white			Lower-class white			Lower-class black		
Age:	3	4	5	3	4	5	3	4	5
N:	103	95	103	22	24	27	23	36	27

(a) *What she did next* _____.

Past tense copula + verb or adjective (*was wipe it up, was nice*)	3	1	9	0	0	0	0	0	0
Present tense copula + verb or adjective (*is wipe it up, is nice*)	6	10	10	0	0	7	0	3	0
New sentence: pronoun + past verb (*she wiped it up*)	42	37	19	27	33	41	17	19	22
No copula, past verb (*wiped it up*)	22	22	23	18	33	22	22	25	48
No copula, uninflected verb (*wipe it up*)	17	15	13	55	29	26	52	47	30
Copula + past verb (*is/was wiped it up*)	8	12	24	0	0	4	0	0	0
Progressive (*is/was wiping it up, wiping it up*)	1	1	0	0	4	0	11	6	0
N:	105	100	104	26	24	27	22	34	27

(b) *What he did then* _____.

Past tense copula + verb or adjective (*was jump in, was fun*)	1	3	7	0	0	4	0	0	0
Present tense copula + verb or adjective (*is jump in, is fun*)	6	5	15	4	0	0	4	4	4
New sentence: pronoun + past verb (*he jumped in*)	42	38	34	39	25	33	17	13	19
No copula, past verb (*jumped in*)	15	23	17	8	8	19	17	16	11

Table 21—continued

	Middle-class white			Lower-class white			Lower-class black		
Age:	3	4	5	3	4	5	3	4	5
N:	105	100	104	26	24	27	22	34	27
No copula, uninflected verb (jump in)	22	15	7	43	58	30	57	61	63
Copula + past verb (is/was jumped in)	12	14	17	0	0	7	0	0	4
Progressive (is/was jumping in, jumping in)	2	2	3	8	8	7	4	4	0

Standard English Acquisition: Middle-Class White

Target. The target structure, PAST TENSE COPULA + VERB OR ADJECTIVE, was used by few children in this group. However, the structure in its present tense form, *is nice* or *is jump in*, appeared more often and reached the 15 percent level by age 5.

Variants. *Omission of the copula:* One of the characteristics of this construction which was tapped by the items we used is that the clauses on either side of *be* are in some sense equated by it. *What she did next* (Action 1) can be described as equivalent to *wipe it up* (Action 2). *Be* provides identity, and Action 2 provides detailed information about Action 1.

The responses of the children who gave no copula can therefore be interpreted in at least two ways. First, it may be that the pseudo-cleft property just described was noticed by even the children who omitted the required copula. Their responses may be interpreted as not having met the constraint of coding the identity of the clauses through using *be*. The variants omitting the copula do in fact meet the criterion of Action 2 being equated to and providing information about Action 1, and this understanding may underlie some of these stem completions.

An alternative explanation is that some of the responses omitting the copula may have been based on an interpretation of the stem as a *wh*-question. It is not possible with the present frame to know how many children were processing *What she did next* as something like *What did she do next?* This could be explored experimentally by using an alternate stem of, for example, *The thing she did next*, and comparing the responses on each of the formulations.

Of the specific types of responses that omitted the copula, the most common, especially in the younger children, was a NEW SENTENCE (*She cleaned it up, He went swimming*). This is the clearest instance of a response that may well reflect an interpretation of the *wh*-nominalization as a *wh*-question, such as *What did she do next?*

Another common no-copula response was a PAST VERB (*wiped it up*). In addition to the two possible explanations mentioned above, there is another alternative for this response which we examined. As noted earlier, it would be possible for an adult to interpret the story stem in a way that would evoke a different construction in which the clause was subject of the verb (not a copula), as in *What he did next cooled him off*. In such an interpretation, the correct response would not require a copula, and the past tense agreement would be incorporated in the main verb—in this case, *cool*. Since a number of children gave responses involving VERB + PAST, it was critical to determine whether they were in fact using the subject nominal clause construction. In particular, the response *cleaned it up* on Item 17a seemed ambiguous. It could represent a subject nominal clause construction, meaning that Carol's action (expressed in the nominalization) cleaned it up. On the other hand, it could represent interpretation of the sentence frame as a *what* question with deletion of the optional noun or pronoun subject, meaning that Carol cleaned it up. This ambiguity threatened to confuse developmental issues.

Our principal means of assessing these alternatives was a semantic one. We looked at the verb + past tense responses on both items and classified them into categories of (1) clear cases of interpretation of the clause as the subject of the verb, as in *What she did next* (*tired her out*); (2) clear cases of interpretation of the child in the story as subject of the verb, as in *What she did next* (*wiped it with a rag*); and (3) ambiguous cases, as in *What she did next* (*cleaned it up*). There were no examples of Category 1 in the data. Therefore, we classified the Category 3 ambiguous cases as examples of Category 2. As Table 21 shows, our confidence in this categorization is supported by the developmental trends. The target copula structure tended to increase with age, but neither the responses we assumed to be *wh*-question answers (*she cleaned it up*) nor the ambiguous responses (*cleaned it up*) showed comparable trends. We think it probable, therefore, that children giving ambiguous responses were interpreting the frame as a question and responding with the child as subject, not interpreting it as a subject nominal clause.

A less common no-copula response involved an UNINFLECTED VERB, as in *clean it up* or *swim*. Again, this type of response declined with age. It seems similar to but more primitive than the *cleaned it up* responses. The percentages of usage by age level support this suggestion.

Advanced variants: The most interesting variation in the middle-class group was use of the COPULA + PAST VERB (*is wiped it up, was wiped it up*). This response increased significantly with age through the range tested. It is interesting in that children making such a response apparently understood the *what* clause as a nominalization requiring a predicate but did not yet control the syntactic rules for formation of the predicate. All the necessary morphemes are present in such responses—the copula *be*, the past tense for agreement with the verb in the *what* clause, and the verb stem itself—but the past tense marker is misplaced, occurring either in the main verb alone (*is cleaned it up*) or redundantly in both copula and verb (*was cleaned it up*).

A response representing nominalization in the wrong tense, PRESENT TENSE COPULA + VERB OR ADJECTIVE, seemed to be the most advanced error made on the way to development of the Standard English form. It increased with age, though nonsignificantly due to the small percentage of children who could handle the form. As previously indicated, this response was used more often than the target form itself.

Dialect Variation: Lower-Class White

Target and variants. Neither the target PAST TENSE COPULA + VERB OR ADJECTIVE form nor the advanced errors of COPULA + PAST VERB and PRESENT TENSE COPULA + VERB OR ADJECTIVE was characteristic of the lower-class white group; even among the 5-year-olds, only about 10 percent of the children gave these responses, compared to about 40 percent in the middle-class sample. This suggests that the frame nominalization was seldom interpreted as a surface subject requiring completion.

On the other hand, the three responses—*wipe it, wiped it,* and *she wiped it*—that omit coding of identity with *be*, or perhaps suggest interpretation of the *what* clause as a question, were very common. We can conclude that in this group the target structure develops much later, if at all.

Dialect Variation: Lower-Class Black

Target and variants. The pattern of responses for the lower-class black children was almost identical to that of the lower-class white children. Again, no-copula responses were the most common. And it is possible that in this group also the *what* clause tended to be interpreted as a *wh*-question rather than as a surface subject. The target PAST TENSE COPULA + VERB OR ADJECTIVE form was not used at all, and the similar PRESENT TENSE COPULA + VERB OR ADJECTIVE was given by only four percent of the children.

Labov (1972: 76–82) notes that in Black English Vernacular, copulas are frequently deleted in sentences with nominal clause + complement constructions. He cites *All I could do, as' him what he's trying to do* and *What I mean by bein' destroyed, they was brought up into they rightful nature.* Thus, despite the fact that such structures in Standard English require a copula, there is no reason to expect the target copula to develop as a categorical form in children learning Black English Vernacular.

Summary

The two items that required furnishing a predicate for a *wh*-nominal clause were the most difficult on the test. Although the middle-class white children showed gains in the target structure and declines in most alternative structures, *be* + complement was used by only about one-fifth of the 5-year-olds. An interesting variation, which increased with age, was the use of *is* or *was* with a past (rather than an uninflected) verb. This type of response suggests that the children were on the way to acquiring the structure but still could not assign the tense to the correct elements. Most other responses seemed to involve omission of *be* to code identity or perhaps were misinterpretations of the stem *wh*-nominalization as a *wh*-question.

Neither lower-class group gave much indication of acquiring the target structure. We must assume that it does not exist as a categorical form in the two lower-class dialects or that if it does, it is not acquired until a much later age.

Action Nominalization

The items we have labeled action nominalization, such as *Playing ball is fun*, involve gerundives with no surface subject. They are paraphrases of *for-to* constructions such as *It is fun (for one) to play ball*. Stockwell, Schachter, and Partee (1973) suggest an underlying indefinite impersonal subject *one*, which, in the derivation of the gerundive from the *for-to* construction, is obligatorily deleted.

On the pilot test, another item with a nominalization was tested.

Pilot item: Jane dreamed that she could fly. When she woke up, she said, "I dreamed about _____ (flying)."

This item, the responses to which appear in Table 22, had to be dropped because the error of using a *that* clause showed a significant

Table 22

Action nominalization—Percentages of responses on pilot item

	Age:	3	4	5
	N:	24	40	51
I dreamed about _____.				
Verb + ing (*flying*)		44	48	51
That clause (*that she could fly, she could fly*)		16	30	41
Noun (*a bird, a girl*, etc.)		24	15	4
Other		16	8	4

increase with age; the emergence of the clause structure was penalizing the more mature speakers. However, we present the data here as background information to our more successful items, in which the nominalized verb was subject of the sentence rather than prepositional object. We were interested to find that *that* clause responses increased with age even more than the target gerundives. Menyuk (1969: 100) notes that among the most mature deviations she observed was a structure such as *I dreamed about that I was going to school*.

In the items we used on the final test, the child was given a direct or indirect quotation frame and then the nominalization in the subject slot. He had to recognize the nominalization as a subject and give the copula and complement. The following were the items used:

Item 18a: Lee likes to play ball. He says, "Playing ball _____ (is fun)."
Item 18b: Pat has learned how to make a bow. Now she thinks that making a bow _____ (is easy).

The responses on these items are summarized in Table 23.

Standard English Acquisition: Middle-Class White

Target.   Most of the children who used the target construction provided a COPULA + NOUN OR ADJECTIVE, such as *Playing ball is fun.* An infrequent but interesting target response was that of offer-

Table 23

Action nominalization—Percentages of responses on
Items 18a and 18b

	Middle-class white			Lower-class white			Lower-class black		
Age:	3	4	5	3	4	5	3	4	5
N:	106	100	104	26	24	27	23	36	26
(a) *Playing ball* _____.									
Copula + noun or adjective (*is fun*)	14	36	73	4	0	14	0	6	14
Definition (*is throwing it*)	10	5	3	4	4	12	0	0	8
New clause (*he throws the ball*)	17	23	10	17	33	15	39	25	33
No copula (*fun*)	5	8	1	4	0	0	4	11	4
Repetition (*playing ball*)	39	18	10	58	50	44	57	50	37
Other	16	10	3	12	12	11	0	8	4
N:	93	93	102	26	24	27	23	36	26
(b) *Making a bow* _____.									
Copula + adjective (*is easy*)	27	33	78	4	0	21	0	0	3
Definition (*is tying the ribbon*)	14	18	8	0	4	12	4	3	19
New clause (*she's tying*)	15	17	6	29	33	30	22	47	33
No copula (*easy*)	5	8	3	0	4	4	4	3	15
Repetition (*making a bow*)	24	17	4	54	42	26	70	36	26
Other	16	7	2	12	17	7	0	11	4

ing a DEFINITION: *Playing ball is throwing it up in the air.* The action nominalization structure proved to be one of the most difficult structures on the test. The acquisition curve was a steep one, however, so that combined target performance increased from roughly 30 percent to about 80 percent during the age span studied.

Variants. REPETITION of part of the story stem, such as *playing ball* or *play*, was the most common error and decreased with age in all groups. This response probably indicates an inability to interpret the nominalization in the frame as a form that requires a predicate. The child seemed to realize it was his turn to speak, but the unlearned structure suggested nothing to him except the words given. Beginning a NEW CLAUSE, as in *He throws the ball*, probably reflects a similar problem. In this case, it is possible that the gerundive was interpreted as a modifier, and that for some of the children, the structure was (*When*) *playing ball*, . . . However, since this type of response decreased with age, we feel that it probably did not involve such a complicated structure. It seems more likely that it involved a strategy of starting over, so as to stay within structures already controlled.

Dialect Variation: Lower-Class White

Target and variants. The target structure COPULA + ADJECTIVE OR NOUN was used significantly less often by children in the lower-class white group than by those in the middle-class group, although development did occur between ages 4 and 5. DEFINITIONS were given by similar percentages of children. The major substitute was the REPETITION type of response, which was used significantly more often by the lower-class white children. Other types of responses occurred at about the same rates in both white groups.

Dialect Variation: Lower-Class Black

Target and variants. The lower-class black children used the two target structures about as often as the lower-class white children. High proportions of REPETITION and NEW CLAUSE responses probably indicate difficulty in interpreting the gerundive as a form requiring a predicate for completion.

Summary

In general, we may conclude that acquisition of the target form is class-related, with the middle-class group using this structure more often than either lower-class group. The high proportions of new clause responses and repetition of part of the story stem, in all groups, probably indicate that the children who had not yet acquired the nominalization structure found it difficult to interpret the gerundive in the subject slot.

Chapter 6

Negative and Comparative Structures

SIMPLE SENTENCE NEGATION

The most frequent form of negation in English involves placement of a negative element after the subject and auxiliary but before the rest of the predicate, for example, *He will not be available* (Bellugi, 1967). In speech it is usually contracted with the auxiliary form, as in *can't, don't, doesn't, shouldn't, isn't, hasn't, won't*, etc. This form of the negative negates the entire clause. Other forms result if only one element is negated; compare *No happy artist can paint masterpieces, Happy artists can paint no masterpieces,* or *Unhappy artists can paint masterpieces.* The more general form of the negative is contained in *Happy artists can't paint masterpieces.*

The test item under discussion here was designed to elicit the general type of sentence negation, specifically the forms *doesn't* or *hasn't.* Since most of the other test items confounded negation with the particular structure negated, we included this item to elicit a relatively straightforward and frequent negative structure. (Negatives with *any* are discussed in the section that follows.)

The first indication of the development of the concept of negation is described in Piaget's studies as the awareness of object permanence—that objects do not cease to exist when they go out of view.

This sensorimotor understanding of existence-nonexistence precedes the period that Bloom (1970) speaks of, when children begin to incorporate negation concepts into their emerging syntax. Bloom suggests that the first type of negative meaning to emerge in syntax is "nonexistence," as in *No cookie* when the cookies have been eaten up. A second is typified as "rejection," as in *No cookie* when the child does not want a cookie. (Rejection was the most frequent meaning of the isolated nonsyntactic *No*.) The last type to emerge is "denial," as in *No cookie* when someone has claimed a cake is a cookie and the child corrects him. In Bloom's terms, the semantic category of the negative in our item is "nonexistence." Therefore, we can safely assume that even the youngest subject would have been able to handle the cognitive demands of giving some syntactic expression of this meaning, and we can examine the forms produced to see how soon they converge with adult forms.

Slobin (1971) has reviewed Wason's work (1959, 1961, 1965), which deals with the comprehension of negative statements. We may state, generally, (1) that affirmatives are easier to comprehend than negatives and (2) that further transformations *sometimes* add to the complexity of processing. For instance, negatives are easier to process if the truth value of the statement being negated is plausible; for example, *Spiders are not insects* is easier than *Spiders are not flowers*. Slobin concludes that more than the syntax is involved in comprehending negative statements; the truth value must also be evaluated, and this is a cognitive operation.

The item we used to test simple negation was the following:

Item 19a: A bird has legs but a worm _____ (*doesn't, hasn't*).

The responses of the children are summarized in Table 24.

Standard English Acquisition: Middle-Class White

Target. It appears that a large percentage of middle-class 3-year-olds had already acquired the target THIRD SINGULAR INDICATIVE + NEGATIVE forms, or *have* + NEGATIVE + INDETERMINATE and the combined curve of the first two responses stays at 85–95 percent target performance throughout the 3- to 5-year age range.

Table 24

Simple sentence negation—Percentages of responses on
Item 19a

	Middle-class white			Lower-class white			Lower-class black		
Age:	3	4	5	3	4	5	3	4	5
N:	102	100	104	23	22	27	21	35	26
A bird has legs but a worm _____.									
3rd singular indicative + negative (*doesn't, hasn't*)	85	82	89	9	30	48	5	0	11
Have + negative + indeterminate (*has none, hasn't any*)	7	3	7	0	0	0	5	0	4
Uninflected *do* + negative (*don't*)	0	2	1	55	52	48	48	57	46
Double negative (*don't have none*)	6	5	3	18	17	4	24	29	19
Lone negative (*not, no*)	2	8	0	18	0	0	19	14	19

Variants. Only a few middle-class white children used UNIN-FLECTED *do* + NEGATIVE *don't* rather than *doesn't*. This response seems to reflect difficulty with the Standard English irregular third person form of *do*, rather than with the negation operation, which was performed correctly. DOUBLE NEGATIVES were supplied at a low and decreasing rate.

A few subjects used a LONE NEGATIVE element, such as *no*. This response may be related to the type of utterance that Bellugi (1967) describes as characteristic of her first stage, in which the negative element is external to the linguistic structure.

Dialect Variation: Lower-Class White

Target. In the lower-class white group, the curve for the target THIRD SINGULAR INDICATIVE + NEGATIVE *doesn't* rises steadily, from 9 percent of the 3-year-olds to nearly half of the 5-year-olds. *Have* + NEGATIVE + INDETERMINATE did not occur in this group.

Variants. About half the children at all ages have the UNIN-FLECTED *do* + NEGATIVE response *don't*, which again seemed to be related to verb form rather than to the ability to negate. On the items testing the regular third person singular (*cries, catches*) the Standard English form was given by only 50–70 percent of this group of children, so it is not too surprising that only a tenth to a half supplied the Standard English irregular form *does* as the auxiliary to carry negation. *Don't* appears to be a viable dialect form for these children.

A DOUBLE NEGATIVE, such as *don't have none*, was given by 18 percent of the 3- and 4-year-olds and then dropped out. We know from Items 20a and 20b that this type of response was common in this group and even increased with age in the items with indeterminates *any* and *anything* (70–77 percent responded *isn't drinking* [*none*], and 40–67 percent responded *can't do* [*nothing*]). In the present item, 19a, the indeterminate was optional, so not all children would be expected to create structures including it.

After age 3, the LONE NEGATIVE element response, such as *no* or *not*, dropped out in this group.

Dialect Variation: Lower-Class Black

Target. The target structures THIRD SINGULAR INDICATIVE + NEGATIVE (*doesn't*) and *have* + DETERMINATE (*has none*) were the least favored forms in the lower-class black group; only 15 percent of the 5-year-olds gave them.

Variants. The favored form was clearly the UNINFLECTED *do* + NEGATIVE, as would be predicted from adult Black English Vernacular; roughly half the children at all ages used this form. Approximately another one-fourth used a DOUBLE NEGATIVE—*don't* plus a second negative—such as *don't have no legs*. In Items 20a and 20b we see that negative attraction to indeterminates like *any* (yielding forms like *none*) is nearly categorical in Black English Vernacular, as Labov (1972b) claims. In the present item, the children who produced such structures with indeterminates followed the Black English Vernacular rules of negative concord, just as they did on Items 20a and 20b. All of our syntactic response categories—*doesn't, has none, don't*, and *don't* (*doesn't*) + second negative—are acceptable Black English Vernacular forms.

The LONE NEGATIVE, isolated *no* or *not*, was given by a steady proportion of 15–20 percent of the black children. This form is no more acceptable in Black English Vernacular than in Standard English, so its persistence is difficult to explain.

Summary

Despite the fact that this was the last item on the test and should therefore show the strongest fatigue effect, it is clear that all three groups were well on their way to mastery of the forms of negation favored in their dialects. Almost all of the middle-class white children were using the target forms at age 5; about three-fourths of the black children were using *don't*, *doesn't*, or double negatives by age 5. The lower-class white 5-year-olds were evenly divided between *doesn't* and *don't*, which probably also reflects the situation in their linguistic environment. All groups, then, showed early competence with the operations of sentence negation available in their dialects.

Indeterminate in a
Negative Context

The complicated relationships among negative sentences in English continue to attract attention from linguists (Klima, 1964; Stockwell, Schachter, and Partee, 1973; Labov, 1972b). One of the most compelling aspects of negatives is their attraction to certain indefinite quantifiers, such as *either*, *ever*, and *any*, yielding such forms as *neither*, *never*, and *none* (*nothing*, *no one*, etc.). Klima (1964) noted that these indeterminates also co-occur with *wh*-questions and verbs such as *wonder* and, on the basis of these differences, labeled the group "indefinite." In Standard English, expression of negation is attracted to these indefinite forms; it is obligatory when the indefinite is subject. To add negation to a sentence with indefinite subject, such as *Anything goes*, it is necessary to say *Nothing goes* instead of **Anything doesn't go*. If the indefinite is not the subject, negative attraction is optional: *He didn't know anything about anybody* and *He knew nothing about anybody* are both possible. However, even in this type of sentence the negation must go to the first of the indeterminates: **He knew anything about nobody* is not permissible. Quirk et al. treat *any* as a special case of nonassertive (1972:22). The interested reader is referred to that comprehensive discussion.

One fact to note about these sentences is that only one negation is permissible in Standard English, even when indeterminates are present that could normally attract the negation. Thus, **He didn't* *know nothing about nobody* is not permissible in Standard English, although we will see that it is very common in nonstandard white English and, within the clause, practically a categorical rule in Black English Vernacular.

The relationship between the quantifiers *some* and *any* is also a puzzling one. Klima (1964) suggested that *any* in negative sentences was a suppletive alternant of *some;* our items were constructed with this analysis in mind. We expected children to use the indeterminate *some* in place of the indefinite *any* as they acquired this type of structure. Since Klima's article, other linguists have pointed out further semantic complexities. For example, Lakoff (1969) argues that *any* has a negative presupposition and *some* has a positive one; compare the sentences *Do they want to do some work?* and *Do they want to do any work?* Labov (1972) accepts these arguments and describes semantic features that distinguish the two quantifiers, such as whether or not items are considered one at a time (*each, any*) or in the aggregate (*some*). The details of this analysis are not relevant to our items, but it is mentioned in view of the fact that the straightforward relationship between *some* and *any* predicted for our items did not emerge.

Bellugi (1967) notes that the children in her study had not worked out the complex indefinite and indeterminate rules for negative sentences at the time of completion of the study. Multiple negation (*I can't do nothing with no string*) was common, and no restrictions were observed at this age. Few double negatives were used by Menyuk's (1971) group of 3- to 7-year-olds; when they were, they seemed to be cases of negation appearing in both verb and indefinite, as in *I don't want no milk* or *I don't want nothing.*

The items we used to test acquisition of the "any" transformation were the following:

> Item 20a: Here are some dogs and some water. One dog is drinking some. The other dog isn't drinking _____ (any).
> Item 20b: Liz can do lots of things, but Barry can't do_____ (anything).

In Item 20a, Standard English requires *any* rather than *some* or *none;* in Item 20b, it requires *anything* rather than *something* or *lots of things* or *nothing.* The task of the child was to recognize the negative context and to supply the form this context requires. The responses of the children are summarized in Table 25.

Table 25

Indeterminate in a negative context—Percentages of
responses on Items 20a and 20b

		Middle-class white			Lower-class white			Lower-class black		
Age:		3	4	5	3	4	5	3	4	5
N:		99	100	104	23	24	26	25	35	27
(a) *The other dog isn't drinking* _____.										
Indeterminate in negative context (*any, any water*)		37	49	58	9	4	4	0	0	4
Indeterminate substitution (*some, something*)		19	4	2	4	4	4	4	3	0
Double negative (*none*)		32	38	35	70	79	77	65	86	96
Noun phrase (*the water*)		5	5	6	13	8	15	30	3	0
Verb phrase or new sentence		4	4	0	4	4	0	0	6	0
N:		103	99	94	25	24	27	22	35	27
(b) *Barry can't do* _____.										
Singular indeterminate in negative context (*anything*)		40	42	67	12	4	4	4	3	7
Plural or mass indeterminate in negative context (*any*)		3	6	6	0	0	0	0	0	0
Double negative (*nothing*)		20	23	16	40	50	67	45	68	70
Noun phrase (*lots of things*)		4	4	2	0	8	0	4	3	0
Verb phrase (*play*, etc.)		31	24	8	48	38	30	45	26	22

Standard English Acquisition:
Middle-Class White

Target. In the middle-class white group, acquisition of the target
INDETERMINATE IN A NEGATIVE CONTEXT (*any, anything*) showed parallel developmental gains of over 20 percent across both items.

Variants. A few 3-year-olds used the INDETERMINATE SUBSTI-

TUTES *some* or *something* on Item 20a, but the response dropped out by age 4. These children may have been imitating the form given in the frame (*One dog is drinking some*). A similar imitation of the frame sequence *lots of things* was possible on Item 20b but was given by very few children. This pattern is consistent with the view that Standard English indefinite *any* is semantically different from indeterminate *some*, rather than a suppletive variant in certain contexts. If the relationship were closer, one would expect fewer double negatives and more substitutions of *some* or *lots of things*.

The most common variation was the substitution of negative forms yielding a DOUBLE NEGATIVE, as in *The other dog isn't drinking* (*none*) or *Barry can't do* (*nothing*). About one-third of the children gave such a substitution on Item 20a, and one-fifth on Item 20b. The usage peaked at age 4 on both items, but the decline at age 5 was nonsignificant.

Thus the overall pattern on both items was similar. The target *any, anything* forms increased with age, whereas all other variations declined—except for one: the double negative.

On Item 20b, substitution of a VERB PHRASE—usually naming things that Barry couldn't do—was given by one-third of the 3-year-olds and one-fourth of the 4-year-olds; it then dropped to 8 percent. All other responses were rare in this group.

Dialect Variation: Lower-Class White

Target. In the lower-class white group, the target INDETERMINATE IN A NEGATIVE CONTEXT (*any, anything*) occurred at very low rates and showed no increase with age.

Variants. Only one or two children supplied the INDETERMINATE SUBSTITUTE *some* or the NOUN PHRASE *lots of things*, so a simple suppletive relationship between *some* and *any* is again not supported.

The most striking difference between the lower-class white group and the middle-class group was that the DOUBLE NEGATIVE forms (*isn't drinking* [*none*] and *can't do* [*nothing*]), rather than the target forms, increased with age. It is clear from Table 25 that in the dialect these children are acquiring, the more mature form is marked by the negative with *not* after the verb and also with *none, nothing,* etc. in the indefinite pronoun position.

On Item 20b, there was a higher incidence of such VERB PHRASES as *go to sleep* or *can't go downstairs;* this response dropped from 48 percent at age 3 to 30 percent at age 5, thus remaining a common response. A few children at all ages responded with noun phrases such as *the water* on Item 20a; other responses were negligible.

Dialect Variation: Lower-Class Black

Target. The pattern of results for the lower-class black children was even more clear-cut than that for the lower-class white children. The target INDETERMINATE IN A NEGATIVE CONTEXT (*any, anything*) was very rarely used.

Variants. As in the other groups, the INDETERMINATE SUBSTITUTE *some* was very rarely supplied by these children. In contrast, the DOUBLE NEGATIVE responses *none* and *nothing* increased rapidly and significantly with age. All but one or two of the 5-year-olds who did produce an indeterminate in this group gave the negative form, which supports Labov's observation that negative attraction to indeterminates within the clause is practically categorical in Black English Vernacular.

Using a definite NOUN PHRASE (*the water*) in Item 20a was common only at age 3. On Item 20b, supplying a VERB PHRASE was a frequent response, falling from almost half of the 3-year-olds to one-fifth of the 5-year-olds. The children who gave these verb phrases did not supply indeterminate quantifiers (such as *some*) or indefinites (such as *any*) that could attract the semantic negative.

Summary

All of our groups seemed to be aware of the need for some sort of indeterminate concord with the stem negative in our items. In the middle-class white group, one-fifth to one-third of all age groups used a negative form such as *none* or *nothing*, even though these forms are not permissible in Standard English. The percentage of children using the acceptable *any* or *anything* forms increased from 40 percent of the 3-year-olds to 60 percent of the 5-year-olds; it appears that, even in middle-class speech, the *any* form in a negative context is not acquired early. *Some*, which lacks a negative presupposition, was used by very few children.

The two lower-class groups, especially the black group, showed a different pattern. The target form *any* was used by very few children, but strong developmental trends occurred for the negative forms *none* and *nothing*. It is clear that in this context the nonstandard dialects strongly favor negative concord.

COMPARATIVE AND SUPERLATIVE

The comparative and superlative structures in English involve some important features of adjectives and adverbs. One feature is that a number of these modifiers occur in pairs describing opposite poles of the same dimension. Examples are *fast-slow* and *big-little*. Frequently, one member of the pair (called unmarked by linguists) has a broader range of usage than the other member, in that it is normally used to refer to the dimension as a whole. In most cases, we ask *How big is it?* Only under very special conditions, in which small size is established as the expectation, do we ask *How little is it?* Either member of a pair, however, can be used to indicate a point or direction of comparison on the scale. We can say either *He is shorter than she* or *She is taller than he*. In the items we constructed for the test, all the target adjectives were of the more general, unmarked type, so that the development of the structures we were testing would be more comparable across items.

Adjectives have also been divided into ordinal scale adjectives, such as *beautiful*, which have an "absolute" reference point or standard, and ratio scale adjectives, like *big*, which do not imply such standard points (Huttenlocher and Higgens, 1971). Our target items were all of the ratio scale type.

In addition to these distinctions, which are specific to modifiers, adjectives and adverbs also vary in semantic complexity. For example, words that refer to distance alone (*long-short*) may be simpler than words that refer to an interaction of distance and time (*fast-slow*).

Along the dimension described by a given adjective or pair of adjectives, several types of statement can be made to relate two things on that dimension. The simplest involves only the uninflected form, as in *John is big and Bill is big too*. An equative *as . . . as* statement claims that two things are equal on that dimension: *John is as big as*

Bill. The negation of an equative statement implies not only inequality but inequality in a particular direction: *Bill is not as big as John*. Another way to express inequality in a particular direction is by comparison: *John is bigger than Bill*. Finally, the superlative establishes the most extreme point of any number of points on the dimension: *John is the biggest of all*. (These last two are expressed with *more* and *most* for certain adjectives: *John is more impressive than Bill, John is the most impressive of all*.) Although adults occasionally use superlatives when only two items are being discussed, the common pattern is to use the comparative form for two things and the superlative for more than two.

We constructed four items to test the development of comparatives and superlatives. The target modifiers were all in the category linguists call unmarked (*tall, big, fast*) and all took the inflections *-er, -est* rather than the *more* + adjective/adverb or *most* + adjective/adverb form required for some adjectives and adverbs. Our comparative items consisted of one adverbial *-er* item and one adjectival negative equative *not as . . . as* item; the two superlative items were identical in form.

COMPARATIVES

The items we used to test the comparative forms were the following:

Item 21a: Ronnie and Paul had a race. They both ran very fast but Paul won because he could run _____ (faster).

Item 21b: Here's Debbie and her sister. Debbie's a big girl, but she's not as big _____ (as her sister).

The responses of the children to these items are summarized in Table 26.

Standard English Acquisition:
Middle-Class White

Target. In the middle-class white group, acquisition of the COMPARATIVE WITH *-er* target shows a steady increase, from about one-third of the 3-year-olds to about two-thirds of the 5-year-olds.

The most surprising result is that the COMPARATIVE WITH *as* tar-

Table 26

Comparatives—Percentages of responses on Items 21a
and 21b

	Middle-class white			Lower-class white			Lower-class black		
Age:	3	4	5	3	4	5	3	4	5
N:	106	100	104	21	24	27	22	36	26
(a) *Paul won because he could run* _____.									
Comparative with −er (*faster, better*)	31	57	63	33	17	26	9	19	33
Uninflected adverb (*fast*)	29	19	16	24	50	37	17	58	44
Uninflected adverb with modifier (*very fast, as fast as him*)	9	10	3	5	8	7	4	3	0
Superlative (*fastest*)	4	8	15	0	4	4	0	0	4
New clause (*yes, because . . .*)	26	8	2	38	21	26	65	19	15
N:	106	100	100	23	24	26	21	34	27
(b) *She's not as big* _____.									
Comparative with *as* (*as her sister*)	71	85	90	22	54	85	14	44	67
Omission of *as* (*her sister*)	6	4	1	4	4	4	14	12	4
New clause (*and she . . .*)	11	3	3	26	8	4	19	18	7
Other	11	8	6	48	33	7	52	26	22

get form (*as her sister, as her, as the other one,* etc.) on the negative
equative item (21b) was used with much greater frequency at all ages
than was the comparative with -er (*faster, better,* etc.) on Item 21a.
The *not as . . . as* form is less frequent in speech and has the further
disadvantage of including a negation, which in younger children often interferes with the production of linguistic structures otherwise
uttered successfully (Bloom, 1970:165). Studies with adults (Slobin,
1971; Sherman, 1969; Clark, 1973) also have shown greater difficulty
in comprehending sentences with negatives.

   Three item differences might help explain the higher frequency
of target use in the *not as . . . as* comparative. In Item 21a, the child

was required to produce the adjective as well as the inflection -er. In Item 21b, the child was given a frame that included the beginning of the comparative and the adjective (*as big*). It may be easier for children to supply the missing term along a given dimension of comparison than to produce the dimension itself. In addition, more of the structure was provided in Item 21b, and the response that was called for thus seemed more obvious and more constrained.

Another possibility is that *big* may be controlled earlier than *fast;* relative size may be simpler to judge than relative speed, which involves both spatial and temporal dimensions. A size superiority is also more easily presented in a static picture, it would seem, than a speed superiority, and it may be more perceptually salient. This kind of salience difference might extend to a considerable number of adjectives and adverbs. Finally, noun modifiers may typically be simpler for children than verb modifiers.

Variants. The most frequent variant on the -er form was use of an UNINFLECTED ADVERB, such as *fast,* or of an UNINFLECTED ADVERB WITH MODIFIER, such as *very fast, too fast,* or *as fast as him,* that may have been an attempt at intensification or comparison. An intensifying mechanism, which we noted in some of the younger children but were unfortunately not set up to record adequately, was the use of stress and loudness: *They both ran very fast but Paul won because he could run (FAST!!!).* We hope that future work on the development of comparative forms will investigate these various attempts at intensifying adjectives/adverbs, which may be an early step in expressing comparisons.

The SUPERLATIVE *fastest* was used by few (15 percent or less) of the children. It seems to be a linguistically more advanced error than the uninflected form. As will be seen, in a superlative context, a few children made the opposite substitution, that of a comparative form.

It is interesting that one variant which did not appear was *more fast,* on Item 21a, a response that would seem a natural overgeneralization of the sort common in child language.

A common variant for these two items was giving a NEW CLAUSE, a response which probably means that the child assumed the sentence was already complete. A few children OMITTED *as* in Item 21b, responding *her sister,* and a few gave irrelevant forms or repetitions of words in the frame, like *big.* On Item 21a, some children responded with agreement (*yes*) or repeated the clause (*because he could run*). The errors on Item 21a were more diverse and more mature (*fastest, very fast, as fast as him*) than those on Item 21b; a number of responses seemed possible other than the -er comparative. On the negative equative item, if the child did not produce the target, what he did was more primitive and implied a total lack of structure.

Dialect Variation: Lower-Class White

Target. In the lower-class white group, the COMPARATIVE WITH -er target form showed no significant developmental change over the 3- to 5-year age range. The COMPARATIVE WITH *as* target form, in contrast, showed a rapid developmental trend; the gap decreased between this group and the middle-class group to the point of statistical equivalence by age 5.

Variants. A common response on Item 21a was the UNINFLECTED ADVERB *fast*, which may involve naming the dimension rather than comparing points along that dimension. This latter form was given by one-fourth to one-half of the children at every age. Again, possible attempts to intensify the adjective via loud, stressed pronunciation may be included in the category. Other types of intensification, such as *very*, were fairly infrequent, as were superlatives.

On Item 21a, a common response was supplying a NEW CLAUSE, which may mean that the child interpreted the frame as already complete. As in the case of the middle-class children, the most common variants on Item 21b seem to indicate a lack of comprehension of the comparative structure already begun. NEW CLAUSES at age 3, and irrelevant forms or repetitions from the frame story (such as *big*) at ages 3 and 4, were given by one-fourth or more of the children.

Dialect Variation: Lower-Class Black

Target. The lower-class black group used the target COMPARATIVE WITH -er at a frequency similar to that of the lower-class white group, although a developmental increase seems to be suggested among the black children but not among the white.

The negative equative item also resulted in similar responses in both lower-class groups. Rapid acquisition of the target COMPAR-

ATIVE WITH *as* in these groups indicates that the lower-class children, despite about a year's developmental lag, were well on their way to a high rate of usage by age 5.

Variants. Again, a common response on Item 21a was the UN-INFLECTED ADVERB *fast,* sometimes with added stress for intensification. Only a very few children (one at each age) gave an UNINFLECTED ADVERB WITH MODIFIER (*very,* etc.) or gave a SUPERLATIVE.

Despite the higher frequency of NEW CLAUSE responses among 3-year-old black children, in this and other respects their responses on both items were not significantly different from those of the lower-class white group.

Summary

The two comparative forms tested, the -er form, as in *he could run faster,* and the negative equative form, as in *not as big as her sister,* were acquired steadily by all children tested, except for a lag in the lower-class white group on the -er form. The negative equative target form, surprisingly, was used at higher rates than the -er target form by all groups. This might be an effect of having more of the structure given in the sentence frame, or it might be related to the different lexical items involved, or it might reflect differences between adjectival and adverbial use. The two lower-class groups used the target forms less frequently at all ages, although rapid development of the negative equative seems to indicate they were catching up on this item. No important racial differences were found.

SUPERLATIVES

The items used to test the superlative were the following:

Item 21c: Kathy's balloon is big, Jake's is even bigger, but Tony's is the
_____ (*biggest*)
Item 21d: Jimmy is tall, and his sister's even taller, but his father's the
_____ (*tallest*)

The responses of the children to these items are summarized in Table 27.

Table 27

Superlatives—Percentages of responses on Items 21c
and 21d

	Middle-class white			Lower-class white			Lower-class black		
Age:	3	4	5	3	4	5	3	4	5
N:	106	100	104	24	24	27	23	35	27
(c) *Big . . . bigger . . .* *the* _____.									
Appropriate superlative (*biggest*)	52	64	91	8	25	63	22	28	39
Inappropriate superlative (*littlest*)	6	13	2	0	4	0	0	0	2
Uninflected adjective (*big*)	22	11	5	44	54	19	57	43	30
Comparative (*bigger*)	13	9	2	44	17	11	9	25	26
Noun (*balloon*)	6	3	0	4	0	7	13	3	4
Verb phrase	0	0	0	0	0	0	0	0	0
N:	106	100	104	22	23	26	22	35	26
(d) *Tall . . . taller . . .* *the* _____.									
Superlative (*tallest*)	63	84	96	9	48	65	9	46	50
Uninflected adjective (*tall*)	16	6	0	23	26	15	50	39	27
Comparative (*taller*)	14	8	3	55	21	19	18	6	19
Noun (*father, boss*)	3	1	0	14	4	0	9	6	4
Verb phrase (*got on glasses*)	2	1	0	0	0	0	14	3	0

Standard English Acquisition:
Middle-Class White

Target. In the middle-class white group, the SUPERLATIVE form
-*est* shows a consistent development across test items, from 52 and
63 percent among the 3-year-olds to 91 and 96 percent among the
5-year-olds. Some of the children who gave the -*est* response supplied an adjective at the opposite pole of the size dimension, as in
littlest or *smallest*, especially on Item 21c. It is possible that these
children misunderstood the picture and thought that Tony was the
girl with the small balloon; however, the administrator pointed to
the balloons as the story frame was read, so misunderstanding of this

kind was minimized. A more interesting possibility is that the children had acquired the names for the dimension as a whole (*big-little*) but were still unable to label the poles correctly, a phenomenon reported frequently in child language (Clark, 1973). Finally, the children may have been responding to the linguistic signal *but* in the frame stories, which frequently signals polar differences (*Tony's is big but Kathy's is little*), as well as to the more subtle degree differences of these items.

Variants. The most common variant was use of an UNINFLECTED ADJECTIVE, either alone (*Tony's is the* [*big*]) or with a noun or pronoun (*Tony's is the* [*big one*]). The second response is the more advanced one because it takes the article *the* into account, although the comparatives in the frame story are ignored.

A decreasing proportion of children used the COMPARATIVE (*bigger, taller*) instead of the superlative form. Finally, a few children—perhaps responding to the definite article *the*—gave NOUN responses not related to the size dimension stressed in the frame story. For the most part, these seemed to be immature labeling responses (*the father*), although we find it difficult to quarrel with the semantic structure expressed in *Jimmy is tall, and his sister's even taller, but his father's the* (*boss!*).

Dialect Variation: Lower-Class White

Target and variants. As was frequently the case in other structures, the lower-class white group used the target SUPERLATIVE structure less often than the middle-class white group at all ages, although the two groups had parallel patterns of acquisition.

Except for an increase at age 4 in the use of an UNINFLECTED ADJECTIVE (*big, big one; tall, tall one*), other responses also tended to parallel those of the middle-class children.

Dialect Variation: Lower-Class Black

Target and variants. Even at age 5, no more than half of the black children were using the target SUPERLATIVE *-est* form.

The fluctuations in proportions of children using the various responses never became significantly different from those of the lower-class white group, except that the 3-year-old white children tended to use the comparative form (-er) more often than did black children of the same age.

Summary

The two items testing the superlative showed developmental trends across classes and races, although the middle-class children used the target -est more frequently at all ages. No important racial differences were found

Control of superlatives was higher in most groups than was that of the -er comparative, but it about equaled control of the negative equative *not as* . . . *as* comparative. Several possible explanations were offered. First, modification of nouns may be acquired before modification of verbs. Second, it may be that superlatives are easier for children and that only the added help of having the tester give the first half of the negative equative enabled children to do well on Item 21b. Third, it should be noted that superlatives and comparatives can both appear with or without the article (*He is taller, He is the taller; He is tallest, He is the tallest*), yet, in our items, *the* appeared with the superlative and not with the comparative. Possibly, production of the comparatives would have been facilitated by including the article; but colloquial usage does not favor article + comparative constructions, and more difficulty may have resulted instead. Finally, the speed dimension (*fast*) used for the -er comparative item might have been more difficult in itself than the size dimension (*big, tall*) used for the negative equative and superlative items.

Chapter 7

Patterns of
Language Growth

In the preceding four chapters we have examined the children's responses on individual structures and items. In this chapter our attention is focused on several aspects of the data that emerge across structures. One obvious point of interest is the order in which the various target structures are acquired. We next look at the data as a whole in relation to social class and racial dialect questions. It is useful to consider, across the diversity of structures, what differences can be seen among the three groups tested, particularly the effects of variants in the adult dialects on acquisition patterns. Finally, we discuss the data in quite a different light, as they reflect the children's knowledge of conversational rules and the contingency demands of language interaction. The children's ways of coping with unfamiliar structures on the test provide new information on the intermediate stages of structure acquisition.

STRUCTURE ACQUISITION

We begin by presenting the overall order of structure acquisition by the middle-class children to serve as a reference point for the rest of the discussion. As we pointed out in many of the individual items, the specific item contexts apparently varied in difficulty even when basically similar structures were being tested. We cannot rely on the items to give us more than an approximate idea of the difficulty of a given syntactic structure, since contextual factors were also affecting the children's responses. Most of these factors were discussed in Chapters 3–6. Nevertheless, it is worthwhile to summarize the order of acquisition of the various structures tested within these particular contexts. Table 28 presents the structures ordered along the dimension of easiest to hardest. Where parallel items existed for a structure, the easiest of the items was used in order to minimize the effects of contextual complexity. The effect is also to highlight the sequence of syntactic development across a variety of structures.

The table shows a general developmental increase in complexity of structures controlled, although there are some notable exceptions. For example, we would not expect noun plural or past progressive to be as late in developing as they appear in the present data. The specific contexts for these items are probably contributive to this outcome, as suggested in the individual structure discussions. Only one item was given for each of these structures, and each was particularly complex. The other factor which emerges from the table is that operations on entire propositions are not necessarily acquired later than operations involving smaller phrases. Infinitive complements (*He wants his brother [to fix it]*) and simple negation (*A bird has legs but a worm [doesn't]*) are controlled by young children. In Chapter 8, we will look at several more refined hypotheses concerning the determinants of order of acquisition.

Because of the even greater contextual and dialect influences on the two lower-class samples, we feel that an overall presentation of the order of structure acquisition for these groups would be meaningless. However, the data for these children reveal aspects of their syntax that deserve further examination. We turn therefore to a consideration of some issues in relation to these dialect groups.

As pointed out earlier, a major purpose of the language production technique was to gather data on the emergence of syntactic structures: to study the stages of their acquisition in middle-class children and to use the opportunity the technique offered to explore development in children from other language environments. It is important to look at the data from the two lower-class samples (white and black) within the context of the adult dialect of each group. Where relationships seem to exist between the adult dialect and the children's responses, these have been suggested in discussing the acquisition of each structure. Now, looking across the individual

Table 28

Age of acquisition of target structures by middle-class white children*

					75% criterion level attained			
	Noun phrases		Verb phrases			Propositions†		
Age of acquisition	Item	Structure	Item	Structure		Item	Structure	
3 years	2b	Noun + possessive (92%)	8a	Habitual present	(76%)	14b	Infinitive complement	(88%)
			9a	Simple past	(89%)	19a	Sentence negation	(92%)
			11a	Present progressive	(77%)			
4 years	4a	Subject pronoun (86%)	10a	Subject-copula agreement	(75%)	15a	Relative clause	(80%)
	6b	Indirect object (75%)	13a	Modal auxiliary	(90%)	21b	Comparative with *as*	(85%)
						21d	Superlative	(84%)
5 years	1a	Noun plural (85%)	12b	Passive	(92%)	16b	Secondary conjunction	(84%)
	6d	Indirect object + direct object (86%)				18b	Action nominalization	(86%)
				75% criterion level not attained				
	3a	Possessive pronoun	11b	Past progressive		17b	Nominalization	
	5a	Mass noun or count noun	13e	Modal (indirect question)		20b	Indeterminate in a negative context	
	7a	Reciprocal				21a	Comparative with -er	

*Using best item if parallel items were present.

†Our comparative-superlative structures included adjectival subject complements and adverbial complements, and could also be used in noun phrases or verb phrases or to modify clauses. Similarly, the negative structures related to sentence negation, object noun or pronoun negation, and indeterminates in a negated clause. For our purposes here, it seemed most appropriate to classify these items as structures involved in "propositions."

items and structures, we will consider the language development trends of the lower-class groups at a more general level.

It should be noted that when examining the lower-class white language data we are dealing with issues that are not well understood. Although dialect studies of lower-class white samples are by no means rare, it is difficult to generalize from the data collected in one geographical area to those collected in another. Regional differences in Black English Vernacular are also documented (Labov, 1972a); but because of its history, Black English is far more homogeneous across regions. Numerous common features are found across localities. It is quite likely that in the lower-class white population sampled in this study a variety of different dialects are represented. It is often difficult to separate developmental from dialectal differences. When little is known about the dialect or dialects to which a group of children have been exposed, the task is even more difficult. This is especially true with cross-sectional data. Thus, the greatest usefulness of the data from the lower-class white sample probably lies in noting where the responses do and do not diverge from those of the lower-class black sample. In addition, hypotheses may be generated for further research on the language development of lower-class white children.

When we speak of our three samples as being exposed to different language systems, we must remember that in the case of Black English Vernacular, and probably in the case of lower-class white dialects as well, it is not merely a case of children learning different categorical rules. Many rules that are obligatory in Standard English are variable in other dialects. Where variable rules permit forms other than the Standard English target, we have noted this fact in our discussion of the individual structures. However, there are two additional issues. The first is the question of how the process and rate of learning a language system are affected by the variability of the rules in the input. A slower acquisition curve would probably be one predicted outcome of the higher degree of variability in the input, and such a difference in rate is common in our data.

In addition to the factor of variable rules that are a part of the dialect of the child's home and neighborhood, we must also consider the fact that the children in our study, like most children growing up in the United States today, had been exposed to Standard English. They were in preschools and day care centers where Standard English was spoken. Moreover, television and radio were part of the children's lives from an early age.

Given that our subjects had been exposed to Standard English, what effects would we expect this to have on their responses to the language production test? We knew from the pilot data that the lower-class children tended to produce more nonstandard forms than did the middle-class children. Though some of this discrepancy in producing Standard English forms on the language production test may be developmental, the most reasonable assumption is that the lower-class children produced forms in their own dialects. This does not mean, however, that the children were producing language just as they would have in their homes and neighborhoods. The social context of the situation in which the subjects were tested was clearly one with Standard English overtones. Testing and other situations with adult interviewers have been found to inhibit children's natural speech, both in amount (Pasamanick and Knobloch, 1955; Resnick, Weld, and Lally, 1969) and in degree of formality and/or use of Standard English (Labov, Cohen, Robins, and Lewis, 1968). In addition, the subjects in our study were hearing Standard English frame sentences from white experimenters. Thus, if code-switching did operate in our subjects, we can be fairly sure that it was in the direction of more Standard English responses than the child normally would use.

It is also possible that the older children, with a growing awareness of social constraints, did more code-switching than the younger children. If this is true, some obtained increments in target forms with age might represent increased code-switching rather than acquisition. Labov (1964) places the acquisition of the vernacular roughly in the age span of 5 to 12 years. As for the perception of the social significance of dialect characteristics, Labov does not attribute this to the child before early adolescence. However, there is some evidence that children are sensitive to such situational factors as formality or "testness" by the age of 3 (Resnick, Weld, and Lally, 1969). In view of the cognitive and social developments that take place in the age span 3 to 5, it is reasonable to suggest that sensitivity to the occasions that call for Standard English might be increasing. Further research on this question would be of interest.

In summary, whereas the middle-class white children have grown up hearing largely a single dialect—one with categorical rules for the structures included on the language production test— the lower-class children have been living in language environments typified, to a greater degree, by variable rules and by the prominent presence of a second dialect (Standard English). With these differences in mind, let us turn to the structures on the language production test and survey the responses of the lower-class white and black groups in relation to those of the middle-class white group.

Structures Associated with Class Difference

On some of the structures tapped by the language production test, the two lower-class groups show a similar developmental pattern but one that differs from that of the middle-class children. On other structures, the lower-class black group differs substantially from the two white groups.

One of the structures in our study on which the two lower-class groups show similar development is the double negative—a feature frequently noted in the literature. The double negative clearly emerged in our data on items with the indeterminate in a negative context, for example, *nothing* instead of *anything* (Items 20a and 20b), and on the simple sentence negation item (19a), where providing an indeterminate was optional. Middle-class children also produced double negatives in this age range but did so significantly less than either lower-class group; they increased in their use of the indeterminate *any, anything,* while lower-class groups showed no such increase.

Another structure on which the two lower-class groups performed similarly is the relative clause. On the items in which the relative clause modifies the subject (15a and 15b), the middle-class white group supplied the relative pronoun significantly more often than the lower-class groups. On one of these two parallel items (15a), the lower-class white children showed evidence of acquiring the relative pronoun; on the other item (15b), the two lower-class groups performed very similarly, with a steady one-third of the subjects omitting the relative pronoun across the entire age range. The results on Item 15a suggest the possibility that the relative pronoun may not be omitted as frequently in lower-class white dialects as in Black English Vernacular; however, in both lower-class groups there appears to be widespread omission of the relative pronoun.

Several structures show acquisition curves that are similar for the two lower-class groups but indicate development that is considerably later than or at a different rate from that of the middle-class group. One such structure was the reciprocal. Lower-class white and black children gave evidence of acquiring this structure during the

3- to 6-year age range, but they were far behind the middle-class subjects. It is not clear whether this class difference was the result of difficulties with the conceptual aspects of reciprocity or with its linguistic expression. Other items on which the two lower-class groups acquired the target structures, but more slowly or at later ages than the middle-class children, were the superlative and the comparative (Items 21a, 21b, 21c, and 21d), action nominalization (Items 18a and 18b), the secondary conjunction (Items 16a, 16b, 16c, and 16d), and the passive (Items 12a and 12b).

Where the target Standard English form is required in the adult form of the dialect, there is a feature in one or both of the lower-class dialects that might explain a slower learning of the target structure. For example, *be* is required in passive sentences (e.g., *These pictures have to [be finished]*) in both lower-class dialects. However, the inflected auxiliary *be* is frequently deleted in other contexts in these dialects, as in *The picture (finished)* instead of *The picture (is finished)*. Consequently, there would not be as many *be* + participle forms in the language the children normally hear. This lower frequency of *be* in variable contexts could affect acquisition of the *be* form in obligatory contexts as well.

Item 1a provides an example of the two lower-class groups responding differently from the middle-class group on the basis of a phonological feature. Although both lower-class groups were significantly behind the middle-class group in their use of /-ɨz/ at all age levels, this should not lead us to conclude that the lower-class children had not yet acquired the plural and/or present tense morpheme. It was clear from the item we eventually used for warm-up (see section on noun + plural in Chapter 3) that the easier /-z/ allomorph was controlled by almost all subjects, including the lower-class children, at age 3.

Structures Associated with
Black English Vernacular

Turning next to structures on which the lower-class black children were markedly distinct from the other two groups, we find that many of the familiar features of Black English Vernacular were operating in the children's responses. The lower-class black group showed the predicted dialect features on these structures: deletion of -s on the habitual present items (8a and 8b); deletion of *be* on the progressive item (10a and 10b); deletion of the copula (Item 11a); and the use on the modal auxiliary items (13a and 13b) of a variety of forms acceptable in Black English Vernacular, including omission of the auxiliary.

In the category of differences that could be called phonological, we find -*ed* deletion on the past tense items (9a and 9b) and dropping of the future tense -*'ll,* as on the future-conditional item of the modal auxiliaries (13a).

When considering structures that elicited similar responses from the two lower-class groups, we remarked on a situation (with *be* in the passive) in which a form obligatory in the dialect might, because of related characteristics of the dialect, be learned more slowly. At least one other such possibility appears among the structures on which the black group differed from the white groups. On the possessive items (2a, 2b, and 2c) either an elliptical or a full form of the possessive could be provided, for example, *the monkey's (food), the baby's (toy).* In Black English Vernacular the possessive inflection is required in such elliptical constructions, although it is deleted in possessive + noun constructions. Yet even in the elliptical form we find omission of the -'s by the lower-class black children. With fewer possessive occurrences to learn from, lower-class black children may learn the form later or may generalize a context that permits deletion in Black English Vernacular to others that do not.

On the basis of the language production test, we find that there are some structures for which Black English Vernacular has acceptable forms that deviate from Standard English, and some structures for which there are no such variants. We decided to compare the performance of the lower-class black children and middle-class white children on these two types of structures. We expected that the difference between the groups would be greater on the structures where there is an alternative form employed by adult black speakers than on the structures where there is no alternative available in the dialect. Trying to confine our comparison to structures that could be assigned to one of these sets without question, that is, structures that either had a variant or did not, we made the division as shown in Tables 29 and 30.

In order to minimize item differences other than those resulting from variants in the adult dialect, the middle-class percentage of target use was used as a baseline, and the difference between middle-class and lower-class black percentages was used as the measure for testing differences. At each age level, the differences between the

Table 29

Structures with Black English Vernacular variants—Percentages of target responses given by middle-class white and lower-class black subjects*

Structure	Item	Middle-class white			Lower-class black			Percentage difference (MCW-LCB)		
	Age:	3	4	5	3	4	5	3	4	5
Simple sentence negation:										
doesn't, has none	19a	92	88	96	10	0	15	82	88	81
Indeterminate in a negative context:										
any	20a	37	49	58	0	0	4	37	49	54
anything	20b	40	42	67	4	3	7	36	39	60
Habitual present:										
cries	8a	76	92	100	13	31	22	63	61	78
catches, throws	8b	74	89	90	8	11	14	66	78	76
Past tense:										
combed	9a	89	96	99	8	30	33	81	66	66
washed, put	9b	68	70	84	22	42	58	46	28	26
Copula:										
are	10a	66	75	82	14	9	15	52	66	67
Progressive:										
is eating, 's eating	11a	73	70	70	9	8	22	64	62	48
Future-conditional modal:										
will/'ll get hurt, might, going to	13a	73	90	89	22	37	44	51	53	45
Nominalization:										
is/was wipe it up	17a	9	11	19	0	3	0	9	8	19
is/was jump in	17b	7	8	22	4	4	4	3	4	18
Mean percentage		58.7	65.0	73.0	9.5	14.8	19.8	49.2	50.2	53.2

*The percentages given represent all answers acceptable in Standard English, including loophole responses.

groups (MCW-LCB), on the with-variant set of structures and the without-variant set were compared by use of a*t*-test. The differences were significantly larger on the with-variant set of structures for the 4- and 5-year-olds: $t_{(20)} = 2.40$, $p < .05$; and $t_{(20)} = 2.51$, $p < .05$, respectively.

As expected, where Black English Vernacular contains a permissible form other than the Standard English target, the gap between extent of target usage in middle-class white and lower-class black groups is significantly wider than where both dialects require the same form. In Chapter 8 this issue of variable rules is discussed from a theoretical standpoint.

In the results for the two lower-class groups there is an abundance of raw material suggesting hypotheses for further research, which is particularly important in view of the limited number of items representing each structure on the test. Especially in cases where there is a variable rule, future investigations can benefit from systematic context variation and the use of many parallel items. Though it is clear why the technique, as it stands, should not be used for assessing the language development of lower-class children, it is clearly useful for eliciting production of linguistic structures. Investigators wishing to assess children's language development in their own dialect should modify the test accordingly; such an instrument could be very useful to those who teach and develop curricula for dialect-speaking children. Like the middle-class children, the lower-class children seemed to enjoy playing the game, caught on easily to the idea of supplying the ending to each "story," and appeared not to interpret the situation as a test. It will be recalled that we alerted the reader to the possibility of code-switching where a situation is perceived by the child as formal or testlike. However, the language production technique appeared to be unusually good at putting children at their ease. This would clearly be an advantage in adapting the instrument for use with children who speak nonstandard dialects.

INTERMEDIATE STAGES IN STRUCTURE USAGE

Throughout this book, we have been assuming that the changing patterns of responses to our items are indicative of developing linguistic skills. We have claimed that even the nontarget responses

Table 30

Structures without Black English Vernacular variants— Percentages of target responses given by middle-class white and lower-class black subjects*

Structure	Item	Middle-class white			Lower-class black			Percentage difference (MCW-LCB)		
	Age:	3	4	5	3	4	5	3	4	5
Comparative:										
faster	21a	31	57	63	9	19	33	22	38	30
as . . . as	21b	71	85	90	14	44	67	57	41	23
Superlative:										
biggest, littlest	21c	58	77	93	22	28	41	36	49	52
tallest	21d	63	84	96	9	46	50	54	38	46
Subject pronoun:†										
he	4a	73	86	94	52	61	67	21	25	27
	4b	65	80	87	26	56	63	39	24	24
Determiner + count or mass noun	5a	17	31	37	4	21	48	13	10	−11
Modal + negative:										
couldn't, didn't	13b	65	80	93	10	61	54	55	19	39
Counterfactual modal:										
couldn't	13c	64	73	91	0	47	41	64	26	50
Reciprocal:										
each other	7a	25	37	63	0	20	31	25	17	32
Mean percentage		53.2	69.0	80.7	14.6	40.3	49.5	38.6	28.7	31.2

*The percentages given represent all responses acceptable in Standard English, including loophole responses.
†The percentages given represent the subjects who gave either of the subject pronouns. That is, gender confusions were not considered failures to give the subject pronoun and were pooled with the target responses.

give evidence of increasing linguistic ability—that structure acquisition is not an all-or-nothing process. This claim assumes that the children were bringing all their linguistic knowledge to bear on the task. In this section we would like to explore this assumption more carefully and look at the types of nontarget responses we found throughout the test. The demonstration of important skills by the children, even when they did not control the target structures, seems to substantiate the usefulness of the technique in tapping children's linguistic knowledge at these ages.

Prerequisite Interactive Skills

Before looking at the types of responses which indicate that children have varying degrees of control of the linguistic structures we tested, we would like to explore the very general interactive skills the children brought to this task.

Preschoolers' ability to adapt to listener requirements has been shown both in free speech (Shatz and Gelman, 1973; Spilton and Lee, 1977) and in structured situations (Maratsos, 1973; Peterson, Danner, and Flavell, 1972). In the present study, we were able to explore only one type of interactive situation and so are reluctant to generalize to others. We would like to mention briefly some frameworks for looking at this task in terms of interactional requirements. One interesting framework is that provided by researchers exploring linguistic function. For example, Dore (1974) reports that even holophrastic children (children aged 1:3 to 1:7) appear to use language in several clearly defined interactive functions. Drawing on Searle's (1969) discussion of "speech acts," Dore lists a set of "primitive speech acts," such as labeling, repeating, answering, requesting action, requesting answer, calling, greeting, protesting. The situation set up in the language production test produced several types of responses that might be classified as labeling, repeating, or answering, in addition to those that functioned to complete the adult's sentence.

A second, more descriptive framework is provided by Bloom, Rocissano, and Hood (1976). Their subjects were older than Dore's holophrastic subjects, but younger than our sample, and the development they report in free-speech interactions with adults is of interest in interpreting our results. They found an increasing proportion of speech that was contingent on the nonverbal or verbal context of the interactive situation, and a decreasing proportion of imitative speech in which the child added no new information to the adult's statements. Within the category of contingent speech, responses contingent on the linguistic input from the adult increased more than those contingent on the situation alone. These researchers conclude that even their youngest children appear to know the basic rules of conversation. The philosopher Grice (1975) has discussed numerous principles of conversation, which include such basic features as taking turns and saying things that are relevant to the topic. Bloom and her colleagues appear to have evidence of early acquisition of some of these interactive skills.

Coping with Unfamiliar Structures

Assuming, then, that our subjects had attained these basic conversational skills, we can look at their responses to our task from a conversational point of view. We can assume that they knew (1) that they had to take turns and (2) that their answer should be contingent upon the linguistic and nonlinguistic context provided by the adult. As we have seen, when target responses were contingent upon all the features of the context, they increased reliably in nearly all of our items. The interesting responses, from this point of view, are the ones in which the child did not control the linguistic structure and thus was not able to furnish the "ideal" answer.

Bloom's information suggests that with increasing age children would give increasingly contingent responses, utilizing all the information they could. At some stages they might only be able to imitate or repeat, or they might add information from the picture that was not linguistically contingent. At more advanced stages they might use both environmental and linguistic information, even though they did not yet control the target response. How did our children cope with situations in which the linguistic demands were beyond them, but the interactive demands clearly called for a response? First, we should note that there were several things that the children did *not* do. With rare exceptions, they did not refuse to respond (which indicates acceptance of the turn-taking demand) and they did not change the subject (which indicates acceptance of the contingency demand). However, they made a variety of other responses, which illuminated for us not only *whether* they controlled a given structure but also, in many situations, *how close* they were to controlling it.

Noncontrol. In some cases, the child's response suggested that the linguistic story stem was syntactically uninterpretable by him. In obedience to the basic turn-taking requirement of the situation, a response was produced, but it did not fit the story stem. Instead, the child would repeat part of the adult's utterance, ignoring the relationship of speech to picture and adding nothing new to the discourse. Or the child would simply label a feature of the picture. The adult's speech might enter into the situation in a crude way—for example, as a list of items already labeled—but the full linguistic structure of the utterance was ignored. For example, on the present progressive item, *"Not now,"* says Sam's mother, *"because (he's eating),"* some children responded *food.* These responses appear to be especially primitive according to Bloom and her associates, since the simple imitative and situationally contingent responses tended to decrease rather than increase with development. In Dore's terms, too, these responses appear to be most similar to "labeling" or "repeating" speech acts.

Another response to this situation was to start a new sentence. In these instances, the children ignored the linguistic stem but often produced a response that was relevant to the picture; these responses may have been somewhat more advanced forms of labeling. Finally, an infrequently occurring response that should be mentioned is *I don't know.* This might be a response that acknowledges both the adult's utterance and the picture, and explains the child's inability to come up with an answer that suitably takes both into account.

Interpreting Unfamiliar Linguistic Forms. The responses discussed thus far all appear to be efforts to cope with a situation in which the child is unable to interpret the linguistic requirements for a response. A second group of responses suggests that the child utilized information in the unfamiliar stem as a basis for a more familiar interpretation. Sometimes, part of the linguistic input was verbally altered by the child in her response, which enabled her to use another form in its completion. On the indirect object item 6b, for example, some children restated the stem: *She got some peanuts and gave them (gave him peanuts).* The child did not stay within the structure presented but used much of the information in it for the response.

In other, related, cases, the child did not openly restate the stem but still appeared to be using some of the information in it to derive a familiar structure to respond to. For example, on the nominalization stem, *What he did next (was go swimming),* some children apparently misinterpreted the stem as a question, *What did he do next?* The responses *Went swimming* or *He jumped in his pool* seem to indicate this interpretation.

It is interesting that children—like adults—seem to be able to edit out "mistakes" in the speech around them. Perhaps, like adults, they assume that they did not hear something correctly, or that the speaker unintentionally made a mistake. (In the examples given, of course, the "mistake" was not an error in the adult's grammatical system, but, from the child's point of view, a form not yet in his own system might seem like some deviation.) Chomsky and others have stressed the achievement of children in acquiring grammar from speech that is often ungrammatical. While others claim that ungrammatical utterances in speech are not as frequent as Chomsky supposed (Labov, 1970), the fact remains that we are able to edit out false starts, stammering, etc. and understand one another even when the unedited string of words appears ungrammatical. Once again, Grice's work stressing the "cooperative principle" of conversation is relevant. In his view, this very basic principle assumes that one's partner as well as oneself will follow the various rules for conversation, such as semantic relevance. If a conversational rule is flouted, the cooperative principle suggests that it is flouted for a reason and that the meaning of the speaker should be sought implicatively. The active and cooperative building of meaning from both linguistic and situational information is stressed in this view. If basic conversational principles are indeed acquired early, consider the implications for the young child having an incompletely developed grammatical system and thus encountering a high proportion of adult speech that is uninterpretable by his system. Piaget's notions of assimilation and accommodation may be relevant to the processes by which a child interprets (or misinterprets) some of the speech forms around him, and then eventually works them into his own grammatical system. Essential to these processes is the child's assumption that the adult means something by the statement, even though it is in an unfamiliar form. By editing (assimilating) to a more familiar structure, the child is able to produce a response relevant not only to the semantic situation but to some of the formal features (such as the word *what*) in the input.

We suggest that cases of this type occurred especially with the subjects from the lower-class dialect groups, and that many of our items were "edited" into different structures by these children. As we have noted in the individual item discussions, the Standard English item frequently was ambiguous or anomalous in terms of Black English Vernacular, and probably in terms of lower-class white dialects as well.

Partial control. A third type of response indicates a further point along the continuum of structure acquisition. In these cases, the stem was interpreted correctly but the child was not yet in complete control of the structure. The clearest examples are from the difficult items such as nominalization or secondary conjunction. On the nominalization item, for example, some children responded *What he did next* (*is went swimming*). On secondary conjunction items we got such responses as *This girl is running and so* (*did that one*) or *This baby can't walk and neither* (*is she*). These and other responses suggest partial control of the structures but clearly with a few details still missing, at least in production.

One of the striking features of the responses is that the children apparently attempted to stay within the required interactive framework—giving an "answer" relevant to both linguistic and semantic context—even in the cases where a target response was not yet within their competence. They frequently were able to utilize at least some of the linguistic information, and the decreasing proportions with age of less appropriate responses such as labeling or repetition suggest that there was a tendency to utilize all the information possible.

Thus, although not all of our items elicited unequivocal evidence of these intermediate types of responses, we feel justified in claiming that there is no clear-cut distinction between control of a structure and noncontrol. The apparent early control of basic conversational rules demanded that our subjects respond and that they make their responses as relevant as possible. Consequently, in addition to our polar situations of noncontrol (evidenced by repetition, labeling, or new sentences) and of good control (evidenced by target responses), we find intermediate degrees of control, as the children tried to maximize the relevance of their contributions.

Summary

In this chapter we have stepped back from the individual structures and looked at a number of aspects of the overall picture of syntactical development that emerge from the data. There was a general developmental increase in the complexity of structures controlled. The performance of both groups of lower-class children reflected the presence of permissible variants in the adult dialects.

A technique such as the language production test, in presenting to every child a range of structures, creates a situation in which children encounter structures unfamiliar to them. Confronted with this situation, they coped in several ways, demonstrating at least three levels along a continuum prior to structure control. In so doing, the children also manifested impressive functional conversational skills. These skills seemed to be employed in maximizing the relevance of responses to both situational and linguistic factors.

Chapter 8

Exploring Theoretical Conceptions

In developmental psycholinguistics a common procedure is to gather an extensive language corpus from each of a small number of children. Many of the most intriguing theoretical proposals of recent years have been derived from this kind of data base. Our data consist of a far more limited and structured sampling of a large number of children. This difference in the type of language data seems to provide a good opportunity to examine some of the paradigms that various psycholinguists have proposed and explore how they might apply to the language production of a very large number of children. Seeing some areas in which our methodology is potentially useful, and knowing about the performance of these 473 children, should aid other researchers in locating questions of interest and in constructing items to test these questions.

We were not able to explore all the issues we wanted to. In addition to the issues discussed in this chapter, we attempted to look at the effects of phenomena like embeddedness, conjoined clauses, and negation in the input. We believe that these effects can be investigated by the methodology reported here, but larger sets of items, controlled for extraneous variables, will have to be constructed for each question.

Our collection of items does furnish some information on several other issues. We focus here on some of the more recent ideas about how language develops, without attempting to be exhaustive and with the knowledge that our data are better suited to discovering problems than to answering questions. We will consider two types of theories. The first type deals with speech production, looking at order of acquisition as a function of complexity, particularly syntactic and semantic complexity. The second type focuses on speech comprehension and hypothesizes that there are strategies of perception that may or may not resemble deep linguistic rules. The two approaches are probably not mutually exclusive. In addition, we will look at the issue of variable rules and their effects on language acquisition.

Roger Brown:
Cumulative Complexity

Roger Brown, in *A First Language* (1973), investigated several factors that might affect the order of acquisition of certain morphemes. He concluded that cumulative semantic complexity of the morpheme or cumulative grammatical complexity or both were determinants of order of acquisition, rather than frequency of the morpheme in parental speech.

Our data are quite different in kind from Brown's. He had only three 2-year-old subjects, but each spontaneously produced a large number of obligatory contexts in free speech for all of the 14 morphemes he studied. We had 310 somewhat older middle-class subjects but only one or two obligatory contexts for each morpheme. Furthermore, on some of the morphemes Brown studied, the language production test was systematically biased toward more difficult items. For example, the very first morpheme acquired by Brown's subjects was the progressive -*ing* form of verbs. We had two contexts for -*ing* on the language production test, a present progressive in a direct quotation in a subordinate clause: "*because (he's eating)*" and a past progressive in a subordinate clause: *he saw that his brother (was watching TV)*.

The -*ing* form was given by less than 90 percent of our 3-year-old middle-class white subjects (still fewer furnished the correct auxiliaries). Brown's subjects, however, had been using -*ing* in 90 percent of the obligatory contexts from a younger age. We suspect that our items must be among the more difficult contexts for -*ing*. This suspicion is supported by the fact that a third item on the original testing, *I see a man* (*painting*), was completed correctly by 100 percent of those subjects—and therefore had to be eliminated from the final instrument. Similarly, the only noun plural item retained for the final version of the test required the allomorph /-ɨz/ (*glasses*), which Brown shows to be the most difficult allomorph of the plural. Direct comparisons of the order of emergence of different structures cannot be made from this particular set of items because of this systematic bias against the simplest items; however, the methodology should lend itself easily to investigating the problem with a wider range of contexts for each structure.

Despite this problem of bias favoring difficult contexts, we were interested in testing our results against Brown's notion of cumulative complexity. Brown's technique involved analyzing each structure into semantic features (such as "number" or "possession"). His predictions of order of acquisition were made on the basis of cumulative complexity. For example, if a given structure, A, had semantic feature X, and another structure, B, had feature X and also feature Y, the prediction was that A would be acquired before the more complex B. However, a third structure, C, which had yet another semantic feature, Z, could be compared with neither A nor B, since there is no way to compare difficulty of different semantic features.

Transformational complexity is calculated in the same way. If structures A and B share transformation X, and B also involves transformation Y, then B is more complex than A. However, they cannot be compared with structures that involve other transformations.

Brown's predictions, which were impressively borne out by his three subjects, are listed in Tables 31 and 32 and are contrasted there with the order of structure acquisition demonstrated by our middle-class white sample. Where there were multiple items for a structure, we have used the item that was easiest for the children, to minimize contextual effects. Where Brown's predictions are supported by our data, we list a plus (+); where they are not supported, we list a minus (−).

Despite the fact that our data are based on very few examples of each structure, some unusually difficult, we find that Brown's semantic predictions are frequently supported by our data. Semantic complexity, as he defines it, predicts two-thirds of the 3-year-old results. Had we included a simpler plural form, the predictions would probably be even better supported. Berko (1958) found over 50 per-

Table 31

A comparison of Brown's (1973) predicted order of
structure acquisition based on cumulative semantic
complexity with order of acquisition as demonstrated on
the Potts Language Production Test

Brown's predicted order of acquisition		Percentage difference between predicted earlier structure and predicted later structure in language production test data*		
Acquired earlier	Acquired later	Age: 3	4	5
Plural	Copula	+3	−7	+3
Past	Copula	+23	+21	+17
Plural	3rd regular	−7	−24	−15
Past	3rd regular	+13	+4	−1
Plural	Auxiliary	−8	−10	+1
Past	Auxiliary	+12	+18	+15
Progressive -ing	Auxiliary	+11	+12	+9
Copula	Auxiliary	−11	−3	−2
3rd regular	Auxiliary	+1	+14	+16

*Acquisition percentage on predicted earlier structure minus acquisition percentage on predicted later structure. Data relate to our middle-class white sample only.

Table 32

A comparison of Brown's (1973) predicted order
of structure acquisition based on cumulative
transformational complexity with order of acquisition as
demonstrated on the Potts Language Production Test

Brown's predicted order of acquisition		Percentage difference between predicted earlier structure and predicted later structure in language production test data*		
Acquired earlier	Acquired later	Age: 3	4	5
Simple progressive -ing	Auxiliary (contractible)	+11	+12	+9
Simple progressive -ing	Auxiliary (uncontractible)	+44	+41	+21

*Acquisition percentage on predicted earlier structure minus acquisition percentage on predicted later structure. Data relate to our middle-class white sample only.

cent difference between simple allomorphs /-s, -z/ of the plural, as in *wugs* or *biks*, and the complex type /-ɨz/ that we used, as in *gutches*.

The transformational complexity predictions involving the progressive are also supported. Brown notes that other grammatical predictions are possible, but they involve irregular forms. He feels that the regular-irregular dimension has not been adequately worked out in the Jacobs and Rosenbaum (1968) grammar he used, and that these predictions are not useful for testing the idea of cumulative transformational complexity. We looked at these predictions (such as past irregular acquired earlier than past regular), but our figures do not support the predictions, and we note that Brown's subjects show some exceptions also. We agree that useful predictions cannot be made until the grammar proposed is more complete.

Like Brown, we are unable to disentangle semantic from syntactic complexity. However, our data support Brown's work in general and suggest that further work with semantic features would be fruitful even with children older than Brown's subjects. The predictive value of transformational complexity is more problematical. First, as Brown suggests, some vital details have not yet been adequately described. Second, as we will see in our discussion of variable rules, there may be major reorganizations of rule systems in development, so that adult derivational complexity will be a mediocre predictor of order of acquisition.

DAVID MCNEILL:
TRANSFORMATIONAL SCOPE

McNeill (1970a, b) suggests that the scope of a syntactic structure helps determine its order of acquisition. For example, the /-s, -z, -ɨz/ allomorphs are the realization of three different morphemes: plural, possessive, and third person habitual present. The plural operates within a single word; the possessive relates two words within a single constituent; the third person verb ending marks a relation between different constituents. McNeill concludes:

> The order of development in English morphology is inversely related to the scope of the inflection. What take time and therefore appear late are rules that cover a range of structures within a single sentence. Besides the -s inflections mentioned before, which among themselves show this principle, English em-

beddings, tag questions, and complements develop relatively late (at four or five years) and each involves the correlation of two or more structures within a sentence. What take little time and therefore appear early, are rules that extend to a large number of different sentences without exception. Rules that cover several structures within a single sentence are typically rules of restriction—e.g., concord. Rules that cover different sentences are typically rules of generality—e.g., all sentences must have subjects and predicates. We thus again have an example of generalization appearing more readily than restriction. (McNeill, 1970a: 86)

The language production test includes a wide variety of structures with varying scope, and we felt it would be appropriate to investigate McNeill's suggestion. Our approach was to consider a wide range of items. As we explained in our discussion of Brown's cumulative complexity, the bias against easy items, which was required by test development, made us hesitant to draw conclusions from our data that leaned too heavily on these individual items. For example, we felt that looking at the plural, possessive, and third person singular morphemes would not be appropriate, although the methodology used here could easily be adapted to test these morphemes systematically. Instead, we compared the acquisition of structures requiring concord *within* a phrase or clause to the acquisition of structures that relate constituents *across* clause boundaries. We omitted certain borderline cases, where it was not clear to us whether the required relationships were within or across boundaries. Structures that had to be omitted on this basis were comparatives and superlatives (Items 21a, 21b, 21c, 21d), modal auxiliaries (Items 13a, 13b, 13c, 13d, 13e), simple negation (Item 19a), such verb phrases as progressive (Items 11a, 11b) and passive (12a, 12b), and infinitive complement (Item 14a). The problem with many of the items omitted was that the frame sentence contained a subordinator or coordinator, such as *if* or *but,* that influenced the target structure concord.

A *t*-test was performed at each level to ascertain whether or not the proportion of subjects producing the within-clause scope structures differed from that producing the across-clause scope structures. For the 3-year-olds, the across-clause structures were significantly more difficult than the within-clause structures $(t_{(29)} = 2.70, p < .05)$. The differences for the 4- and 5-year-olds were

Table 33

Acquisition of structures as a function of scope*

| | Item | Age: | Percentage giving target response | |
			3	4	5
Structures with within-clause scope					
Noun + plural	1a		69	68	85
Noun + possessive	2a		75	82	92
	2b		92	93	98
	2c		58	61	88
Possessive pronoun	3a		25	30	47
Subject pronoun	4a		73	86	94
	4b		65	80	87
Count/mass noun	5a		17	31	37
Indirect object	6a		56	73	92
	6b		57	75	75
Indirect object + direct object	6c		65	66	82
	6d		69	72	86
Reciprocal	7a		25	37	63
Habitual present	8a		76	92	100
	8b		74	79	90
Simple past	9a		89	96	99
	9b		68	70	84
Copula	10a		66	75	82
Indeterminate in a negative context	20a		37	49	58
	20b		40	42	61
Mean percentage			59.80	67.85	80.00
Structures with across-clause scope					
Restricted relative	15a		67	80	91
	15b		73	80	89
	15c		54	73	65
Secondary conjunction	16a		49	71	81
	16b		50	72	84
Secondary conjunction + negative	16c		21	37	80
	16d		24	43	80
Nominalization	17a		9	11	19
	17b		7	8	22
Action minalization	18a		24	41	76
	18b		41	51	86
Mean percentage			38.09	51.55	70.27
Difference within-across			21.71	16.30	9.73

*Again, data reflect responses of our middle-class white sample only.

not significant at the .05 level $(t_{(29)} = 1.94$ and $t_{(29)} = 1.25$, respectively).

We see that averaged across a large number of items, McNeill's hypothesis receives some support here. If difficulty of context could be equalized, we might find it in smaller subsets as well. The variation in acquisition *among* the structures within each scope category in Table 33 indicates again that transformational scope is only one of the factors influencing the order of acquisition.

It would be interesting to investigate the decreasing difference with age between control of the within-clause structures and of the across-clause structures. In the adult Standard English speaker, of course, we would expect only slight variations from 100 percent for both types of structure in these highly constrained contexts. In children, it would be interesting to see at what point the two types converge. Our preliminary test here suggests statistical equivalence by age 4.

Before leaving the topic of transformational scope, we would like to touch on a further complicating factor. Some of the items we have listed as within-clause structures are actually sensitive to other clauses. The items testing for verb tense provide a good illustration. Our pictures were "timeless" in that the activity pictured could often be described by a number of tenses—present, past, progressive, etc. The linguistic stem alone gave the information necessary to choose the correct Standard English tense form. For example, in Item 8a, the habitual present was specified by *is* in the frame *Every day, when this baby is tired and hungry, he* _____. In Item 9a, the simple past was specified by *woke* and *gave* in the frame *This morning mother woke Tom up and gave him breakfast. Then she* _____.

As noted earlier, the children were also sensitive to other types of parallelism. Note, for example, the possessive pronoun item, 3a: *The turtle is hers, the bird is his, and the dog is* _____. Dogs can be described in many ways. For example, we can say *The dog is brown* or *The dog is a Scottie.* Many children did not yet control the target *theirs,* but most of them—even 3-year-olds—attempted to identify the possessor. Again, on the count/mass item, 5a, order-of-mention parallelism appeared to take precedence over syntactic agreement.

McNeill's hypothesis, then, must be qualified as it applies to our data. Linguistic operations that embed or otherwise subordinate whole propositions to other propositions are indeed learned later.

However, even our youngest children appear to be able to coordinate linguistic forms across clauses in the short discourses of the language production test.

LOIS BLOOM:
VARIATION AND REDUCTION

Variable rules are relevant to two aspects of the work presented in this report. First, Labov has shown that they are useful in describing differences among dialects, and we have discussed this aspect in terms of our social class and racial groups. Second, Brown (1973) has suggested that they may provide a fruitful way of looking at developing grammars, and Bloom, Miller, and Hood (1975) have presented a model of variation for the speech of very young children. Let us examine our data in the light of these suggestions.

Optional rules have been incorporated into transformational grammars almost from the beginning, along with obligatory rules, which must always apply to a given structure. Relative clauses provide illustrations of both types of rule in Standard English. If the relative pronoun is the subject of its clause, it must always be obligatorily included: *Those are the people that run the city.* If the relative is the object of its clause, however, it may be included or optionally deleted: *Those are the people that she appointed, Those are the people she appointed.*

Labov (1973) has refined the notion of "optional rule" further. He suggests that a deletion rule may occur in a fixed proportion of cases over time, and that this probability of deletion is part of a speaker's internal rule system. Further, he suggests that a variety of contextual factors—semantic, syntactic, and phonological—may contribute to the probability of deletion. In our examples, it might be that speakers delete *that* more often after a simple noun phrase (such as *people*) than after a noun phrase including a postposed modifier (such as *people from urban areas*):

     a. Those are the people she appointed.
     b. Those are the people that she appointed.
     c. Those are the people from urban areas she appointed.
     d. Those are the people from urban areas that she appointed.

In sentences like *a* and *b*, *that* deletion may occur 50 percent of the time. In sentences like *c* and *d*, deletion may occur only 10 percent of the time. (The figures are hypothetical.) In a complete Labov-type grammar, all such rules would have a complete set of contingencies stated.

At first glance, assuming that children have a Labov-type set of deletion rules seems counterintuitive, because it implies that an earlier stage of language, which includes a rule that deletes forms variably, is more complex syntactically than a later stage, in which the forms appear categorically. Bloom's (1970) original account of a "reduction transformation" in some toddler linguistic systems was questioned on these grounds by Brown (1973) and others. However, as Bloom, Miller, and Hood point out, variable rules and reduction of number of constituents, as in ellipsis, are characteristic of adult grammar as well. They state:

> Rather than drop out, the process of reduction undergoes its own development and changes as the child grammar is progressively elaborated. Further, the fact of reduction is implicit in adult grammar and operates in conjunction with many derivational and transformational constraints. Thus, rather than being an expediency for explaining the interpretation of utterances, the reduction that occurs in the child grammar is a linguistic process that interacts with the integration and organization of categories and rule relations in the linguistic system. [Bloom, Miller, and Hood: 41]

The authors go on to suggest a model in which grammatical, lexical, and discourse factors act as variable constraints in structure production.

Until a more complete developmental grammar is proposed, we do not know if Bloom's hypothesis will solve the problem of earlier stages appearing to be more complex than later stages. In fact, if rules are taken to be descriptions of the child's knowledge at a given stage, rather than descriptions of processes directly involved in production, it is not surprising that early fragmentary knowledge requires more elaborate description than later, deeper knowledge. We are left with the situation of individual categorical rules apparently becoming simpler as speakers mature, although the total system may well be becoming more complex. Further, Bloom and her associates were discussing primitive linguistic rules, which are quite different from the mature variable deletion that Labov studied. However, it is worth stressing that this type of phenomenon is found in language throughout development and into adulthood. We believe that this analysis of linguistic development as a complex interaction of many developing rules, but with no fundamental discontinuities, is a more fruitful approach than views that stress distinct qualitatively different stages of development. No doubt major restructurings occur and some categories and structures are acquired rather suddenly. But Bloom's view suggests that even rapid changes may involve reorganizations of exactly the same types of linguistic processes that characterize earlier stages.

Two types of evidence from the language production test seem relevant to the theoretical points raised by Labov, Brown, and Bloom. First, we can look at variability within individual children across parallel items, to see if the structures are produced categorically (as in adult speech) or variably in these early linguistic systems.

We looked at our youngest middle-class white group, the 41 children aged 3:2 to 3:5, in order to maximize the comparability to Bloom's subjects. There were seven structures with pairs of items that were appropriate for this comparison. (Other structures—such as subject pronouns, which differed in gender—were considered only partially parallel, and the nominalization pairs were eliminated because they were extremely difficult.) For each pair of items, we sorted our 41 subjects into those that got both right $(++)$, the first right but not the second $(+-)$, the second right but not the first $(-+)$, or both wrong $(--)$. The results are shown in Table 34.

On each structure, the majority of the children performed identically on the two parallel items, but there was a steady minority of one-sixth to one-third of the children who demonstrated variability. The minority was not consistently made up of the same individuals; no child was always inconsistent, and only seven were always consistent. The inconsistencies might, of course, reflect random lapses of attention or individual peculiarities, but they might also demonstrate systematic effects of the constraints Bloom, Miller, and Hood suggested, such as differing discourse context or differing lexical familiarity (differing grammatical complexity was minimized in this particular comparison). The technique of the language production test might be utilized for a systematic comparison of contexts that

Table 34
Individual variability on parallel items

Item	++	+−	−+	−−	Total consistent	Total inconsistent
Indirect object + direct object (6c and 6d)	17	5	8	11	28	13
Simple past (9a and 9b)	24	11	4	2	26	15
Passive (12a and 12b)	13	5	3	20	33	8
Modal: indirect speech (13d and 13e)	7	5	3	26	33	8
Infinitive complement (14a and 14b)	29	1	8	3	32	9
Restrictive relative (15a and 15b)	21	5	10	5	26	15
Superlative (21c and 21d)	17	5	8	11	28	13

vary in Bloom's constraints, for further investigation of her suggested model.

A second issue that interested us was the acquisition of rules that are variable in the adult dialect. Most linguistic studies, including ours, have stressed categorical rules because they have been more completely studied. However, if Bloom's model of continuity in linguistic processes is correct, the acquisition of rules that remain variable in adult speech becomes even more interesting.

Since most of our items involved rules that are categorical for middle-class white speakers, we could not extract very much information about the issue from this group alone. The only items we could compare were the relative clause items, where subject relatives are categorically included in Standard English but object relatives are variably supplied. The results are shown in Table 35. Variability in the adult dialect looks as though it may relate to both the age of acquisition and the rate of usage by the most mature middle-class white children.

An even better comparison of the acquisition of variable as opposed to categorical rules can be found by looking at our lower-class black sample. As we have stressed throughout this book, the language production test items are widely varying in the degree to which they are appropriate for speakers who are acquiring Black English Vernacular. However, this very characteristic of the items is useful in the present question, enabling us to compare the acqui-

Table 35

Categorical and variable rule learning—Percentages of middle-class white target responses on relative clause items

	Age:	3	4	5
Categorical:				
Item 15a		64	79	91
Item 15b		72	80	88
Variable:				
Item 15c		54	73	65

sition of categorical rules to the acquisition of variable rules.

The reader is referred to Tables 29 and 30. Only in the first three items of Table 29 (which test simple sentence negation and indeterminates) is the Black English Vernacular variant nearly categorical in adult speech (for example, a speaker *must* say *I don't see none*, and never *I don't see any*). For all the other items listed, the target structures in Table 29 are variably supplied in adult speech, while the structures in Table 30 are always supplied by adult Black English Vernacular speakers. We performed a *t*-test on the reduced set of items, deleting the indeterminate and sentence negation structures and again minimizing item difficulty by measuring the difference between the lower-class black percentages and the middle-class white percentages. Among the 4- and 5-year-olds, a significantly greater percentage produced the target structures in the categorical rule set than in the variable rule set ($t_{(17)}$ = 1.97 and 1.86, p < .05). The differences for the 3-year-olds were not significant, although the means favor the categorical rule set. The lack of significance at these levels may reflect a floor effect, in which few target structures of any type are produced by these children, or it may reflect wider variability in the younger groups.[1]

As we have pointed out in the item discussions, the more mature black children are not just omitting Standard English targets; they appear to be actively supplying valid Black English Vernacular variants. Two examples are repeated here, as Table 36, to underscore our point.

---

1. It should be noted that for the 3-year-olds the variance was significantly greater in categorical than in variable rules, ($F_{(8,9)}$ = 11.2, p < .01).

Table 36

Percentages of responses to structures with categorical
rules in Standard English and variable rules in Black
English Vernacular

		Middle-class white			Lower-class black		
Age:		3	4	5	3	4	5
Past tense (Item 9b):							
combed (acceptable in both Standard English and Black English Vernacular)		89	96	99	8	30	33
comb (acceptable only in Black English Vernacular)		6	3	1	78	69	59
Present progressive (Item 11a)							
he's eating (acceptable in both Standard English and Black English Vernacular)		77	78	84	9	14	33
he eating (acceptable only in Black English Vernacular)		4	1	1	36	50	52

It is clear from the high rate of usage among the most mature
speakers of Black English Vernacular that the deleted -ed and -s
forms are equally or even more acceptable than the full form in these
items.

The results of our preliminary investigation suggest that variability in the adult dialect has a powerful effect on the acquisition of
rules. However, conclusions about the exact nature of the effect on
individual linguistic development will require more detailed analyses of individual systems. As stressed both by Bloom, Miller, and
Hood (1975) and by Labov (1973), variable deletion and reduction
transformations require evidence from within the same system of the
existence of underlying forms that are deleted. Without this evidence, it is more reasonable to assume that the form is not part of
the system at all. A refined and detailed set of items with many repli-
cations of structures would be necessary to explore individual systems in enough detail to discover whether a given instance of non-
occurrence of a structure reflected deletion or nonacquisition.
However, the evidence we have presented about variability within
children, and the differential supplying of variable structures by
even our most mature subjects, suggest that variability is an important area for further exploration by researchers in linguistic
development.

T. G. Bever: Perceptual Strategies of Comprehension

Bever's (1970) influential article on perceptual strategies, along with a variety of experiments and observations by Turner and Rommetveit (1967), Ervin-Tripp (1973), Menyuk (1971), Sinclair and Bronckart (1972), and others, has awakened interest in another approach to the study of language development. Rather than starting with adult derivational descriptions and attempting to account for child language phenomena in terms of these descriptions, the perceptual strategy approach starts with child perceptual abilities and with surface structure forms, and attempts to account for child language phenomena by proposing rules for interpretation of these surface forms. The rules proposed so far have little resemblance to the derivational rules normally proposed in generative grammar, although the statistical overlap in sentences accounted for is obvious. For example, one of the strategies proposed by Bever (Strategy D) states: "Any *Noun-Verb-Noun* (NVN) sequence within a potential internal unit in the surface structure corresponds to "actor-action-object" (1970: 298). It is clear that using this strategy to interpret language will very frequently lead to a correct conclusion, as in *Joe pushed Bill.* It is also clear that from time to time it will fail, as in *Joe was pushed by Bill.* Children who have only Strategy D thus have difficulty with passive sentences. At a later stage, when they know more about the world, some actor-action-object interpretations are rejected as implausible. For example, in such a nonreversible passive as *The pony is ridden by the girl,* pony-ride-girl as actor-action-object is implausible to a child who knows about usual relations between girls and ponies, so it is correctly reinterpreted as an object-action-actor sequence (McNeill, 1970b). However, such reversible passives as *the dog is chased by the cat* are systematically misinterpreted, since dog-chase-cat is a plausible actor-action-object sequence. Only later do children interpret reversible passives correctly (McNeill, 1970b).

The language production test contained three sets of structures (eight items) that seemed relevant to investigating a perceptual strategy hypothesis. Obviously, researchers interested in the topic will want to do more extensive tests; our purpose here is only to pull together the preliminary indications of perceptual strategy effects that this test revealed. We had no adequately matched pairs of structures through which to compare agent-action with action-agent surface structures, but four pairs of items furnished information on the action-object versus object-action order.

The following structures and items were compared:

1. *Auxiliaries*

Action-object: Item 13b (modal + negative): He stretched and he stretched but _____ (he couldn't get them, he didn't get them).

Object-action: Item 13a (Future-conditional): If they fall out of the tree now, _____ (they might be hurt, they'll get hurt, etc.).

2. *Verb + to + passive or active infinitive*

Action-object: Item 14a (infinitive complement): Boys, I want you _____ (to put them away, to clean them up, etc.).
Item 14b (infinitive complement): He wants his brother _____ (to fix it, etc.).

Object-action: Item 12a (passive): In 5 minutes those pictures have to _____ (be finished, get done).
Item 12b (passive): It has to _____ (be washed, get cleaned, etc.).

3. *Relative clause*

Action-object: Item 15a: These are the children _____ (who ride the bus, etc.).

Object-action: Item 15c: This is the house _____ (that he lives in, where he lives, etc.).

The results of comparing these items are summarized in Table 37.

We find that the items with action-object order tend to be easier than those with object-action order, just as strategy theories would predict. The exception is the auxiliary structures at ages 3 and 4; perhaps the negative + past item, 13b, is more difficult in other ways for the younger children than the future-conditional item, 13a (see discussion of modal auxiliaries in Chapter 4 for details).

While this particular test is not extensive enough to furnish conclusive support for the hypothesis that particular orders such as subject-verb-object operate as acquisition strategies for children, our preliminary figures are compatible with such a hypothesis. We suggest that further information about the importance of surface sequence strategies in acquisition may be obtained by using methodology similar to that reported here.

Table 37

Percentages of target responses on action-object versus
object-action structures*

	Action-object				Object-action		
Age:	*3*	*4*	*5*		*3*	*4*	*5*
Auxiliaries:							
Item 13b (negative)	65	80	93	Item 13a (conditional)	73	90	89
Verb + *to* + *passive* or active infinitive:							
Item 14a (active)	81	84	90	Item 12a (passive)	36	63	88
Item 14b (active)	88	89	98	Item 12b (passive)	48	59	92
Relative clause:							
Item 15a	64	79	91	Item 15c	54	73	65

*The data given here reflect responses of the middle-class white children only.

SUMMARY

We have considered the compatability of our results with four theoretical suggestions made by developmental psycholinguists in recent years: Brown's notion of cumulative complexity, McNeill's proposal of transformational scope, Bloom's variation model, and the
perceptual strategy approach of Bever and others.

Brown (1973) investigated factors affecting the order of acquisition of selected morphemes. His predictions of order of acquisition
were made on the basis of an index of cumulative complexity. We
looked at our results in light of Brown's cumulative complexity idea
and made the possible comparisons with our own findings. We
found that given the limitations of data comparability, Brown's semantic predictions were frequently supported by our data. In our discussion, we tried to point out where the data did not support the predictions and where additional work with semantic features is
necessary.

McNeill's work (1970a, b) suggests that the *scope* of syntactic
structures helps determine order of acquisition. Averaged across a
large number of items, we were able to substantiate McNeill's hypothesis to some extent. We pointed out, however, that the hypothesis must be qualified as it applies to the data of this study. While the
operations that linguistically embed or subordinate propositions are

the ones that are learned later, even the young children of this study were able to coordinate linguistic forms across the clauses represented in the language production test.

Bloom, Miller, and Hood (1975) argue for the continuity of variable deletion as a process in child and adult language. They suggest that variability in children's structure usage is a function of the systematic effects of grammatical, lexical, and discourse factors. This conception relates to our data in two ways: (1) we can look at the parallel items for a single structure in the test to examine children's variable production where rules are categorical in adult Standard English, and (2) we can compare children's production of categorical versus variable rules. Regarding the first relationship, we did find the kind of variable production of parallel items that Bloom, Miller, and Hood's thesis would predict. As to the second relationship, a comparison of the data revealed that variability in the adult dialect seemed to relate to acquisition by middle-class white children. For lower-class black children as well, variability in the adult dialect seemed in our data to be related to rule acquisition. To answer the more difficult question of whether the missing forms are deleted or are not a part of the child's system at all, a detailed investigation of individual systems is needed. The methodology used here seems useful for this enterprise.

Among the perceptual strategies that Bever and others have hypothesized, the only one we investigated was the processing of noun-verb-noun sequences as actor-action-object (Bever, 1970). Looking at the limited number of items on the test that relate to this proposed strategy, we found that items with action-object order tend to be easier than those with object-action order.

For each of the four theoretical conceptions examined, our results provide general support and indicate ways in which further investigation through systematic use of the sentence-completion technique would be fruitful. In addition, we hope to have suggested a portion of the wealth of new problems and possibilities that emerged from these findings.

Epilogue

In Chapter 1 we stated that we would avoid linguistic and psy-cholinguistic controversies and present our data within the context of other theoretical frameworks only where such overlap was appar-ent. We have not engaged in hypothesis testing, nor have we at-tempted to couch our findings in terms of a particular theoretical viewpoint. In our Chapter 8 discussion of four current perspectives in the field, we pointed out that the data and technique reported here can be put to use in pursuit of a variety of interests. In this conclud-ing section we should like to suggest some further directions. While we delimited our own task as one concerned with the structural fea-tures of language, it would be an understatement of the usefulness of the technique to leave the reader with the impression that there are no further domains to be explored by this means.

Our discussions of the individual structures included several dif-ferent perspectives on the data whenever such vantage points seemed directly relevant to understanding the results. First, we fre-quently looked at the data from the perspective of the child's psy-chological processing, specifically with the processing rules re-quired by these structures. Second, we often needed to discuss linguistic factors, especially those usually categorized within the phonological and syntactic domains. And third, we found it appro-priate to point to possible factors implicated in the linkage between the conceptual and linguistic aspects of producing particular structures. We would like to point out now that these three perspectives on the study of language could serve as the principal thrust of future research studies—studies designed to gather the data necessary for building a theory of language development.

Each of the structures we tested could be plumbed for its potential contribution to all three approaches. To simplify discussion, we would like to outline briefly how a few structures might be focused on from one or another of these vantage points.

In terms of psychological processing, young children's language has interested many psychologists as a rich source of information about early rule learning. Examples that shed light on the nature of rule learning abound in our data, and readers can see how the technique could be used to map out more exhaustively the learning of any one rule network. Let us consider only one example of how the data allow us to sketch in a little of what rule learning is like for a single structure.

Both rule learning and variable rule learning are evident in the data collected for the present study. While one might be inclined to think of such a syntactic element as the subject pronoun as reflecting "simple" rule learning, a developmental analysis of the error patterns from age 3 to age 5 indicates that its acquisition is not altogether straightforward. Among the rules involved in acquiring the use of the appropriate subject pronoun are learning to designate gender and learning to use the proper case. We can see by examining the data that some children were correct in gender usage but made an error in case. Others used the correct case but had not mastered the gender rule completely. On the way to mastery of the rule network pertaining to the subject pronoun, then, we see evidence of points where one rule is controlled and the other is not. Moreover, in addition to learning each of the rules for a single structure, the child also has the task of learning to coordinate these rules. While we will not exhaust the potential richness of the research comparisons in this summary, the data can easily be extended to the study of rule coordination, as distinguished from the abstraction of individual rules.

Moving to another perspective, there would be great usefulness in systematically exploring such data from the vantage point of linguistic concerns. For example, in morphological development, we see variation in our data in the use of the possessive allomorph /-z/ in frames that differ on several dimensions. These include phonological (/-iy/ in *monkey* and *baby*, /-aʷn/ in *clown*); contextual (type of possessive, if any, in frame); and syntactic (whether the task was of the sentence-completion or question-answer type). Linguists wishing to investigate systematically the relationship of these variables to the acquisition of possessive allomorphs could examine them further by means of this technique.

Another type of linguistic question raised by the present data is exemplified by the children's responses to the direct and indirect object structures. When children had the opportunity to give either the direct object + *to* + indirect object (*Dad gave a balloon to him*) or the inverted indirect object + direct object (*Dad gave him a balloon*), the great majority at all ages gave the latter. This is not what would be expected in view of the traditional linguistic description of the inverted form as derived from the direct object + *to* + indirect object. Although more extensive investigation would be needed to be certain of the course of acquisition, this finding illustrates the way linguistic formulations could be examined in the light of developmental data collected through the use of the language production method.

Moving to the third perspective, the exploration of conceptual and linguistic relations, the structures of negation are very appealing territory for cognitive psychologists—full of possible relations among cognitive processes and linguistic structures. Other researchers have examined some of the ways negation affects sentence processing and made an initial investigation of the interlocking development of the conceptual system of negation and the linguistic expression of it. Yet, many questions remain to be answered in the area of the production of negatives and underlying cognitive competence.

In the present data there is strong evidence that middle-class children frequently produce double negatives, despite their lack of exposure to that form from adult models. When Standard English–speaking children produce the double negative, it is usually attributed to overgeneralization. No attempt has been made, however, to look at the relationship of these occurrences to what is being said. One could generate a number of hypotheses about this relationship, some syntactic, some semantic, and some nonlinguistic. Perhaps, for example, the concept embodied in *anything, anyone, anywhere* is a more difficult one for the young child than the corresponding negative equivalents, *nothing, no one, nowhere*. This sort of hypothesis would be accessible to examination by means of the methodology used here.

The technique has already given impetus to new research from the cognitive perspective that attempts to validate psychological constructs across both verbal and nonverbal domains (Cocking, 1976). This approach takes cognitive variables such as those proposed by Piaget (e.g., causal relationships, temporal relationships, and negation) and looks for their concomitants in verbal structures (such as—in the case of causality—causal connectives, *if* clause conditionals, and simple future tense structures).

The technique on which this book is based provides a natural interchange as a context for collecting data about children's knowledge of language. And, as we have pointed out, these data are not limited to any one theoretical perspective for interpretation or to any one discipline for usefulness. Identification of the psychological, the linguistic, and the cognitive tasks implicated in complex structures, such as some of those tested here, may enable us to focus better on language development at advanced levels. Recent work is moving toward exploration of the interface between syntactic strategies on the one hand and semantic and pragmatic strategies on the other. We hope to have offered some possibilities for furthering such research.

Appendix

Tables Relating to
the Methodology

Table A-1

Means and standard deviations of mental age (MA) and
IQ, as measured by the Peabody Picture Vocabulary Test:
middle-class sample

Age group	N	MA $\bar{X}$	SD	IQ $\bar{X}$	SD
Early 3's	41	50.73	9.75	112.63	13.52
Late 3's	65	58.37	12.25	112.14	12.01
Total	106	55.42	11.90	112.33	12.55
Early 4's	45	61.38	13.31	108.78	12.88
Late 4's	55	69.38	14.48	110.24	12.97
Total	100	65.78	14.46	109.58	12.88
Early 5's	49	76.06	12.41	112.57	11.30
Late 5's	55	83.06	11.37	109.84	10.25
Total	104	79.76	12.32	111.13	10.79
Total sample	310	66.92	16.34	111.04	12.12

Table A-2

Means and standard deviations of mental age (MA) and
IQ, as measured by the Peabody Picture Vocabulary Test:
lower-class sample

Group	N	MA $\bar{X}$	MA SD	IQ $\bar{X}$	IQ SD
Lower-class whites:					
3-year-olds	26	38.92	9.75	88.89	16.04
4-year-olds	24	48.96	10.56	86.25	33.14
5-year-olds	27	62.19	13.51	91.59	15.01
Total sample	77	50.21	14.92	89.01	22.33
Lower-class blacks:					
3-year-olds	23	37.78	5.74	90.87	13.06
4-year-olds	36	47.00	11.55	77.08	42.67
5-year-olds	27	52.93	19.39	81.59	25.06
Total sample	86	46.40	14.57	82.19	31.90

Table A-3

Means and standard deviations of total raw scores on the
language production, comprehension, and Peabody
(PPVT) tests: middle-class sample

Age group	N	Production $\bar{X}$	Production SD	Comprehension $\bar{X}$	Comprehension SD	PPVT $\bar{X}$	PPVT SD
Early 3's	41	42.49	16.37	63.35	6.41	42.27	8.18
Late 3's	65	52.35	15.57	65.33	5.94	47.39	8.02
Total	106	48.54	16.53	64.58	6.14	45.41	8.42
Early 4's	45	55.29	15.28	67.88	5.70	48.98	8.68
Late 4's	55	61.49	14.57	66.77	7.49	53.75	7.71
Total	100	58.70	15.14	67.30	6.64	51.60	8.46
Early 5's	49	73.74	12.85	71.32	3.98	56.92	6.06
Late 5's	55	72.71	9.62	71.44	4.31	60.35	5.06
Total	104	73.19	11.21	71.38	4.11	58.73	5.79
Total sample	310	60.09	17.67	67.74	6.35	51.87	9.40

Table A-4

Means and standard deviations of total raw scores on the
language production, comprehension, and Peabody
(PPVT) tests: lower-class sample

Group	N	Production $\bar{X}$	SD	Comprehension $\bar{X}$	SD	PPVT $\bar{X}$	SD
Lower-class whites:							
3-year-olds	26	17.08	11.15	55.25	7.44	30.50	11.22
4-year-olds	24	34.63	19.75	48.08	24.32	40.75	9.25
5-year-olds	27	50.15	20.71	70.21	3.19	49.44	8.54
Total sample	77	34.14	22.28	58.88	17.69	40.34	12.45
Lower-class blacks:							
3-year-olds	23	12.96	7.31	51.00	6.68	33.26	13.62
4-year-olds	36	27.58	12.00	57.53	7.03	38.67	10.22
5-year-olds	27	33.44	17.57	54.73	17.84	42.22	14.89
Total sample	86	25.51	15.23	54.58	11.93	38.34	13.06

Table A-5

Item difficulty, by social class and racial group

Structure	Item	MCW	LCW	LCB
Noun + plural	1a	.7387	.5195	.2791
Noun + possessive	2a	.8322	.6364	.4186
	2b	.9452	.6234	.2791
	2c	.6871	.4675	.4419
Possessive pronoun	3a	.3387	.2727	.2209
Subjective pronoun: gender	4a	.7677	.5454	.7325
	4b	.8322	.5714	.6047
Determiner + count noun or mass noun	5a	.2806	.2727	.2325
Indirect object *to* + noun phrase	6a	.7322	.4026	.3837
	6b	.4484	.2727	.2325
Indirect object + direct object	6c	.7097	.6753	.1163
	6d	.7452	.6234	.6744
Reciprocal	7a	.4516	.2078	.2093

Table A-5—*continued*

Structure	Item	MCW	LCW	LCB
Habitual present	8a	.8839	.5584	.2325
	8b	.8097	.3636	.1136
Past tense	9a	.9548	.6234	.2558
	9b	.7193	.5974	.4419
Subject-copula: present tense	10a	.7419	.4415	.1163
Progressive	11a	.7806	.4935	.1860
	11b	.5355	.2597	.1395
Passive	12a	.6226	.3766	.3140
	12b	.6613	.3377	.3605
Modal auxiliaries	13a	.8387	.5974	.3488
	13b	.7935	.4805	.4419
	13c	.7613	.3506	.3256
Indirect question	13d	.4871	.2208	.2093
	13e	.4710	.2987	.1744
Infinitive complement	14a	.8322	.4026	.5930
	14b	.9097	.5195	.6744
Relative clause	15a	.7710	.4935	.2674
	15b	.8065	.4286	.3837
	15c	.8581	.8182	.8023
Secondary conjunction	16a	.6742	.2987	.1744
	16b	.6742	.1169	.2442
Secondary conjunction + negative	16c	.4581	.2597	.0349
	16d	.5129	.2727	.1512
Nominalization	17a	.1258	.0260	.0116
	17b	.1226	.0260	.0116
Action nominalization	18a	.4226	.1169	.0814
	18b	.5000	.1169	.0698
Simple sentence negation	19a	.9000	.2157	.0698
Indeterminates in negative contexts	20a	.4774	.0519	.0116
	20b	.4742	.0649	.0465
Comparative	21a	.5000	.2338	.2093
	21b	.7452	.0565	.4070
Superlative	21c	.7613	.3377	.3023
	21d	.9548	.6234	.2558

Table A-6

Means, standard deviations, and test-retest correlations
on language production test: middle-class retest sample

| Age group | N | First administration | | Second administration | | Pearson r |
		$\bar{X}$	SD	$\bar{X}$	SD	
Early 3's	21	44.00	15.93	49.86	15.86	.93
Late 3's	33	53.82	15.59	61.42	13.22	.86
Total	54	50.00	16.31	56.93	15.26	.90
Early 4's	24	56.63	13.00	65.50	11.33	.89
Late 4's	26	62.27	12.88	70.65	10.72	.82
Total	50	59.35	13.17	67.94	11.20	.86
Early 5's	25	74.96	9.35	77.52	6.63	.82
Late 5's	27	73.56	9.89	78.30	7.50	.84
Total	52	74.23	9.56	77.92	7.04	.82
Total sample	156	61.14	16.64	67.53	14.53	.92

Table A-7

Means, standard deviations, and test-retest correlations
on language production test: lower-class retest sample

| Group | First adminstration | | Second administration | | Pearson r |
	$\bar{X}$	SD	$\bar{X}$	SD	
Lower-class whites (N = 34)	40.71	22.80	45.38	23.53	.9366
Lower-class blacks (N = 45)	27.91	15.13	30.56	14.53	.9159

Table A-8

Internal consistency coefficients on
language production test: middle-class
sample

Age group	N	r
Early 3's	41	.882
Late 3's	65	.867
Early 4's	45	.868
Late 4's	55	.860
Early 5's	49	.873
Late 5's	55	.744

Table A-9

Intercorrelations of total raw scores on the language production, comprehension, and Peabody (PPVT) tests

	3-year-olds			4-year-olds			5-year-olds		
	CA	PPVT	Comp.	CA	PPVT	Comp.	CA	PPVT	Comp.
Middle-class whites									
Production test	.23	.45	.69	.26	.60	.37	.04	.45	.47
Comprehension test	.23	.49		−.09	.33		.09	.32	
PPVT	.29			.32			.39		
Lower-class whites									
Production test	.28	.52	.34	.05	.47	.04	.34	.33	.41
Comprehension test	−.14	.74		−.07	.10		.55	.41	
PPVT	.25			.03			.41		
Lower-class blacks									
Production test	.03	−.12	−.20	.12	.51	.33	.32	.41	.54
Comprehension test	−.35	.51		.17	.67		.12	.70	
PPVT	−.03			.22			.45		

References

ANISFELD, M., J. BARLOW, and C. M. FRAIL. 1968. Distinctive features in the pluralization rules of English speakers. *Language and Speech,* 11(1), 31–37.

AUSTIN, J. L. 1962. *How to do things with words.* Cambridge, Mass.: Harvard University Press.

BELLUGI, U. 1967. "The acquisition of negation." Unpublished doctoral dissertation, Harvard University.

BELLUGI, U., and W. HAAS. 1968. *Syntactic structures for modelling in preschool training.* Urbana, Ill.: ERIC Clearinghouse on Early Childhood Education.

BELLUGI-KLIMA, U. 1971. Comprehension test of grammatical structure (1970 Greeley revision.) In C. S. Lavatelli, ed., *Language training in early childhood education.* Urbana, Ill.: University of Illinois Press.

BERKO, J. 1958. The child's learning of English morphology. *Word,* 14, 150–177.

BEVER, T. G. 1970. The cognitive basis for linguistic structures. In J. R. Hayes, ed., *Cognition and the development of language.* New York: Wiley.

BEVER, T. G., J. MEHLER, and V. V. VALIAN. 1970. Linguistic capacity of very young children. Lecture at Graduate School of Education, Harvard University, 1967. Cited in D. McNeill, *The acquisition of language: The study of developmental psycholinguistics.* New York: Harper & Row.

BLOOM, L. 1968. "Language development: Form and function in emerging grammars." Unpublished doctoral dissertation, Columbia University.

———. 1970. *Language development: Form and function in emerging grammars.* Cambridge, Mass.: M.I.T. Press.

BLOOM, L., L. HOOD, and P. LIGHTBOWN. 1974. Imitation in language development: If, when, and why. *Cognitive Psychology, 6,* 380–420.

BLOOM, L., P. MILLER, and L. HOOD. 1975. Variation and reduction as aspects of competence in language development. In A. Pick, ed., *Minnesota symposia on child psychology,* Vol. 9. Minneapolis, Minn.: University of Minnesota Press.

BLOOM, L., L. ROCISSANO, and L. HOOD. 1976. Adult-child discourse: Developmental interaction between information processing and linguistic knowledge. *Cognitive Psychology, 8,* 521-552.

BRAINE, M. 1963. The ontogeny of English phrase structure: The first phase. *Language, 39,* 1–13.

BROWN, R. 1957. Linguistic determinism and the part of speech. *Journal of Abnormal and Social Psychology, 55,*1–5.

_____. 1968a. The development of Wh- questions in child speech. *Journal of Verbal Learning and Verbal Behavior, 7,* 279–290.

_____. 1968b. Derivational complexity and the order of acquisition in child speech. Carnegie-Mellon Conference on Cognitive Processes.

_____. 1973. *A first language: The early stages.* Cambridge, Mass.: Harvard University Press.

BROWN, R., and U. BELLUGI. 1964. Three processes in the child's acquisition of syntax. *Harvard Educational Review, 34,* 133–151.

BROWN, R., C. CAZDEN, and U. BELLUGI. 1969. The child's grammar from I to III. In J. P. Hill, ed., *Minnesota symposia on child psychology,* Vol. 2. Minneapolis, Minn.: University of Minnesota Press.

BROWN, R., and C. HANLON. 1970. Derivational complexity and order of acquisition in child speech. In J. R. Hayes, ed., *Cognition and the development of language.* New York: Wiley.

CANTRIL, H. 1944. *Gauging public opinion.* Princeton, N.J.: Princeton University Press.

CARLSON, P., and M. ANISFELD. 1969. Some observations on the linguistic competence of a two-year-old child. *Child Development, 40,* 569–575.

CAZDEN, C. B. 1967. The acquisition of noun and verb inflections. *Child Development, 39,* 433–438.

_____. 1968. Some implications of research on language development for pre-school education. In R. D. Hess and R. M. Bear, eds., *Early education.* Chicago: Aldine.

_____. 1972. *Child language and education.* New York: Holt, Rinehart, & Winston.

CHOMSKY, C. S. 1969. *The acquisition of syntax in children from 5 to 10.* Cambridge, Mass.: M.I.T. Press.

CHOMSKY, N. 1965. *Aspects of the theory of syntax.* Cambridge, Mass.: M.I.T. Press.

CHOMSKY, N., and M. HALLE. 1968. *Sound patterns of English.* New York: Harper & Row.

CLARK, E. V. 1973. What's in a word? On the child's acquisition of semantics in his first language. In T. Moore, ed., *Cognitive development and the acquisition of language.* New York: Academic Press.

──────. 1974. Some aspects of the conceptual basis for first language acquisition. In R. Schiefelbusch and L. L. Lloyd, eds., *Language perspectives—Acquisition, retardation, and intervention.* Baltimore, Md.: University Park Press.

COCKING, R. R. 1976. "The synchrony in development of psychological constructs across verbal and nonverbal domains." Unpublished manuscript, Educational Testing Service.

COCKING, R. R., and M. POTTS. 1974. "The issue of valid units-of-measurement in children's language productions." Paper presented at the Minnesota Roundtable on Early Childhood Education, Minneapolis, Minn.

──────. 1976. Social facilitation of language acquisition: The reversible passive construction. *Genetic Psychology Monographs,* 94, 249–340.

COPPLE, C. E. 1973. "The comparative ease of processing Standard English and Negro Nonstandard English by lower-class black children." Unpublished doctoral dissertation, Cornell University.

COPPLE, C. E., and G. J. SUCI. 1974. The comparative ease of processing Standard English and Black Nonstandard English by lower-class black children. *Child Development,* 45, 1048–1053.

DORE, J. 1974. A pragmatic description of early language development. *Journal of Psycholinguistic Research,* 3, 343–350.

DUNN, L. 1959. *Peabody Picture Vocabulary Test.* Minneapolis, Minn.: American Guidance Service.

ERVIN-TRIPP, S. M. 1970. Discourse agreement: How children answer questions. In J. R. Hayes, ed., *Cognition and the development of language.* New York: Wiley.

──────. 1973. *Language acquisition and communicative choice.* Stanford, Calif.: Stanford University Press.

FRASER, C., U. BELLUGI, and R. BROWN. 1963. Control of grammar in imitation, comprehension, and production. *Journal of Verbal Learning and Verbal Behavior,* 2, 121–135.

GRICE, H. P. 1975. Logic and conversation. In D. Davidson and G. Harman, eds., *The logic of grammar.* Encino, Calif.: Dickenson.

GRIMES, J. E. 1975. *The thread of discourse.* The Hague: Mouton.

HALLIDAY, M. A. K. 1967. Notes on transitivity and theme in English. *Journal of Linguistics,* 3, 37–81; 199–244.

──────. 1968. Notes on transitivity and theme in English. *Journal of Linguistics,* 4, 179–215.

HOLZMAN, M. 1972. The use of interrogative forms in the verbal interactions of three mothers and their children. *Journal of Psycholinguistic Research,* 1, 311–336.

HUTTENLOCHER, J., and E. T. HIGGENS. 1971. Adjectives, comparatives, and syllogisms. *Psychological Review, 78*(6), 487–504.

INGRAM, D. 1974. The relationship between comprehension and production. In R. Schiefelbusch and L. Lloyd, eds., *Language perspectives— Acquisition, retardation, and intervention.* Baltimore, Md.: University Park Press.

JACOBS, R. A., and P. S. ROSENBAUM. 1968. *English transformational grammar.* Waltham, Mass.: Blaisdell.

JAKOBSON, R. 1960. Concluding statement: Linguistics and poetics. In T. A. Sebeok, ed., *Style in language.* Cambridge, Mass.: M.I.T. Press and New York: Wiley.

―――. 1968. *Child language, aphasia, and phonological universals.* The Hague: Mouton.

KLIMA, E. 1964. Negation in English. In J. A. Fodor and J. J. Katz, eds., *The structure of language: Readings in the philosophy of language.* Englewood Cliffs, N.J.: Prentice-Hall.

KLIMA, E., and U. BELLUGI. 1966. Syntactic regularities in the speech of children. In J. Lyons and R. Wales, eds., *Psycholinguistic papers.* Edinburgh: Edinburgh University Press.

LABOV, W. 1964. Stages in the acquisition of Standard English. In R. Shuy, ed., *Social dialects and language learning.* Champaign, Ill.: National Council of Teachers of English.

―――. 1970. The study of language in its social context. *Studium Generale, 23,* 66–84.

―――. 1972a. *Language in the inner city: Studies in the black vernacular.* Philadelphia: University of Pennsylvania Press.

―――. 1972b. *Socio-linguistic patterns.* Philadelphia: University of Pennsylvania Press.

LABOV, W., P. COHEN, C. ROBINS, and J. LEWIS. 1968. *A study of non-standard English of Negro and Puerto Rican speakers in New York City.* New York: Columbia University. (ERIC Document Reproduction Service)

LAKOFF, R. 1969. Some reasons why there can't be any *some-any* rules in English. *Language, 45,* 608–615.

LANGACKER, R. W. 1968. *Language and its structure: Some fundamental linguistic concepts.* New York: Harcourt, Brace, & World.

LANGENDOEN, D. T. 1969. *The study of syntax: The generative-transformational approach to the structure of American English.* New York: Holt, Rinehart, & Winston.

LOCKE, J. L. 1971. Phoneme perception in two- and three-year-old children. *Perceptual and Motor Skills, 32*(1), 215–217.

MARATSOS, M. 1973. Nonegocentric communication abilities in preschool children. *Child Development, 44,* 697–700.

McNEILL, D. 1966. Developmental psycholinguistics. In F. Smith and G. Miller, eds., *The genesis of language.* Cambridge, Mass.: M.I.T. Press.

————. 1970a. *The acquisition of language: The study of developmental psycholinguistics.* New York: Harper & Row.

————. 1970b. The development of language. In P. H. Mussen, ed., *Carmichael's Manual of Child Psychology, Vol. 1.,* 3d ed. New York: Wiley.

McNEILL, D., and N. McNEILL. 1968. What does a child mean when he says "no"? In E. Zale, ed., *Language and language behavior.* New York: Appleton-Century-Crofts.

MENYUK, P. 1963a. A preliminary evaluation of grammatical capacity in children. *Journal of Verbal Learning and Verbal Behavior, 2,* 429–439.

————. 1963b. Syntactic structures in the language of children. *Child Development, 34,* 407–422.

————. 1968. Children's learning and reproduction of grammatical and nongrammatical phonological sequences. *Child Development, 39,* 844–860.

————. 1969. *Sentences children use.* Cambridge, Mass.: M.I.T. Press.

————. 1971. *The acquisition and development of language.* Englewood Cliffs, N.J.: Prentice-Hall.

MILLER, G. 1962. Some psychological studies of grammar. *American Psychologist, 17,* 748–762.

MILLER, W., and S. ERVIN. 1964. The development of grammar in child language. In U. Bellugi and R. Brown, eds., *The acquisition of language.* Monographs of the Society for Research in Child Development, 29 (92), 9–34.

NELSON, K. 1973. *Structure and strategy in learning to talk.* Monographs of the Society for Research in Child Development, *38* (149).

PASAMANICK, B., and H. KNOBLOCH. 1955. Early language behavior and the testing of intelligence. *Journal of Abnormal and Social Psychology, 50,* 401–402.

PERLMUTTER, D. M. 1968. *Deep and surface structure constraints in syntax.* New York: Holt, Rinehart, & Winston.

PETERSON, C., F. DANNER, and J. FLAVELL. 1972. Developmental changes in children's response to three indications of communicative failure. *Child Development, 43,* 1463–1468.

POTTS, M. 1970. *A test of language production.* Ithaca, N.Y.: Cornell University. (Technical Report)

————. 1971. *A technique for measuring language production in three, four and five year olds.* Ithaca, N.Y.: Cornell University. (Technical Report)

————. 1972. A technique for measuring language production in three, four and five year olds. *Proceedings of the 80th Annual Convention of the American Psychological Association, 9,* 11–13. (Summary)

POTTS, M., and E. LEWTHWAITE. "The development of Standard English among Pakeha, Maori, and Samoan children in New Zealand schools." Report in progress.

QUIRK, R., S. GREENBAUM, G. LEECH, and J. SVARTVIK. 1972. *A grammar of contemporary English*. London: Longman Group.

RESNICK, M. B., G. L. WELD, and J. R. LALLY. 1969. "Verbalizations of environmentally deprived two-year-olds as a function of the presence of a tester in a standardized test situation." Paper presented at the meeting of the American Educational Research Association, Los Angeles.

ROEPER, T. 1973. Connecting children's language and linguistic theory. In T. E. Moore, ed., *Cognitive development and the acquisition of language*. New York: Academic Press.

ROMMETVEIT, R. 1974. *On message structure*. New York: Wiley.

SEARLE, J. 1969. *Speech acts: An essay in the philosophy of language*. Cambridge: Cambridge University Press.

SHATZ, M., and R. GELMAN. 1973. *The development of communication skills: Modifications in the speech of young children as a function of listener*. Monographs of the Society for Research in Child Development, 38 (3).

SHERMAN, J. A. 1969. "Imitation and language development." Unpublished manuscript, University of Kansas.

SHERMAN, M. 1969. "Some effects of negation and adjectival marking on sentence comprehension." Unpublished doctoral dissertation, Harvard University.

SHIPLEY, E., C. SMITH, and L. GLEITMAN. 1969. A study in the acquisition of language: Free responses to commands. *Language*, 45, 322–342.

SIGEL, I. E. 1972. The distancing hypothesis: A causal hypothesis for the acquisition of representational thought. In M. R. Jones, ed., *The effects of early experience*. Miami, Fla.: University of Miami Press.

SINCLAIR, H., and J. P. BRONCKART. 1972. S.V.O.: A linguistic universal? A study in developmental psycholinguistics. *Journal of Experimental Child Psychology*, 14 (3), 329–348.

SLOBIN, D. I. 1966. Grammatical transformations and sentence comprehension in childhood and adulthood. *Journal of Verbal Learning and Verbal Behavior*, 5, 219–227.

———. 1968. Imitation and grammatical development. In N. Endler, L. Boulter, and H. Osser, eds., *Contemporary issues in developmental psychology*. New York: Holt, Rinehart & Winston.

———. 1971. *Psycholinguistics*. Glenview, Ill.: Scott, Foresman.

SLOBIN, D. I., and C. WELSH. 1967. "Elicited imitation as a research tool in developmental psycholinguistics." Berkeley: Department of Psychology, University of California. Mimeo.

SPILTON, D., and L. LEE. 1977. Some determinants of effective communication in four-year-olds. *Child Development*, 48, 968–977.

STARR, S., and S. ESHELMAN. 1975. "Contexts of language: Listener and topic." Paper presented at the biennial meeting of the Society for Research in Child Development, Denver, Col.

STOCKWELL, R. P., P. SCHACHTER, and B. H. PARTEE. 1973. *The major syntactic structures of English.* New York: Holt, Rinehart, & Winston.

STROHNER, H., and K. E. NELSON. 1974. The young child's development of sentence comprehension: Influence of event probability, nonverbal context, syntactic form, and strategies. *Child Development, 45,* 567–576.

TORREY, J. 1972. "The language of black children in the early grades." New London, Conn.: Department of Psychology, Connecticut College.

TURNER, E. A., and R. ROMMETVEIT. 1967. The acquisition of sentence voice and reversibility. *Child Development, 38,* 649–660.

WARNER, W. L., M. MEEKER, and K. EELLS. 1960. *Social class in America.* New York: Harper.

WASON, P. C. 1959. The processing of positive and negative information. *Quarterly Journal of Psychology, 11,* 92–107.

———. 1961. Response to affirmative and negative binary statements. *British Journal of Psychology, 52,* 133–142.

———. 1965. The context of plausible denial. *Journal of Verbal Learning and Verbal Behavior, 4,* 7–11.

WERNER, H., and B. KAPLAN. 1963. *Symbol formation: An organismic-developmental approach to language and the expression of thought.* New York: Wiley.

WETSTONE, H. S., and B. Z. FRIEDLANDER. 1973. The effect of word order on young children's responses to simple questions and commands. *Child Development, 44,* 734–740.

WILKS, S. S. 1940. Confidence limits and critical differences between percentages. *Public Opinion Quarterly, 4,* 332–338.

Index

Structure and Development
in Child Language

Designed by G. T. Whipple, Jr.
Composed by Imperial Litho/Graphics,
in 10 point VIP Melior, 2 points leaded,
with display lines in Melior.
Printed offset by Thomson/Shore, Inc.
on Warren's Old Style, 60 pound basis.
Bound by John H. Dekker & Sons, Inc.
in Holliston book cloth
and stamped in All Purpose foil.

Library of Congress Cataloging in Publication Data
(For library cataloging purposes only)

Main entry under title:
Structure and development in child language.

  Bibliography: p.
  Includes index.
  1. Children—Language. 2. English language—Syntax
I. Potts, Marion.
P118.S8   401'.9   78-10968
ISBN 0-8014-1184-X